FINDING THE RIGHT WORDS

FINDING THE RIGHT WORDS

Essays, Poetics, Critical Fictions Concerning Canadian Culture, Literature, Language, and Personal Identity

JOHN MOSS

IGUANA

Copyright © 2025 John Moss
Published by Iguana Books
720 Bathurst Street
Toronto, ON M5S 2R4

All rights reserved. No part of this publication may be reproduced, stored in a retrieval system or transmitted, in any form or by any means, electronic, mechanical, recording or otherwise (except brief passages for purposes of review) without the prior permission of the author.

Publisher: Cheryl Hawley
Front cover design: Ruth Dwight, designplayground.ca
Front cover photo: Portrait of John with Jack. Photograph by Stephen C. Moss

ISBN 978-1-77180-746-3 (paperback)
ISBN 978-1-77180-745-6 (epub)

This is an original print edition of *Finding the Right Words*.

For Beverley Haun, my lovely and beloved partner.

For Laura Moss and Cynthia Sugars, whose two-volume anthology, Canadian Literatures in English: Texts and Contexts (first edition, Penguin, 2008; second edition, Broadview, 2025, 2026), came out after I could make use of its infinite resources. Laura is my daughter and a professor at UBC; Cynthia is a former colleague at the University of Ottawa.

For Margaret Atwood, for shaping Canadian literature and language as no other; her writing is everywhere here.

For Robert Kroetsch and George Bowering, for Eliot and Yeats, whose impact on my sensibility continues to be profound.

For Jack Morgan, my friend.

ACKNOWLEDGEMENTS

Canada, Impossible. *Originally published in* Apropos Canada *(Frankfurt am Main, 2010).*

Landscape Untitled. *Written as part of a* festschrift *for Clara Thomas, published by* Essays on Canadian Writing, *Summer 1984 Early drafts were delivered as lectures at the Modern Languages Association conference in Erie, Pennsylvania and at the Universities of York and Birmingham, all in 1983.*

Invisible in the House of Mirrors. *The largest part of this was originally published in Canada House Lecture Series #21, edited by Michael J. Hellyer, Canadian High Commission, 1983.*

Haunting Ourselves: Atwood and the Open Eye. *Drawn from* Margaret Atwood: The Open Eye *(University of Ottawa Press, 2006); and* An Interview with Margaret Atwood, *Christine Evain and Reena Khandpur, published in a series called* Canadensis *by the Université de Nantes, 2006.*

Labyrinths and Jigsaw Puzzles. *Parts of this were originally published by the* Associazione Italiana di Studi Canadesi. *It was called "The*

Feminization of Narrative Form." I also draw heavily on an essay published in The Paradox of Meaning, *Turnstone, Winnipeg 1999, as "Mrs. Bentley's Gender"; and on an essay published in* The Journal of Canadian Studies, *"Gender Notes: Wilderness Unfinished," Summer 1998.*

Himmler's Got the King. *Originally published in* Re-Visions of Canadian Literature, *edited by Shirley Chew (University of Leeds Press, 1985). Variants also appeared in* Present Tense *(NC Press, 1985) and* The Paradox of Meaning *(Turnstone Press, 1999).*

Being/Fiction *was originally published by* Essays on Canadian Writing *in Summer 1989 as "Life/Story: The Fictions of George Bowering."*

Exploding Slowly. *Originally published in* Under Fire, *edited by Lorne Shirinian (Blue Heron Press, 2003).*

Invisible Among the Ruins. *From the book of the same title, originally published by University College Dublin Press, 2000, and Cormorant Press, 2000.*

Temagami. *Originally published* in Visions and Voices in Temagami *(Nipissing University, 2000), edited by A.W. Plumstead.*

The Ivory Flute. *Adapted from* To Set the Stone Trembling *(Vanguard Press, 2022)*

Imagine Tahiti. *Originally published in* Lindstrom Unbound *(Iguana Books, 2019).*

Resisting Autobiography. *Originally published in* Being Fiction *(Tecumseh Press, 2001, reprinted 2005, 2007).*

A Particularly Lovely Project: The Journal of Canadian Fiction. *Originally published in* Canadian Literature *#202, 2009, UBC.*

Two from Other Perspectives:

> Shifting Identities: A Conversation with Laura Ferri. *Originally published in* Englishes: Letterature Inglish Contemporanee *(Rome, 2002).*
>
> The End of Allusion: An Essay by Crystal Chokshi. *Originally published here.*

Life, In Short. *Originally published in* To Set the Stone Trembling *(Vanguard Press, 2022).*

CONTENTS

ACKNOWLEDGEMENTS VII
PREFACE.. 1
CANADA, IMPOSSIBLE 3
LANDSCAPE, UNTITLED.. 14
INVISIBLE IN THE HOUSE OF MIRRORS 41
HAUNTING OURSELVES: ATWOOD AND THE OPEN EYE... 76
LABYRINTHS AND JIG-SAW PUZZLES 87
HIMMLER'S GOT THE KING 109
BEING/FICTION 127
EXPLODING SLOWLY 143
INVISIBLE AMONG THE RUINS.. 155
TEMAGAMI 187
THE IVORY FLUTE... 198
IMAGINE TAHITI 231
RESISTING AUTOBIOGRAPHY 239
A PARTICULARLY LOVELY PROJECT: *THE JOURNAL OF CANADIAN FICTION*.. 258
TWO FROM OTHER PERSPECTIVES

   Shifting Indentities:
   A Conversation with Laura Ferri 265
   The End of Allusion:
   An Essay By Crystal Chokshi... 269

LIFE, IN SHORT 276

PREFACE

Over the years I've published in a variety of modes and genres. This book gathers a selection of shorter works that I believe are significant but for the most part are no longer accessible. While they may be read in random order, they in fact move through a particular sequence to explore evolving aspects of Canadian language, literature, and culture from earliest times but focussed especially on the second half of the 20th century. As they do so, critical argument gives way to the allusive complexity of memoir and fiction.

Despite a long preoccupation with the Arctic, about which I have written a great deal, the pieces here are concerned mostly with other matters. The opening essays illuminate the struggle to find ourselves as Canadians and to find the words we could feel were our own. An ongoing fascination with structural differences between writing by men and by women vies with my interest in language throughout, centred on such radically engaged writers as Robert Kroetsch, George Bowering, and, inevitably, Margaret Atwood. Critical analyses give way to critical fiction, which in turn leads to fiction as fiction before veering back to the personal. I have concluded with two pieces which examine aspects of my work from other perspectives, before a few last words of my own.

Most of my literary work can be accessed online, and other scholarly writing can be ferreted out in the depths of academe. In everything here, I have made elisions and emendations, for the sake of both reader and text. I'd like to acknowledge the absence of indigenous and first-generation writers who have surged to the forefront in the years since these pieces were created. My most recent work and undoubtedly my last is a philosophical dystopian thriller called *To Set the Stone Trembling* (2022). That is what I hope to have done here in my own small way: set the stone trembling.

CANADA, IMPOSSIBLE

In the spring of 2006, I was Visiting Professor of Canadian Literature at the Universität Wien and invited to give the opening address at the International Graduate Conference for Canadian Studies in German-speaking Countries in the presence, among other dignitaries, of Mme Gervais-Vidricaire, Canadian Ambassador to Austria. It was published in Apropos Canada *(Frankfurt am Main, 2010). I felt a good way to start this collection is from alien perspectives, before diving into the evolution and achievements of Canadian poetics and narrative strategies or sharing the outcome of my own critical-creative endeavours.*

For the past five weeks I have been living in Austria and teaching at the Department for English and North American Studies at the University of Vienna. Through the spring of 1980 I taught Canadian literature in West Berlin. During the early 1960s I spent a lot of time with German sunworshippers and anarchists on Ibiza, long before it became expensive, and back then I travelled in Germany and Austria through several impoverished seasons by what used to be called "auto-stop." In Waterloo County, southwestern Ontario, my great grandparents on my mother's side spoke German, not only at home but in the community. When my Scottish grandmother turned up in

1891, moving from nearby Granton, Ontario, she had to learn German to work as the first telegraphist in the local post office. When I was a child and she was very old, she would gleefully evoke her mother-in-law by speaking English with a theatrical German accent.

It has been a while now, living in Vienna, since I first began dreaming in German. Appropriately, in the city of Freud, when I wake up, I have no idea what I was dreaming about. The German language has become as familiar to me as my own and yet it remains largely a closed dimension in the parallel worlds of my mind. No matter how carefully I listen, whether to people speaking around me or to my echoing genes, German refuses to make sense. I have no facility with languages at all. Even English often leads me into obscurity and confusion. Therefore, it is humbling to stand before a gathering of people who speak not only English but German, and probably French, and perhaps other languages, as well.

I am here as a Canadian. That seems to be my primary credential. Many of you at this conference know more about aspects of Canadian culture and Canada as a geophysical presence, about Canadian politics, history, economics, natural resources, native peoples, bicultural symbiotics, immigrant statistics, multicultural anomalies, postcolonial angst. But I know about *being* as a Canadian, although that only has meaning in the Heideggerian sense. *Dasein.* My awareness of my own existential condition is from a particular and unique Canadian perspective. This might qualify me to speak as a representative human in the world but not as an exemplary Canadian, a collectivity wherein I exist as a person of no great genius or eminence, although with a penchant for the public display of modesty which is a particularly Canadian characteristic.

A good part of my academic career has been devoted to making generalizations about Canada, usually in the disguise of informed opinions; sometimes, especially in more recent years, these opinions are embedded in poetry and fiction. Imagination has been necessary because there is no such thing as Canada. This makes Canada an existential singularity — its non-existence proof that Canada exists. Canada in the Heideggerian sense exists in being what it is not.

Samuel Beckett would have understood: Canada is an impossibility. My authority for saying this is that I am Canadian.

"You can write whatever you want about Vienna, it will always be true." This was written by the Viennese writer Hans Weigel in a marvel of dialectical redundancy, proving by making his statement that his statement, in fact, is the truth. He wrote this, of course, in German and perhaps meant something quite different. What we understand, here, together, in English, might not be what he meant. And if you are quietly translating my English translation of Hans Weigel back into German, you might not even see the Canadian connection.

Perhaps we should take a different approach. Canada is not a blank slate. Just because quite possibly there is no such thing as Canada and just because whatever you say about Canada is true, no matter how contradictory, no matter how contrary, Canada is not *tabula rasa*. Nor is it a whole that is either more or less than the sum of its parts. Nor is it what is left of North America when you take away the United States and Mexico. In fact, if the U.S. ceased to exist, Canada would collapse as a ribbon of desiccated snow along the north bank of the Rio Grande. If you were to arrange what each of you knows about, believes in, desires from Canada, the result would not be a mosaic signifying Canada from a Germanic perspective. It would be more like the proverbial elephant, described by a cohort of the blind from a variety of perspectives. Each of you might be correct; the chances of assembling your separate visions into an elephant, however, or a mosaic representing an elephant are infinitesimal.

In Austria, history and geography converge. The same might be said of all the nations in what we peremptorily call "the old world." "The old world" is a term that seems to mean those parts of the planet wherein historical texts were devised to record the progress of what is determined by textual analysis to be "civilized." Given that the indigenous people of Australia settled there some fifty-thousand years ago, long before the endangered cave drawings were inscribed at Les Escaux, long before Europeans exterminated their Neanderthal cousins, given that the native peoples of America were likely there for at least twenty thousand years before the Vikings landed at L'Anse aux Meadows in New-found-land, it seems odd to call their worlds "new." Yet, we name those people aboriginals as if they were a geographical feature of the landscape, with a past but no story. And if history is text, not heritage, then perhaps that is true. In real nations, such as Austria and Scotland, history and geography are virtually inseparable, the shifting boundaries and diverse causes of generations indelibly inscribed on the bruised and battered surface of the earth.

In the United States, history subdued geography, drew it into submission through grand schemes like the Hoover Dam and a manifest destiny in which conquest was not of other nations but of the land itself. With armies and engineers, farmers and entrepreneurs, Americans staked out the heart of a continent and imposed a revolutionary history upon everything within its grasp. In parts of Central and South America, history has yet to bring the natural world into submission, but not for want of trying. There are vast areas of rainforest that will not surrender, yet they, too, will finally dwindle to dust in the face of global atrocities. History, like cancer, will eventually kill off what it cannot control.

Canada, subject to the same threats, is different. History is one thing, geography another. If, in the U.S., geography was subdued by history, and in the Old World, from Ireland to Israel, Japan to Viet Nam, geography has been subsumed by history, in Canada it was the imposition of geography as a system of measurement, of incising distance and direction upon the land, that made history possible. If elsewhere, history and geography ultimately converge, in Canada they refuse to do so. We have history, yes. Much of it was written by surveyors as they superimposed new names over old, making every map of Canada a palimpsest — native names that endured five hundred generations were suddenly over-written by strangers with an alien tongue. Some of it was written in the ledgers that trading post storekeepers sent 'home,' with notes on market conditions; some was scripted by permanent tourists like the Strickland sisters, or by subversives like Anna Jameson and Mina Hubbard. And much of our history happened somewhere else, on the battlefields of Europe, in South Africa, in Singapore, among foreign diplomats at Paris and Ghent.

Attempts have been made to trace our national narrative, most famously through the fur trade, and in popular accounts through the building of the railroads, or the distribution and ultimate uses of Eaton's Catalogue. But a cursory survey of Canada today reveals how inadequate these historiographic paradigms actually are. For a story to become history, it must make the collective enterprise seem its inevitable outcome. One can believe the United States would be otherwise, but for the Wild West. Yet, in Canada's case, millions of amphibious rodents slaughtered to make hats for European gentry are nothing in romance or myth upon which to found a nation, and their sacrifice bears little on the minds of contemporary Canadians. It is the difference between metaphor and metonym. Beavers no more embody the story of our past than the seal hunt does of our present, or the slaughterhouses of Chicago do of the American dream.

History and geography in Canada form an uneasy alliance. One of the reasons is time. In Canada we are never far from reminders of how ancient is the universe and our human place within it. We are aware, even from the city's edge, of the vast excoriated surface of the Earth gleaming under the sun through five and a half times zones (Newfoundland declaring its difference on the half hour); we talk endlessly in Tim Hortons over coffee, in offices and schools, over neighbourhood fences and to complete strangers, of weather systems rolling for days, even weeks, across our sovereign landscape; we are aware of how fragile is our tenure on the planet, by virtue of our vast wilderness, which the native peoples call home. We are a very old country, geographically. Yet our history has no roots. It is like lichen on Arctic boulders, a mixture of algae and fungus, with no reality of its own, clinging to the surface of the rock.

Ask Canadians about history. They will tell you about the Greeks and the Persians. Hebrews and Egyptians are pushed a little to the side as religion and myth. They might tell you about Rome, or the interminable quarrels of Europe, or the European imperial project abroad; or inform you that the Gettysburg address was Abraham Lincoln' postal code during the Revolution. We sometimes get confused. You might hear of Chinese dynasties or Mogul empires. Or of conquistadores and buccaneers. Ask Canadians about history: you will hear almost nothing of Canada. For a few minutes on November 11th every year, we celebrate our valiant warriors, but this is nostalgia, not history. We make other gestures, we celebrate Queen Victoria's birthday, we celebrate our hockey victory over the Soviets in 1972, we celebrate the brief life of a one-legged runner, Terry Fox. It is not that things did not happen in Canada, but rather that, for the most part, we choose to forget.

This is in part our colonial legacy; by definition, history happened elsewhere. In part, it is due to our evolutionary progress toward democratic sovereignty, such as it is; there were no signal events, only significant dates. Partly, it is because we live so close to 'concept America'; it is difficult to see our reflection mirrored in the rocket's red glare. And finally, perhaps for these other reasons, we now erase ourselves in a bland mixture of humility and arrogance under the aegis of multiculturalism: do not fear assimilation for we are so empty as to be infinitely accommodating.

Is there such a thing as culture if no-one knows about it? As a postmodernist, I'm used to telling jokes no-one gets. It is almost a measure of my humour's success that it goes unappreciated, and I tend to feel a vague sense of disappointment when someone smiles. But if an entire culture goes unrecognized, perhaps it is more than a quirkiness to be overlooked or admired. This is not my judgement, that Canadian culture does not exist, that the term itself, 'Canadian culture,' is apparently an oxymoron. It is probably not the judgement of people working for the National Film Board or activists funded by the Canada Council in one or another of its various guises; it is probably not the judgement of Canadian Studies specialists, such as yourselves, each of whom has a different notion of what Canadian culture is and why it is difficult to grasp; nor the judgement of professional Canadians working for the Canadian Broadcasting Corporation. Otherwise, you will be hard pressed to find someone who admits to Canadian culture as an empirical fact.

Culture has enlivened the Canadian sensibility from the beginning, of course, when, following the arrival of Europeans to our illimitable shores, we first conceived ourselves a separable place in the world. Culture washed across us in waves — from France, the British Isles, Germany, from Eastern Europe, from Japan, China, Southeast Asia, from what we awkwardly know as the Indian subcontinent, and always from the south, where Americans commodified populist culture as a major export, and increasingly, rising like springwater from below, from the people, the First Nations, who were here when the others arrived; culture washing over us seems only to have worn us away. Perhaps, the only thing distinguishing our culture is that, like Atlantis beneath the sea, it haunts by its absence and is under constant erasure.

Only a few years ago, a minister for cultural affairs in the federal government declared there is no such thing as Canadian culture. I cannot remember who she was — to do so is like remembering an assassin's name while forgetting the victim's — but I documented her precise words in a book called *The Paradox of Meaning*. In any case, so many other politicians have urged upon us the same facile and cowardly denial of Canada as a cultural entity that there is nothing extraordinary in the minister's unseemly effacement. It seems a characteristic of the political profession, in Canada, to cast no shadow. This happens, of course, either when there is wondrous illumination or there is absolute darkness.

Do not think it is only federal politicians who stand shadowless and gaze into mirrors in an inversion of vampires, seeing only their own reflection, the background being utterly void. Last year the Government of Ontario considered granting, *ex cathedra,* legal jurisdiction to Sharia Law within a self-defining community throughout the province.

Quebec, of course, for all its sad legal battles over language, has a culture. Only a few years ago we almost tore the country apart, and left indelible scars, by refusing to allow Quebec the constitutional designation, 'distinct.' We would be damned if Quebec is a distinct society, we would be damned if it is not! And the rest of Canada, each region, each federal riding, is for electoral purposes distinct, emphatically so, so long as that appellation is not donned as a mantle of disaffection. You can see what I mean about the paradox of meaning: cultural distinctiveness is not to be confused with political difference. Politicians might allow Quebec its undeniable personality, based on the confluence of time, space, and being, or, to put it less grandly, on the coming together of history, geography, and culture over an extended period, sufficient to make it distinct. But Canada as a whole, which paradoxically includes Quebec, is simply — not family, not community, not alliance — Canada is simply a consensus.

Let me clarify. We are a very cultured people. Well, no, we are not a people. Let me say that again: we are very cultured, notwithstanding our lack of peopleness. 'Notwithstanding' is a very Canadian word. Those familiar with our constitutional documents will vouch for that. Perhaps, if we are to uncover evidence for Canadian culture we should start with the word, 'notwithstanding.' There must be some idea of Canada that can *stand* for the whole. We are highly educated, we are well informed, we are relatively open-minded. But if we cannot imagine ourselves in the world, how can we expect the world to imagine us?

I think it would be safe, even in such a cultural treasury as Vienna, to say that the term 'culture' in relation to national being does not refer to the arts, to enlightenment and the refined sensibility. Rather, it describes the depth of shared values and social behaviour by which a particular people experience their collective existence. In the past, such values and behaviour have been determined by racial or ethnic homogeneity, religion, language, common laws, continuity of customs — all usually, but not always, circumscribed by geographic limits and historical continuity. Quebec, by these cultural measures, is certainly a nation. Each tribal unit of native peoples in Canada, as determined by negotiated or imposed boundaries, is known as a First Nation. Some of these consist of thousands, others of only a handful of people. The Inuit of Canada, who participate in a circumpolar genealogy, are not a nation, since their borders for convenience are the same as those of the country to which they are host. Most Inuit would probably refuse the contained and limiting implications of the term. They are free people upon the land, ownership of which is a logical absurdity. They are proof, perhaps, that while a nation must certainly have or be a culture, a coherent culture is not necessarily a nation.

What, then, is Canada, if not impossible. Austria is an idea that can be held in the mind, without knowing exactly what that means. If someone were to challenge the notion, our several definitions would inevitably overlap. One can have an idea of Austria, and Mozart and Freud, the Habsburg dynasty, World Wars, alpine scenery, the governor of California, these will all be there. An idea of the United States, diverse as it may be, and often idealized as 'the American dream,' will include Washington and the Constitution, Lincoln and the Civil War, the Kennedys, cowboys, gangsters, Marilyn, the Mississippi, James Dean, Dr. Martin Luther King, Jr., and probably the governor of California, as well.

What about the idea of Canada? What are the iconic names, images, conditions or events that converge in our collective awareness of ourselves, in your conception of us as a singular entity? Superman and Austin Powers originated in Canada, but we don't think of them. Mounties and mountains? Many Canadians have seen neither. Maple leaves, Maple Leafs — foliage of trees unknown in most of the country except on a flag designed by a political party, a hockey team as much reviled as revered. The North? North is a direction determined by the Earth's axis. Despite the opinion of many, especially in Canada, it is not a place. Moral vision? We are fiercely polite. Political vision? No. Our federal political system is of accidental design and incidental efficiency. Is there an idea of Canada based on nostalgia — not really, when the past seems vaguely an embarrassment? On a dream? We dream only, in occasional panic, of having no dreams.

Where, then, does an immigrant to Canada arrive? If we seem a nation only by political expediency, and a country by virtue of adjectives describing our size, our diversity, our weather, and we seem culturally transparent, pathologically reticent about our past or future, diffident about the foundations of our laws and values (as if we had none, before our very recent Charter of Rights and Freedoms), then what are newcomers, who are strongly encouraged to maintain the customs and culture they fled, what are they to become? The answer, of course, is Canadian. In a contemporary world, Canada is emerging as a postcolonial multicultural anomaly. We are the first postmodern nation.

In a world where the pride of nations leads to devastating moral righteousness, after twentieth century nationalisms led to imponderable waste, Canada can serve as the model for difference. The terrible clash of historical inevitabilities will be mute if history, itself, ceases to be of importance. Whoever it was who said, those who do not know history are condemned to repeat it, was wrong, dead wrong. It is those who do know history who are its minions, its slaves, who are driven to rewrite it again and again. History is not the repository of virtue but the breeding ground of folly and vice.

Canada breaks all the rules of what it is to be a nation. Of course, we have a past, but we choose the present. And of course we have a culture, but we live it, day to day. It is not something we think much about, but just try suggesting we join the United States and see where it gets you. Who cares if we mumble about health care and hockey, the right to ban handguns, bilingual cornflakes. We know who we are. We also know we are not an inviolable chorus or choir, but a lovely cacophony of multiple voices. We are not my mother's Canada, which was neo-European, nor her mother's Canada, which was British, nor her mother's, which was pioneer, nor hers, shaped by land-clearing settler-invaders, nor any other, back nine generations to my earliest forbears who fled the American Revolution, my Mennonite grandmother from Pennsylvania. Nor is my own fiercely sovereign Canada that of my children, which is multicultural, multiracial, nor of their children, my six grandchildren, which is yet to be determined. We are a community in motion. It is only in stasis we become dangerous to ourselves or to others.

And, of course, we *are* geography, we're the empty place on CNN weather maps. In Mercator projections we're impossibly large; in geography texts, impossibly variegated, absurdly complex. We have the longest ocean coastline in the world. It would be as hard to miss us on maps as to draw our margins from memory. Perhaps because of size and diversity, perhaps because we have learned from the original peoples whose descendants are still among us, we do not possess the land with borders and boundaries, with laws and deeds and government treaties, and certainly not with walls, which are the greatest geographic folly of all. But we are here: understand this, we are an ancient land, a land unlimited by human consciousness. Geography may have conspired with history to give us our present shape and generated the illusion of ownership, but we are merely custodians. And even without maps, we know *where* we are.

Many of you who are experts in Canadian Studies have been to Canada. Once there, you were in no doubt where you were. From Vancouver to Halifax, Comox to Heart's Content, there is something about Canada that says you are there. Is it because we drink double-doubles, admire cops, smoke pot, smile a lot, hate winter, love snow, reject -isms and -ologies, and always say thank you? We break the rules of what it means to be a nation. Somehow the word "country" might seem more appropriate, but we break the rules of what it is to be a country, as well. Yet, when you cross from the U.S. into Canada you know you are there; when you get off the plane or the ship from elsewhere, you know you are there.

Imagine dreaming in English, and waking up to realize you only speak German. Imagine me, in Vienna, surrounded by a language I do not understand, immersed in the baroque splendour of a culture steeped in the past, within national boundaries established by armies and alliances, in a world where maps do not make countries, but countries make maps. I know from its splendid coffees and pastry, Vienna is empirically real, yet so much is encoded in ineffable diction, I cannot make it quite real in my mind. Like music. Like Haydn and Mozart and Schubert — we know these men as a visceral experience but not who they were. Not who they are. As we listen, sensibility and sense, feelings and reason, reach out and touch each other, even caress, but they do not converge. Music, of course, is impossible. If there were no-one to hear, it would not exist. That is what postmodern Canada is like; that is what it is like to be a Canadian.

LANDSCAPE, UNTITLED

How do you make English Canadian? How do you relate to the world when your soul frets in the shadow of a language that paradoxically is your own and yet alien? This essay confronts what has become recognized as a postcolonial condition: it explores procedures through which Canadian poets gradually accommodated English to fit experience for which it was ill-prepared by tradition or usage, in an often subtle revolution that has given to us, finally, a voice of our own. Written as part of a festschrift *for Clara Thomas, published* by Essays on Canadian Writing, Summer 1984. *Early drafts were delivered as lectures at the Modern Languages Association conference in Erie, Pennsylvania and at the Universities of York and Birmingham, all in 1983. It is meant to be a companion piece with the next essay in this collection, "Invisible in the House of Mirrors." Many of the poetry quotations in both essays are from a single anthology. I would like to think this was a result of my conviction that critical consideration of poetry can be only as accessible as the poetry it contemplates. It might also, however, relate to the fact that much of the writing and virtually all checking of citations were done out of the country, where Canadian poetry texts were in short supply.*

Naming is a primary function of poetry. Adam was the first poet, and, to use A.M. Klein's phrase, each poet in his or her turn is "the nth

Adam."[1] In naming, the poet does more than label and take inventory. The poet assumes imaginative control of the world. Through words the poet merges the experience of things and things themselves; defines through words both the centre and the limits of consciousness. If appropriate language is not at the poet's command, then the world from his or her perspective and for those who share it is quite literally beyond comprehension. Such is the case in a colonial context where the poet is bound to use words that are rendered inadequate by geographical transposition.

A language such as English that has served the colonial enterprise so well on a practical or instrumental level can still, in worlds away from its origin, confound the literary sensibility and set the literary imagination askew. The colonial literature of Canada provides ample examples of words simply not up to the demands made upon them in the new environment. The inherent weakness of colonial poetry is not so much a question of poets who, removed from their informing culture, are inadequate to the resources of the language, but rather the reverse. No amount of talent can domesticate alien words that, through a colonial set of mind, are not even recognized as alien. This dissociation between mind and environment is self-perpetuating.

But gradually names and the named become reconciled through an arduous reinvention of the language, word by word. Gradually the new place falls under imaginative control. Then, as in Canada, poetry becomes possible. Then, as poetry, Canada becomes possible.

The nineteenth-century English gentlewoman Susan Moodie, as Margaret Atwood re-creates her, responds to the "New World" on disembarking at Quebec with a plaintive declaration:

> I am a word
>
> in a foreign language.[2]

Before leaving home, Moodie may have thought Canada a foreign word. But as first experienced she finds Canada so substantial and unaccommodating that consciousness itself seems alien, and her own character, so far removed from its originating context, the creation of consciousness. Atwood's conceit is no metaphor: English that has crossed an ocean in Moodie's mind has become in Canada a foreign language, and Moodie, far from being the reservoir of language she was before leaving, has become merely an element within it, a word, herself.

Atwood is one of the few Canadian poets both to recognize and to resolve into poetry the discrepancy between language born of one place and the reality of another. In "Progressive Insanities of a Pioneer" she articulates the disorienting predicament of consciousness in a strange milieu:

> Things
>
> refused to name themselves; refused
>
> to let him name them.[3]

Again, she does not speak in metaphor, but literally. Without naming, there is no "tension/ between subject and object." The mind, without shape or circumference, collapses.

Atwood seldom writes in metaphor. Her tropes are more subtle and more aggressive, particularly when she is trying to make language the bridge between experience or perception and the world experienced or perceived. When she writes of sinking through stone to the knee, or being a mirror, or being a pool ("Think about pools"), she means quite literally what she says — that is the way it is, or *seems*, which is another way of saying *is*. Often, apparent metaphors are in fact image-equations for an emotional state, particularly in poems where the mind in the presence of landscape is forced into confrontation with itself. Language is literal; it is consciousness that is figurative.

Perhaps it is inevitable that a poet who stretches the literal possibilities of language to its limits should be so aware of its limitations. Specifically, Atwood recognizes in her poetry that there are times when language does not fit the experience of things perceived and must be forced, sometimes nearly to the point of incoherence. And when the language simply does not fit, when it remains steadfastly alien, then there is only madness or silence.

Early Canadian writers, bound to use a language ill-suited to conditions in the so-called New World, inadvertently discovered another option: they wrote bad poetry. What the colonial mind, virtually by definition, could not comprehend was that language itself was the problem. It is one thing for Atwood, from a present perspective, to have the fictional Moodie recognize words as a barrier between subjective and objective realities; it is quite another to suppose the historical Moodie could have recognized the same. From the perspective of the historical Moodie, colonial dissociation was not the result of a language depleted and distorted by transposition to a new place; colonial dissociation would more likely have been regarded as the cause itself of verbal misprision, if such had been recognized at all.

Words in a discrete verbal language grow out of the customs and culture, the history and sociology, of people in a particular place. They define and reflect the community by providing what for non-literate peoples is a mystical bond between themselves and the conditions of the landscape that shape their lives. Words are inseparable from the geography in which they have come into common usage. But they are also inseparable from the consciousness that has come into being through their usage. When they are transported in the mind, they carry the conditions of their origin with them. This makes them useful instrumentally, for ordinary discourse, and yet virtually assures that they will be inappropriate in bringing a new world under imaginative control.

Simply knowing the denotative value of a word does not guarantee that it accurately conveys meaning. The word "snow" provides a good example of how English in Canada was, and to an extent continues to be, merely an historically expedient *lingua franca* phoneme. On a January day in Canada, one may look outside and say, "It is very cold out there and the snow is deep." What one might mean, however, is that it is the normal temperature outside for a Canadian January and the snow is of normal depth for this particular part of the world. Yet we feel obliged to say "cold" and to say "deep." The Inuit have dozens of words for snow; the English have only one. Canadians have none.

Without modifiers, Canadian use of the word 'snow' is obtuse and obscure. Adjectives must compensate for the word's Teutonic origin and its evolution into modern usage in a moderate climate. To put the case on a broader base, consider a line from "Acadia" by Joseph Howe, published posthumously in 1874:

> For ages thus, the Micmac trod our soil.[4]

The glaring and inadvertent irony of the line, proclaiming prior possession of the land by virtue of race, nearly obscures the ineptitude of Howe's language. Not only does "our" dispossess the native people of their heritage and history, but it asserts, against their concept of coexistence with the land, the alien and overwhelming principle of land ownership. Their very name in this context is subverted, for Micmac means the people and here its meaning is virtually reversed to stand for an exotic faction. Furthermore, the opening words of the line cast over the aboriginal existence the net of European time: "thus," through the cycles of "our" history, "for ages," they lived in this place. And how so? They "trod our soil." One treads European byways, English meadows, the streets of London. In early Acadia, the geography was not passive, not to be "trod" upon. It was, and in good part still is, active, complex, aggressive. One encounters, experiences, endures, surmounts, submits to, exalts in, lives with the Acadian landscape. One does not tread its soil, an odd and inappropriate synecdoche, suggesting the rich, turned fields of an English countryside.

Joseph Howe was not a poet by trade, but as a journalist and politician he was a professional in the use of words, very much at home with the English language. The language he was born to, however, like the sentiments he expressed, was founded in a different place. Reading "Acadia," one reads in fact of an England strangely transformed, and not of a particular Canadian region.[5]

Everywhere that English travelled as the language of colonization, people shared Howe's problem. Generations after settlement took place, consciousness and sensibility continued to be shaped by words and by syntax that sustained the dissociated colonial set of mind. The genius of Twain and Whitman was their revolutionary re-creation of the English language as an American idiom; but it should be remembered that their contributions only came about many decades after the American War of Independence. In Canada, a similar process, without benefit of an ideological base, has extended through more than two centuries, accomplished for the most part by poets whose intentions outreached their achievements, and it is not yet complete.

Ineptitude early in the Canadian tradition was inadvertent, and therefore difficult to counter, although evidence suggests that one or two poets tried to turn an awareness of their limitations to advantage. Archibald Lampman is one of the best Canadian poets of the past century. With rare sensitivity, he allows language to be the expression of his experience with landscape, rather than using it in an effort to make the land submit. Yet even he, upon occasion, loses out in the struggle towards poetic coherence. The following mixture of awkward personification, inflated rhetoric, and comically inappropriate words is the opening stanza of his 1888 poem "Storm":

> Out of the gray northwest, where many a day gone by
> Ye tugged and howled in your tempestuous grot,
> And evermore the huge frost giants lie,
> Your wizard guards in vigilance unforgot,
> Out of the gray northwest, for now the bonds are riven,
> On wide white wings your thongless flight is driven,
> That lulls but resteth not.[6]

In a grot, unforgot. Thongless. Such awkwardness is unusual in Lampman's poetry, an aberration. There are poetasters in the Canadian tradition, however, who never rise above such doggerel. Consider the images and conceits in the following excerpt from an

1842 poem by the Canadian (as opposed to his Irish namesake) Standish O'Grady:

> In winter here, where all alike contrive,
>> And still withal few animals survive,
>> Till summer's heat, so potent and so quick,
>> Enough to make *the Crocodile grow sick*;
>> With vile mosquitoes, lord deliver us,
>> Whose stings could *blister a Rhinoceros*.
>> If on the living insects are thus fed,
>> How ill must fare the worms when we are dead![7]

O'Grady died before his poem saw print, which may have been a critical judgement.

Being aware of a problem does not necessarily mean the solution is at hand. In the following, a sonnet by Wilfred Campbell published in 1893, the poet seems to recognize that the only way he can get into the picture — that is, find language that will effectively merge consciousness with the landscape — is quite literally to climb in. The effect is bizarre, and only a little redeemed from the ridiculous by the wistful hope that his irony is intentional:

> I sit me moanless in the sombre fields,
> The cows come with large udders down the dusk,
> One cudless, the other chewing of a husk,
> Her eye askance, for that athwart her heels,
> Flea-haunted and rib-cavernous, there steals
> The yelping farmer-dog. An old hen sits
> And blinks her eyes. (Now I must rack my wits
> To find a rhyme, while all this landscape reels.)
> Yes! I forgot the sky. The stars are out,

> There being no clouds; and then the pensive maid!
> Of course she comes with tin-pail up the lane.
> Mosquitoes hum and June bugs are about.
> (That line hath "quality" of loftiest grade.)
> And I have eased my soul of its sweet pain.[8]

Sometimes the line between catharsis and a laxative is rather fine.

The next excerpt, from an 1894 poem by Bliss Carman, shows no regard at all for the function of language in the poetic merging of self with natural process. The result is disconcerting.

> Only make me over, April
> When the sap begins to stir!
> Make me man or make me woman,
> Make me oaf or ape or human,
> Cup of flower or cone of fir;
> Make me anything but neuter
> When the sap begins to stir![9]

According to OED, the meaning of "sap" as a simpleton was long established before Carman used it here.

Bliss Carman wrote some memorable lines of poetry. He is widely regarded as a major Canadian poet. He also wrote some very bad lines, abusing both language and the landscape, in his effort to express a discursive sensibility in what he took to be a unified world.

Poets somewhat more responsive to the problems inherent in the poetic use of English in a Canadian context had no better solutions. As early as 1825, the Canadian Oliver Goldsmith published in *The Rising Village* a spirited celebration of British North America in which he rather crudely acknowledges the need for episodic stimulation to make the lyric aspects of his poem take root. Thus, he inserts the maudlin story of Albert and Flora into what is otherwise a hybrid pastoral-epic-chronicle vision. Most of the descriptive passages in the poem are given narrative quality through extensive use of personification, but this only makes the awkwardness of his descriptive language seem more graphic when it falters.

At his best, Goldsmith delivers such innocuous lines as the following with aplomb:

> And where the forest once its foliage spread,
>
> The golden corn triumphant waves its head.[10]

But to this couplet the poet appended a note which ponderously explains that the process of clearing land is actually a good deal more difficult than his verse allows. He does not add that by corn he really means grain, for then as now corn in the North American sense of the word is "Indian" maize and in the field at harvest is not golden but a deep luxuriant green.

Howe, in "Acadia," a generation later, uses similar personification in an attempt to vitalize language that otherwise renders the Canadian landscape virtually opaque. He makes the "Indians" an extension of the land, then explosively transforms both into myth through a graphic depiction of the slaughter of innocents — that is, of English settlers. He also catalogues, naming tree types, for example. He surveys and documents, naming the qualities of a flower, lamenting the expulsion of the French from their Acadian homeland. He spins tales, brief and timeworn stories, to give the place a life of its own. Instead of using words to define the Canadian landscape, perhaps through naïveté Howe reverses the procedure, using characteristics of place to rework the language, to make it pliable, plausible, if not quite new. In this, he anticipates the best and most revolutionary aspects of poetry by Charles G.D. Roberts, Archibald Lampman, and Isabella Valancy Crawford in the next generation. Without seeming to recognize the extent to which language itself stood between imagination and the world he wished it to convey in his poetry, Howe left us with work the best of which seems eccentric and the rest simply not very good. To his credit, or perhaps because he was a closet poet, Howe avoided the tendency among his contemporaries to reduce language in their poetry to literary artifact, especially in the description of a landscape that seemed to elude or refuse definition. The result of this tendency was poetry that for the most part was mediocre and derivative.

As Daniel Wilson suggests in an 1858 review of Charles Sangster's *The St. Lawrence and the Saguenay*, that particular poem suffers because it "more frequently re-echoes the songs that are to be gathered amid the leaves of the library shelf, than under those with which the wind sports among the branches whereon songbirds warble their nuptial lays."[11] Ironically, Wilson commits the very offence for which he rightly admonishes Sangster. As the 'poetical' enters his prose, the words seem estranged from their Canadian context. Wilson's recognition that the path to success for the poet of the New World lies not in the direction of "literariness," does not guarantee that he knows a better route himself.

II

There are worlds of difference between English words in the poetry of Charles Sangster, Joseph Howe, Wilfred Campbell, Standish O'Grady, and Oliver Goldsmith and those same words, Canadian words, in poetry by Margaret Atwood, George Bowering, Robert Kroetsch, and their contemporaries, writing now. The process by which English is becoming a Canadian language is infinitely complex. It might be illuminated by passages arranged, not to develop an argument, but to reveal idiosyncrasies in the changing function of language as the process occurs. Each quotation is accompanied by a brief commentary. The quotations are in chronological sequence, dated, and identified by author. They are otherwise set free of context to avoid formal or thematic intrusions on a consideration of the word as word, image as image, trope as trope. Most were originally selected from the 1974 edition of Klinck and Watters' *Canadian Anthology*, affirming that they have been drawn from the mainstream. All passages, as a concession to orderliness, are based on a single and quintessentially Canadian motif — winter.

Begin with Oliver Goldsmith, 1825.[12]

> though around thy shore
> Is heard the stormy wind's terrific roar;
> Though round thee Winter binds his icy chain,
> And his rude tempests sweep along thy plain,
> Still Summer comes, and decorates thy land
> With fruits and flowers from her luxuriant hand …

The words are nonspecific; innocuously opaque. The images are cosmetic jewellery. Generalization is made concrete through arbitrary personification. However, metaphoric activity is jarringly aligned with image rather than personality. The result is somewhat obscene: if Winter holds the place as a *being* in chains, then the parallel structure of the trope suggests that what he is doing, sweeping her plain, is indeed, as the poem says, quite "rude." One-half of a conceit cannot reasonably insist on place as a person while the other half limits it to geography.

• • •

> Thou barren waste; unprofitable strand,
> Where hemlocks brood on unproductive land,
> Where frozen air on one bleak winter's night
> Can metamorphose *dark brown hares to white!*

— Standish O'Grady, 1842[13]

Words in the first two lines are charged with emotions to chill a speculator's heart, but the landscape is generalized beyond recognition. The sentiment is quite in keeping with the hyperbole of the second two lines, though not with the wit. The poet's lack of restraint has led him to at least one memorable image, "frozen air," in which a single word is virtually redefined by the conditions it describes. "Frozen" air is Canadian English.

•••

> We worship the spirit that walks unseen
> Though our land of ice and snow ...
>
> — Thomas D'Arcy McGee, 1858[14]

Words in the second line are nearly emptied of meaning, so much are they a cliché; yet cliché becomes metaphor. "Land of ice and snow" is not Canada — it is a trope that stands for Canada. George Orwell has written of metaphors that in a state of exhaustion cease to be metaphors, but here we have the opposite, a generalization so vapid it can only have meaning as metaphor.

•••

> What though the northern winds that o'er thee blow
> > Borrow fresh coolness from thy hills of snow,
> > and icy Winter, in his rudest form,
> > Breathes through thy vallies many a chilling storm ...
>
> — Joseph Howe, 1874[15]

Again, imprecision, personification, gender stereotypes, and again, the vulgarity of Winter, this time rudely blowing his cold breath along Acadia's valleys. To his credit, the poet tries to make the imagery conform somewhat to actuality, but the closer his images come to the lyric, to a descriptive function, the more inadequate seem his words.

A "chilling" storm is commonplace and redundant; a winter storm in Canada could hardly be otherwise. The idea in the first two lines that wind draws cold from snow is diminished by the word "coolness" from clever insight to quaint conceit. Neither sentiment nor syntax is strong enough to transform the word "coolness" to make it new. It lingers inappropriately, undermining both the lyric and narrative values of its immediate context.

•••

>From his far wigwam sprang the strong North Wind
And rush'd with war-cry down the steep ravines,
And wrestl'd with the giants of the woods;
And with his ice-club beat the swelling crests
Of the deep watercourses into death,
And with his chill foot froze the whirling leaves
Of dun and gold and fire in icy banks;
And smote the tall reeds to the harden'd earth;
And sent his whistling arrows o'er the plains,
Scatt'ring the ling'ring herds …

— Isabella Valancy Crawford, 1884[16]

How vivid the plain, here, and real, compared to Goldsmith's. Mythic rather than generalized personification fuses image with metaphor so powerfully that the language itself is wonderfully precise, even when the landscape is occasional diffuse.

•••

Never a bud of spring, never a laugh of summer,
    Never a dream of love, never a song of bird;

> But only the silence and white, the shores that grow chiller and dumber,
> Wherever the ice-winds sob, and the griefs of winter are heard.
>
> — Wilfred Campbell, 1889[17]

Personification for description and mood alone. Generalization is not in the description, but of the described: bud of spring, laugh of summer, dream of love, song of bird. These are flaccid things, generic images, good words reduced to inadequacy through evasion. And the shores, what shores? How silent, if winds and winter "sob" against them? These are only words, words that draw meaning not from the landscape that the poet wishes to describe, nor obliquely from the resources of language, but from common usage. Dictionary words.

•••

> Here by the gray north sea,
> In the wintry heart of the wild ...
>
> — Bliss Carman, 189[18]

This is winter from a nice warm study, a literary convenience, image transformed into a metaphor — honest perhaps to emotion but a distortion nonetheless. If "wintry" and "heart" have literal meaning at all, then the opening line, "by the gray north sea," must not; or conversely, if the poem is set close by the sea, then it cannot on the same literal level also be set in the "heart of the wild." If one line is taken to be metaphor and the other literal, then the image will serve. The landscape, however, has then been reduced to poetic device. (I realize, here, I am leaning into the meaning of the transmogrified Canadian word, "wild," to mean "wilderness.")

∙∙∙

> I sat in the midst of a plain on my snowshoes with bended knee
> Where the thin wind stung my cheeks,
> And the hard snow ran in little ripples and peaks,
> Like the fretted floor of a white and petrified sea.
>
> — Archibald Lampman, 1893[19]

The plain — as real as being there. The perspective is participatory; poetic consciousness is a presence within the landscape. What happens, what is felt, what is seen, what it is like — these are fused into a wholeness of "what is" by the consciousness that contains them, by the poem itself. Consciousness and text are virtually one and the same. The effect on language is spectacular. The simple authenticity of the first line, the striking precision of the last, both descriptions of stillness although one is purely narrative and the other a lyric trope, contain between them, like parentheses, the simplest of images in the simplest of language and lend each word new and vital meaning. "Thin" and "hard," in particular, have been remade through resolutely Canadian usage. "Thin" wind is what stings the cheeks of any winter traveller, who would be still in contemplation at that place, in that moment of time. "Hard" snow runs in "little" ripples on the frozen surface of the winter. "Thin" and "hard" have become Canadian words.

∙∙∙

The following passages are taken in sequence from "The Skater" by Charles G.D. Roberts, a poet whose best work fuses language and landscape as no other had before him. However, the originality and quiet splendour of his diction occasionally provide a licence to err.

My glad feet shod with the glittering steel
I was the god of the winged heel.

...

And the woods hung hushed in their long white dream
By the ghostly, glimmering, ice-blue stream.

...

A spinning whisper, a sibilant twang,
As the stroke of the steel on the tense ice rang;

...

And I turned and fled, like a soul pursued,
From the white, inviolate solitude.

— Sir Charles G.D. Roberts, 1896[20]

Apart from the mildly awkward metonymy of "glad feet," these couplets read well and carry with them an aura of authenticity. "Ice-blue" stream, on reflection, seems more poetic than actual, although the sounds of steel on ice are convincing, and the fearsome intensity of winter isolation is real enough. But! When, ever, in Canada or elsewhere, is it possible to have deep drifts of snow, woods hushed in snow, and a stream of open ice to skate upon? If the ice is clear, then the snow has yet to come. Every outdoor skater knows, with snow come shovels. The words seem authentic, but the scene is fake.

•••

All the lake-surface
Streamed with the hissing
Of millions of iceflakes
Hurled by the wind;

...

> Then on the third great night there came thronging and thronging
> Millions of snowflakes out of a windless cloud;
> They covered her close with a beautiful crystal shroud,
> Covered her deep and silent.
>
> — Duncan Campbell Scott, 1905[21]

Descriptive precision combines with narrative intensity to create a very effective dramatic scene. Snow lying like a crystal shroud is a beautiful image, though more authentic for its metaphoric value than its descriptive accuracy.

•••

> If our eyes wed close, then the lashes froze, till sometimes we couldn't see;
> It wasn't much fun, but the only one to whimper was Sam McGee.
>
> — Robert Service, 1907[22]

Winter here is solely a setting for narrative action; it has neither lyric nor metaphoric value. The snow is Styrofoam; the cold, a dramatic necessity.

•••

> Now the old folded snow
> Shrinks from black earth.
> Now is thrust forth
> Heavy and still
> The field's dark furrow.
>
> — F.R. Scott, 1936[23]

The diction is simple and direct, the images precise. Only in the peculiar dynamism of the verbs is there a hint of personification which suggests this passage might be part of a larger metaphor.

• • •

What of the winter? Half the year is winter.

— E.J. Pratt, 1940[24]

Winter: reduced and simplified; narrative exposition.

• • •

and the voice draws their pencil
like a sled across snow …

— P.K. Page, 1946[25]

Winter is a fact of life; snow itself has become the metaphor.

• • •

till the chilled nail shrinks in the wall
and pistols the brittle air …

— Earle Birney, 1949[26]

Old words, here, made new. 'Chilled' has never before meant what the poet makes of it in these two lines; "pistols" and "brittle" have been remade entirely. Other meanings of these words have not been abandoned but, rather, subsumed. Each key word in these brief lines makes every other a new and different word. The chilled nail shrinks;

it pistols the brittle air. A dictionary could not explain what here explains itself.

•••

> I would take words
> As crisp and as white
> As our snow …

— A.J.M. Smith, 1954[27]

A commonplace image made extraordinary through a logical inversion; snow may be routinely described as crisp and white, but it is entirely new that words should be described that way. The metaphor takes the nature of snow for granted, especially of "our" snow, but turns familiarity to wonder through its precision in defining a particular quality of language, of "words." A sort of self-fulfilling prophecy, this passage is a fine example in itself of the concept it seems meant to convey:

> I would take words
> As crisp and as white
> As our snow …

•••

> after a while wind
> blows down the tent and snow
> begins to cover him …

— Al Purdy, 1968[28]

Snow is snow; it is what it is, does what it does. Word and element are one.

•••

the rustle of the snow

...

thistles bright with sleet

...

At night the house crackled.

— Margaret Atwood, 1970[29]

No metaphors. Images precise, striking, authentic. Consciousness re-creates the language. The house *does* crack, the snow *does* rustle, and thistles sometimes *are* bright with sleet in the Canadian winter. Words and the experience are one.

•••

We took the storm windows/off
the south side of the house
and put them on the hotbed.
Then it was spring. Or, no:
then winter was ending.

...

No trees
around the house.
Only the wind.
Only the January snow.
Only the summer sun.

— Robert Kroetsch, 1977[30]

Pure meaning. No modifiers; no metaphors. Winter is a season defined by the experience of the people the poem addresses; the snow of January is self-explanatory, a condition familiar in the experience the poem addresses. This is a Canadian poem. The words are regional, substantial, authentic. They are inseparable, ultimately, from experience or consciousness; accessible, ultimately, to anyone, and, once grasped, they carry the potential of universal significance.

III

Canada is a word (think about words).

POSTSCRIPT

There is a whole area of language as deep and secret as the psyche that to date has gone largely unexplored. No one looks at the word that seems to mean the same from place to place, speaker to speaker, that might have the same lexical definition, yet means differently — sometimes radically and profoundly so. "Queen," to the American, the Canadian, the English: fairy-tale romance, constitutional ambiguity, tradition. There are other meanings, besides, which extend beyond cultural boundaries, related to being in drag, to chess, to apiary, to bed size. But Queen with a capital Q means differently to Americans, Canadians, and English.

Studies in dialect and idiom tend to quantify the obvious. Cross-cultural studies dwell on functional communication or on idiosyncrasy. Linguistic, semantic, and semiotic studies deal with relationships. Systems prevail. Lévi-Strauss, building on Saussurean principles of verbal structure, recognized the profound impact of language on the development of the individual within society. Lacan, rather violently imposing Lévi-Strauss and Saussure on a hapless Freud, deduces the importance of language on the development of the individual within the species. Chomsky discounts to a large extent the experience of the individual in the acquisition of language, and

Steiner, likewise, in the imposition of silence. The function of language in relation to consciousness and to the world is a matter of considerable interest and much theorizing. Yet theory for the most part attends to structures, to syntax, to planes of meaning, linear and spatial, and pays little attention to the discrepancies of meaning within the words themselves, discrepancies that may arise due to the very structures of language and consciousness that they sustain.

Because language is a system, and meaning is systemically determined, words can evade or subvert lexical and allusive meaning, can render speech or writing a secret code, perhaps inimical with, and perhaps in service to, the speaker/writer's desire to say. A number of feminist writers have recognized language itself as a source of repression and not just through Lacanian syntactical and symbolic ordering but deep within the words themselves. Sadly, in the verse preceding entry into Judy Chicago's symbolically extravagant feminist oeuvre, *The Dinner Party*, she writes that "Lo," when women are heard and recognized at last, our species will return to "Eden."[31] Could she have used words less appropriate, resounding as they do with both literary and theological traditions of female subjugation?

Simone de Beauvoir in 1949 called her inquiry *The Second Sex (Le deuxième sexe)* with obvious confidence, knowing that the meaning of words would be determined, or redetermined, by awareness of their source: "second" is historically appropriate, temporal acknowledgement of an ordered primacy; but second is also emphatically an ironic rejection and, with more subtle irony, second alludes to the future, the new chance to get things right, the end of practice, of God's first and failed experiment, were there a God. If de Beauvoir's title had been on a book by Norman Mailer, the words would have meant quite differently; used as it is, it usurps linguistic misogyny.

Another French writer, in words reminiscent of Atwood's Moodie, declares that her language, "although it is mine, is foreign to me." Asserting the feminist necessity to reinvent language without rejecting it, without receding into incoherence or silence, Madeleine Gagnon declares: "I am a foreigner to myself in my own language and I translate myself by quoting all the others."[32]

A half century earlier, James Joyce acknowledged in *A Portrait of the Artist as a Young Man* much the same problem from an Irish perspective. His response within context is an ironically naïve declaration of passionate commitment, and beyond text, in subsequent texts, it is the reclamation of language not through passion but erudition. In *Portrait,* Stephen is in a discussion of words with the dean of studies:

> He felt with a smart of dejection that the man to whom he was speaking was a countryman of Ben Jonson. He thought:
>
> — The language in which we are speaking is his before it is mine. How different are the words home, Christ, ale, master on his lips and on mine! I cannot speak or write these words without unrest of spirit. His language, so familiar and so foreign, will always be for me an acquired speech. I have not made or accepted its words. My voice holds them at bay. My soul frets in the shadow of his language.[33]

Joyce in the shadow of his given language; woman, as Julia Kristeva says, "estranged from language"[34] or, as Gagnon might say, "foreign to it"; theorists enthralled with its apparent and elusive systems; Canadian poets like Kroetsch and Atwood, George Bowering and bp Nichol, forcing upon old words new and radically unequivocal ambiguities; all demand of us a reassessment of the language we use so casually to comprehend our relations in and with the world and ourselves.

If we have not the words, then we are estranged from every one and every thing. Such estrangement, at least from the landscape, is seen to diminish as language is reinvented by our poets, reassessed by their readers. This procedure may parallel developments in the major tradition that, arguably, constitute neither improvement nor deterioration. The gradual shift from ornamentation and metaphoric analogy to the unadorned metonymic representation that characterizes so much of the best contemporary poetry is, however, empirically and emphatically an improvement in the Canadian context.

Especially in the twentieth century, arguments have been put forth which parallel and reflect the development towards possession of an alien and only language by some who think we all — not only women, Irish, working class, Canadians, other neo-or post-colonials who are bound to use contemporary language for more than diversion and the exchange of goods — we all find soul and psyche more alienated than appeased by what language has become, by what words imprisoned in syntactical structure and rigid traditions have become.

Through much of her life, Gertrude Stein argued that writers must work back in the English language to the "excitingness of pure being," where word and thing were virtually one.[35] As William H. Gass describes it, words become things in her writing, are in effect real, on their own, "as physical as statuary."[36] Stein and Gass argue for, and in their own writing offer by example, words that are artifact and object and conceptual presence all at once, complete in themselves and yet, discontinuous from context, hint of other worlds, other things. Along with Robert Kroetsch, the most articulate and aware speaker in Canada of his own adventures with language in literature, they urge that language move away from vapid cliché and from the indulgence of idiosyncratic originality. Meaning will no longer be conveyed by image or vision, by complex analogical construct; meanings will accrue, rather, amid the discontinuities of word-things, through shared experience between writer and reader of the possibilities provided by text.

Kroetsch's lines are real:

> Only the January snow.
> Only the summer sun.

The words are real, the poem, the snow and sun are real. January, summer, only, only, the — all are real.

NOTES AND WORKS CITED

1. A.M. Klein, "Portrait of the Poet as Landscape," in *Canadian Anthology*, ed. Carl F. Klinck and Reginald E. Watters, 3rd ed. (Toronto: Gage, 1974), p. 347.
2. Margaret Atwood, "Disembarking at Quebec," in *The Journals of Susanna Moodie* (Toronto: Oxford University Press), 1970, p. 11.
3. Margaret Atwood, "Progressive Insanities of a Pioneer," in *The Animals in That Country* (Toronto: Oxford University Press, 1968), p. 39.
4. Margaret Atwood, "Tricks with Mirrors," in *You Are Happy* (Toronto: Oxford University Press, 1974), p. 27.
5. Joseph Howe, "Acadia," in *Nineteenth Century Narrative Poems*, ed.
6. David Sinclair (Toronto: McClelland and Stewart, 1972), p. 25.
7. At least Howe acknowledges a native population. As recently as 1954 a poet as sensitive to social issues as F.R. Scott could write of Canada before white settlement being "empty as paper," the landscape just waiting for the "language of life," "the full culture of occupation, "to "turn this rock into children" (F.R. Scott, "Laurentian Shield," in *Canadian Anthology*, pp. 276–77). Less surprising, both Catharine Parr Traill and her sister, Susanna Moodie, a century before Scott, erased indigenous culture from the landscape, even if they begrudgingly admitted the spectral presence of the people themselves.
8. Archibald Lampman, "Storm," in *Canadian Anthology*, p. 124.
9. Standish O'Grady, "The Emigrant," in *Canadian Anthology*, p. 29.
10. Wilfred Campbell, "At Even," in *Canadian Anthology*, p. 96.
11. Bliss Carman, "Spring Song," in *Canadian Anthology*, p. 113.
12. Oliver Goldsmith, "The Rising Village," in *Nineteenth Century Narrative Poems*, p. 3.

13. Daniel Wilson, "Review of Sangster's The St. Lawrence and the Saguenay," in *Canadian Anthology*, p. 70.
14. Goldsmith, "The Rising Village," p. 25.
15. O' Grady, "The Emigrant," p. 28.
16. Thomas D'Arcy McGee, "The Arctic Indian's Faith," in *Canadian Anthology*, p. 61.
17. Howe, "Acadia," p. 19.
18. Isabella Valancy Crawford, "Malcolm's Katie," in *Canadian Anthology*, pp. 88–89.
19. Wilfred Campbell, "The Winter Lakes," in *Canadian Anthology*,
20. P. 94.
21. Bliss Carman, A Northern Vigil," in *Canadian Anthology*, p. 110.
22. Archibald Lampman, "Winer Solitude, in *Canadian Anthology*,
23. Sir Chares G.D. Robert, "The Skater," in *Canadian Anthology*, p. 104.
24. Duncan Campbell Scott, "The Forsaken," in *Canadian Anthology*, pp. 152–53.
25. Robert Service, "The Cremation of Sam McGee," in *Canadian Anthology*, p. 208.
26. F.R. Scott, "March Field," in *Canadian Anthology*, p. 261.
27. E.J. Pratt, "Brébeuf and His Brethren," in *Canadian Anthology*,
28. P.K. Page, "The Stenographers," in *Canadian Anthology*, p. 435.
29. Earle Birney, "Man Is a Snow," in *Canadian Anthology*, p. 299.
30. A.J.M. Smith, "To Hold in a Poem," in *Canadian Anthology*, p.273.
31. Al Purdy, "Lament for the Dorsets," in *Canadian Anthology*, p. 405.
32. Margaret Atwood, *The Journals of Susanna Moodie*. The first two lines are from "Resurrection," p. 58; the third is from "Thoughts from Underground," p. 54.
33. Robert Kroetsch, *Seed Catalogue* (Winnipeg: Turnstone Press1977), pp. 11, 13.
34. Judy Chicago's "The Dinner Party" was on exhibition at the Art Gallery of Ontario, Toronto, May 22-July 4, 1982.

35. Madeleine Gagnon, "Corps I," trans. Isabelle de Courtivron, in *New French Feminisms: An Anthology*, ed. Elaine Marks and Isabelle de Courtivron (Amherst: University of Massachusetts Press, 1980), p. 179.
36. James Joyce. A Portrait of the Artist as a Young Man (London:
37. Jonathan Cape, 1952), p. 194.
38. Julia Kristeva, "Oscillation du *'pouvoir'* au *refus*," interview by Xaviére Gauthier, trans, Marilyn A. August, in *New French Feminisms: An Anthology*, p. 166.
39. Gertrude Stein, *Four in America* (New Haven: Yale University Press, 1947), pp. v-vi.
40. William H. Gass, *Fiction and the Figures of Life* (New York, Knopf, 1970), p. 20.

INVISIBLE IN THE HOUSE OF MIRRORS

This was originally delivered in November 1983, as one of two lectures I gave at Canada House, Trafalgar Square. The other, called Arctic Landscape and the Metaphysics of Geography, *I did in October of 1991 as part of a larger work called* Enduring Dreams: An Exploration of Arctic Landscape *(Anansi, 2004). In the early sixties, I lived in London and Canada House was the centre of my threadbare world. I picked up mail there, read* The Toronto Telegram, *and overheard people speaking like me. Lecturing there felt like a homecoming. Both times. "Invisible in the House of Mirrors" is a companion piece with the essay preceding this ("Landscape, Untitled"), likewise concerned with the struggle by our poets to make English an authentic Canadian language.*

I

Language is of course Borgesian, a labyrinth of labyrinths. Words are reflecting surfaces within a closed, enclosing system. They offer an illusion of depth. The infinite possibilities of their syntactical arrangement are a maze of corridors, each giving way to another and another. Words reflect words, refract and repeat without limit, within the fixed walls of the finite house. This is not a metaphor. There are no metaphors inside a labyrinth.

Now, imagine yourself surrounded by mirrors, lost in the funhouse. Imagine yourself, like Dracula, with no reflection. Abandoned by Barthes and Barth, you search for yourself among the mirrored planes, but you are nowhere to be found. Knowing you are there is not enough. Descartes was wrong.

We are born into language, as Wittgenstein says. It precedes us; we come into an awareness of ourselves not only through language but within it. Language provides the dimensions of our consciousness, both individual and communal. To the extent that as structuralists we are apt to say, with a somewhat different concept in mind, that we are the creations of linguistic convention, we are separated by words from the world. When Adam named the world on our behalf, he placed himself apart from it. He became the words he spoke and set poets forever after the task of transcending the limitations of language to assert the reality of their own existence and, by implication, ours as well.

Poetry is the perverse and necessary art by which language is turned upon itself to yield up the very presence, in the world, of the substantial self which it denies. In Canada, poets in English must use a language that evolved into a coherent system in some other place than our own, through time upon the surface of which we float, the jetsam of an alien history. The sense of individual being within both the spatial and temporal landscape can sometimes in Canada be so ephemeral as to make the place, our place, seem virtually uninhabited. Consequently, many Canadian poets show a special interest in naming the New World, as if for the first time. Their poetry yearns to fuse consciousness with the landscape, words with things, with the object-world; their poetry yearns to affirm their being, our being, to make us be, in the world.

A few, most notably Margaret Atwood, recognize futility in the attempt to re-create ourselves in a place that seems intrinsically opposed to our presence, through language that belongs somewhere else, words that won't fit, word arrangements that render us mute. "Our flag," she says, in "Two-Headed Poems," "has been silence, /which was mistaken for no flag." Later in the same poem she argues:

> You can't live here without breathing
> someone else's air,
> air that has been used to shape
> these hidden words that are not yours.[1]

So acutely aware is she of the problem we share, Atwood seems at times to submit. Yet she makes of our absence, and her own, fine and haunting poems.

Others, Robert Kroetsch, Daphne Marlatt, George Bowering foremost among them, refuse both invisibility and silence. They reinvent the language; one word at a time, they make it ours. They don't struggle with words to define the landscape and thereby somehow take possession of it, as other poets have so often tried to do, and so often failed. Rather, it is the land they use to redefine the language. Their experiences of and in the world, their consciousness of the landscape within which they find themselves, translates in their poetry, through the force of their poetic chutzpah, into words so substantial as objects, inseparable from the things they signify, that we, among them, reading the poem, reading ourselves — *écriture*, to use Derrida's term for it — become equally as substantial. Through words, we become ourselves; we become real.

It was only toward the middle of the last century that Canadian poets discovered their inability to establish a lyric presence within the Canadian landscape had more to do with the nature of language than with the natural world or the authenticity of their experience within it. Our early poets personified the land — unable to infuse it with consciousness in the manner of their Romantic counterparts, they gave it personality on its own, sometimes using "Indians" as its embodiment, more often simply turning it into an unwieldy concatenation of improbable giants. Sometimes they reduced the land to the stuff of documentary, in prolix passages which seemed meant by their density to prove that it existed at all.

One or two of the best, late in the nineteenth century, did manage to fuse the landscape with self through the sheer lucid precision of their poetry. Few poets have captured the existential condition of being in winter with words more evocative than Archibald Lampman's, in such phrasing as "frost than stings like fire," or "winds that touch like steel."[2] Not, however, until A.M. Klein's magnificent poem of 1948, "Portrait of the Poet as Landscape," did a Canadian poet acknowledge through poetry the importance of words themselves in the relationship between being and the world:

> For to praise
> the world — he, solitary man — is breath to him. Until it has
>   been praised, that part has not been. Item by exciting
>   item —
> air to his lungs, and pressured blood to his heart, —
> they are pulsated, and breathed, until they map,
> not the world's, but his own body's chart![3]

"Look," he says of the poet, earlier in the same poem, "he is/the nth Adam ... in a world but scarcely uttered, naming, praising". It is by words the poet becomes real, each poet in turn.

In her 1960 poem, "Butterfly Bones," Margaret Avison shows the limitations of language evident in poetic usage, moved as it is "towards final stiffness" within the forms of literary convention.[4] The real and vital world of words that is our natural heritage, what she calls "Adam's lexicon," is "locked in the mind." We no longer have access to words that once spoke for the living relationship between self and other, Adam and the world he named. Whether this is due to the seemingly fixed nature of literary forms (the alternate title of the poem is "Sonnet Against Sonnets"), or because literature draws attention to our loss in a world which we impale with words in order to comprehend, is in the poem indeterminate. But Avison is a poet, writing, not mute; the very existence of her poem suggests our problem originates not so much in poetry as in language itself.

Many other Canadian poets have written *about* words, made words and the problems of words for the poet, for all of us, the subject of their poetry. Adam appears time and again: the original Canadian. Sometimes, as in Jay Macpherson's whimsically serious poem, "The Fisherman," he seems to embody the role of language in separating us from the better world. Naming is simultaneous with the Fall from Eden:

> Old Adam on the naming-day
> Blessed each and let it slip away.[5]

David Helwig, in a whimsically haunting poem, "The Bugbear," relates language to the Fall into mortality — which, with a Heideggerian twist, is what makes things real. Of the child-scaring bugbear he ironically intones:

> A hundred times
> we wish that Adam
> had named him
> so that he might be real and die.[6]

If each poet is the nth Adam, Adam is the algebraic root of n, the primal poet. It is as a failed Adam that Atwood's prototypic Canadian in "Progressive Insanities of a Pioneer" is overwhelmed, in a place where consciousness and the landscape were (are) mutually impenetrable, where

> Things
> refused to name themselves; refused
> to let him name them.[7]

Words for Atwood may be as solid as flesh or a flight of stones. They thicken the tongue, swell "with other words, with blood."[8] fall away from the bone, make spells, make poems, but most important of all they provide an environment in which to live, the palpable dimensions of our lives. When they will neither adhere to the world nor become it, the object-world where we have our object-being, what I call the "landscape," then we in effect live in two worlds — and always with the risk that we may fall into the abyss between, which is madness or silence.

Atwood's concern for words and the paradox of language, especially in this/that place named Canada, is shared by so many that it seems endemic. Words about words. Certainly, all poetry is in some measure, as Irving Layton has said, about poetry; art, like language, is self-referential. "Each art," writes Konrad Fiedler, "expresses only itself."[9] But in so doing, art, and in particular poetry, uses divers worlds to make its presence known and felt. And, curiously, in Canada Mallarmé's assertion that poems are not made of ideas but words has a special and literal relevance, for it is words themselves, not language with its unlimited syntactical possibilities, but words as words, that so often provide the subject and rhetorical objective of Canadian poetry.

A.J.M. Smith wrote in "To Hold in a Poem," in 1954:

> I would take words
>
> As crisp and as white
>
> As our snow; as our birds
>
> Swift and sure in their flight;[10]

And for four more stanzas of a single sentence, he hangs all the weight of words and place on that opening phrase: I would. I would take words, I would hold in verse, austere. I would; a yearning for what exceeds his grasp, escapes his capacity to achieve. His poem, a deconstructionist's delight: its genius in the impossibility of its intent and the unlimited indeterminacy of its significance as it plays with lingual and literary conventions towards that end, to hold in a poem the spirit of a place when its physical presence refuses still to be named.

John Newlove, another generation, Atwood's generation, evokes in "The Pride" a vision of how the land itself will come to us, but not through the stories we tell of it, not until the words are right —

> Those are all stories;
> the pride, the grand poem
> of our land, of the earth itself,
> will come, welcome, and
> sought for, and found,
> in a line of running verse, sweating, our pride;
> we seize on
> what has happened before,
> one line only
> will be enough,
> a single line and
> then the sunlight image suddenly
> floods us
> with understanding, shocks our
> attentions, and all desire
> stops, stands alone;
> we stand alone
> we are no longer lonely
> but have roots,
> and the rooted words
> recur in the mind, mirror, so that
> we dwell on nothing else, in nothing else,
> touched, repeating them,
> at home freely
> at last, in amazement."[11]

In what could be a quotation from Wittgenstein, at least in poetic transliteration, Newlove says: when the right words spring "upon us,/ out of our own mouths,/ unconsidered, overwhelming," then we have roots; "we dwell on nothing else, in nothing else,/ ... at home freely/ at last." What for Wittgenstein is a truth, however burdensome, in Canada is only a possibility. Wittgenstein never envisioned our invisibility in the house of mirrors, but then he was not born into a language that belonged somewhere else.

Language precedes our presence in the world. It is a public place, a communal place within which we live with others of the same family. But the words — words are different. We share them and yet they are personal and sometimes private; inseparable of course from language, they are also inseparable from self. Language and consciousness are not co-extensive, for language contains consciousness. But collectively they co-exist — for language can no more be, without consciousness, than consciousness can be (in the Husserlian sense of awareness of being aware), without language. Words, however, ground consciousness in the world, as Husserl insists. Words can have substance as real as the landscape they signify, as the mind that holds them within. Even as language seems to keep us separate from the world, words have the capacity to join us to it — or also, as we in Canada must sooner or later acknowledge, the capacity to render us insubstantial, not transcendent but invisible, unreal.

To be an individual in the world is to be conscious of oneself within language, separate from the world. Jacques Lacan argues that early language acquisition and the child's sense of otherness are co-incident. As we grow into language we become ourselves. But language is a given, while our relationship with words and the relationship our being in the world sustains between words and the things they signify, are very much open to change. Thus, a poet like Newlove envisions the people of Canada coming alive in the land not through the radical transformation of our whole language but through the as yet unachieved precision of just a few words, a perfect brilliant line or image or unyielding phrase. And Atwood in her poetic projections of collective or prototypic Canadian response to the land, especially in the early volumes, *The Animals in That County* and *The Journals of Susanna Moodie,* and in *Two-Headed Poems,* similarly relates our problems of language not to the body of the whole, its referential and syntactical complexity which in fact she exploits, often with stunning effect, but to the words themselves, and the refusal of individual words to merge with the things they are meant to signify. We remain apart from the landscape because the words by which we know ourselves do not fit it, and the landscape remains outside of us because our words will not contain it. We live within language, and we live within landscape, but the two refuse to coincide.

Atwood ensures that what might be of only parochial interest is given in her poetry universal dimension. The divided self and alienation from the world, both in consequence of being as a condition of conscious-ness, which in turn is the creation of language — and here linguistic structuralism and phenomenological existentialism are intertwined — though endemic in Canada are by no means indigenous to it. In much of her poetry, it is the function of words in relation to private being, more than to public, that dominates, and of course nothing is of more far-reaching significance to the reader than the nature of individual existence.

Gwendolyn MacEwen, contemporary with Atwood and Newlove, writes at times with an eerie passion to illuminate the paradoxical function of naming in relation to being, usually without particular reference to a Canadian context. In fact, in what could easily be taken as an analogue for the alien nature of language in her own country, she writes most effectively in what might be called a transcultural idiom, as an outsider among the rooted cultures of Greece and the Arab world or as an observer within the imagined splendour of ancient Egypt. In a 1966 poem, called "Poems in Braille," MacEwen creates a disconcerting dialectic out of the relationship between words and the substantial world of things. For the "you" of the poem, words precede individual presence:

> all your hands are verbs,
>
> now you touch worlds and feel their names —

> ...
> the chair and table and book extend from your fingers;
> all your movements
> command these things back to their
> places; a fight against familiarity
> makes me resume my distance.[12]

For "you," words are a bond with the world and the means by which you bring it under imaginative control; but for the fearful "I" of the poem, it is only things that precede presence, not words — words come between self and the world. The world has substance, and the self is an image drawn from it like the print from a cast, and is ephemeral and may perish. The real art is in the stone, not the print.

In a particularly resonant set of lines, MacEwen sums up the relationship between 'I' and the object word:

> I name all things in my room
> and they rehearse their names.

Two sides of a schism. In the first line the personal pronoun predominates; in the second, personality has been annihilated. Things, differentiated, seize control of the sentence as they struggle to accommodate names that are not in their nature, not yet. The "I" could almost be Canada, and "you," the embodiment of a relationship with language we must "become," if we are to endure.

MacEwen argues a thing's true name is to be discovered, not given. The image, then, is more to be trusted than the word; an image reveals more than it says, while words may be concealed or obscured by the thing itself. The most enigmatic image, one which recurs often in MacEwen's work, is the word as image, the hieroglyph. MacEwen recognizes that images offer a mode of transcending the limitations of words, and the hieroglyph in this sense is inherently the most satisfying; the image as object as word, a word which literally contains its own meaning.

The relationship in poetry between word and image is infinitely intriguing. An image is more than its constituent words; it uses words to create an analogue with the object world, and as words contribute to an image, they become merely properties of a complex aesthetic construct. Yet an image is also less than its words, for an image works by defining limitations, while words reach always beyond a particular context,

participating in each instance with the whole of language. An image may be given a specific interpretation, but its words will inevitably confound any particular fixed and finite meaning.

In "The Pride," John Newlove creates disturbingly authentic images of the landscape, alive with the "Indian" past. But those are all stories; only stories. When the exact right words come to us — then, then we will become the Indians and they, us, and the land will be ours and we, its living voice. For the Indian, word and image, place and self, were fused. It is they, then, whom Newlove says are "our true forbears,"[13] waiting to be.

In a more private vision, Margaret Atwood shows an abiding concern for the destructive discrepancies between images and the lived-in world, between images and words as we struggle to sustain our individual presence within the world. This is a major motif running through Atwood's poetry and one of the informing principles of her very fine novel, *Surfacing*. In "This Is a Photograph of Me," she gives it a disconcertingly effective ironic twist. The poem opens onto a landscape in a blurred snapshot. There, in the background, the voice describing it says, under the lake, is her own drowned self. If you look long enough, you will see.[14]

Again: a deconstructing poem. It is, of course, absurd to think she has drowned; and yet, if we accept as real the image of the photograph within the poem, and the image within the image, then how can we not accept that same voice when it declares the image illusory, incomplete. The mind swarms with indeterminate possibilities — Atwood's anomaly, the dispossessed queen at the swarm's dead centre.

Seldom has personal absence in the landscape been revealed so graphically. Yet the concept embodied seems to account for certain peculiarities of Canadian poetry. Could the legendary wanderlust of

Earle Birney and Al Purdy, George Bowering and Gwendolyn MacEwen, be argued as the quest for a place in the world to fit their given language, better than their own? Interestingly, little of their work includes England, where their language originates. Could the penchant by Canadian poets for documentary form, noted by Dorothy Livesay, relate to their need to ground experience in the factual, experience which refuses to be rooted in the language they are bound to use? Facts; to compensate for the absence of reality? Could the splendid achievement of contemporary Canadian poets be the result of their confrontation with invisibility and silence? Atwood makes poetry of doubt. Bowering makes poetry out of his cheerful and lonely refusal to fade or be mute.

It's interesting to consider the implications of living within an alien language, bound by habit and usage to words that deny our being in the world. Even the music of our poetry, the often discordant and sometimes melodic rhythms, could be taken in many instances as an expression, not of the inarticulable truth, but of inarticulability itself. "Anglo-Saxon Street," a 1940s poem by Earle Birney, imitates the structures and syntax, the assonance and aural dialectic, of Old English poetry in order, it seems, to draw ironic contrast between displaced English slum-dwellers and both their Canadian context and their cultural heritage. Beyond that, Birney's rhythms make the point that the language he, the poet, must use is also alien, drawn like these people out of its own place and the culture which made it. These people, in Canada: "soaking bleakly in beer, skittleless."[15]

James Reaney makes much the same point about language with more disarming clarity in one particular quatrain of his poem 'The Bicycle,' which fairly leaps from its fluid context in a lovely imitative jouncing, under the duress of suddenly ragged syntax and rhythm:

> The March wind blows me ruts over,
>   Puddles past, under red maple buds,
> Over culvert of streamling, under
>   White clouds and beside bluebirds.[16]

The echoes of Anglo-Saxon, of language used in such a way as to affirm its alien origin, poetry made from the awkwardness of words, all this conveys the exhilaration of adolescence which is what the bicycle means, in the life of the poem.

All of this, the speculation and the fun, derives from the fact that when a language is taken from its place of origin to another place, it ceases to be the same language. Though the words may seem to be the same, even the relationship of the language to those who use it becomes quite different. Just as the culture of the Old World transported from abroad ceases to be an environment and becomes heritage, nostalgia, the instrument by which a lost world is kept alive, so too does language, transported, change from environment to instrument. In Canada we still celebrate Queen Victoria's birthday. And, equally as anomalous, we speak her English tongue — we use it, but we have trouble living with it, living within it, and recognizing ourselves within it.

English in North America crossed over with the earliest settlers and was the established language awaiting more recent arrivals. It not only preceded individual presence but collective presence as well. Deviations from seventeenth and eighteenth century English in the United States, and from nineteenth century English in Canada, followed in the wake of social and cultural change, rather than in anticipation or paralleling them, as in the Old World.

In England, English and the civilization it expresses, as colour is the expression of pigment, are inextricably related. While language and race are not synonymous, a history of the English language illuminates the history of English civilization and the English people. A history of the English language in Wales, Ireland and Scotland as surely illuminates the history of the Welsh, Irish and Scots, for whom the language superimposed on their own is no less rooted in the lost Indo-European dialect which is their common ancestor. But a history of English in Canada is necessarily little more than an account of linguistic peculiarities, and in the United States, a survey of variant usage. It was not superimposed, but transplanted, for, otherwise, there were only aboriginal languages, which were incomprehensible, or a vast silence. In India and Africa, a history of English might somewhat more closely relate to a history of the peoples involved, but then surely to their oppression, to the collapse of civilizations, not to their development. Throughout the English-speaking world, outside of Britain, people share in common not so much a language, which varies remarkably from place to place, but the condition of living with a language that is not in any true sense their own.

Language is the expression of a particular people through time in a particular place. In each word of a language, as a casual reading of the Oxford English Dictionary will reveal, there is history and geography, culture and the complex origins of a civilization. This holds true as much for prepositions and articles as for verbs and nouns. Each word on its own, amplified by its syntactical potential, speaks history, articulates the landscape, the place and the times of its emergence into common usage, whether the speaker is aware or not of its freighted implications.

In my part of south-eastern Ontario, settled through land grants issued to demobilized soldiers after our war with the Americans in 1814, English is thoroughly entrenched as the only language of the area. Yet the village we live in is called, on old maps, Belle Roche as well as Bell Rock and Bellrock; and on some old maps the Depot River appears as Deep Eau — a lingual compromise. But the word I am coming to is far more historically complex. Locally, people refer to the scrubland with which the district abounds as brulie. It is not a word they hear in school or in town or are ever likely to see in print; but it's a word they grow up with, a part of the local topography, inseparable in their minds from the landscape it signifies. Its origin seems to be French, probably from the fur-traders, many of them *bois-brulés* or "Half-Breeds," who travelled the area for two centuries before settlement. I assume it is derived from the French, but its origin is obscured in usage, and, in usage, is irrelevant. Yet when a farmer around Bellrock speaks of brulie, the past and the present converge. However unwittingly, in a single word he is expressing his rootedness in the place he no doubt never questioned might be real, and his own.

Now, consider that every word in the English language is equally as laden with the history of a people in a particular place. Every single word. Without exception. Walking in the English countryside, as surely as one walks amidst history, one walks among words. Reading English poetry, it is impossible to separate language from the social and historical traditions, the geography and the people, the language contains.

In Canada, this then is what our poetry yearns for: words so right for us they become ours, inseparable in consciousness from the world with which they will merge.

> We wanted to describe the snow
>
> the snow here, at the corner
>
> of the house and orchard
>
> in a language so precise
>
> and secret it was not even
>
> a code, it was snow,
>
> there could be no translation.[17]

The alternative, in this poem by Margaret Atwood, is silence: "Our other dream: to be mute."[18] To be dumb, free from the tyranny of language which holds us apart from the world; or mute, masters of language so precise, effortless and vital that it ceases to obtrude as a separate entity between us and the world — words, unspoken, in which we and the landscape are one.

Confronted by silence, Atwood retreats in her poetry into a medley of wit and despair. Refusing the perfect beauty of her words, she dwells instead on the absence they reveal. On the other side of silence, however, other poets wrench language to make it fit their worlds — "so precise/ and secret… there could be no translation." Bowering, Kroetsch, Marlatt, their words become things, a landscape to live within.

Daphne Marlatt has talked of the capacity for language to provide an environment in poetry so palpable and compelling that we and the poet are re-created together within it. In the prefatory remarks to *What Matters* she states it this way:

> ... i was writing poems, both short- & long-line, composing out of a poetic that taught me language, its 'drift', could ground my experience in the turn of a line as tense, as double-edged, as being felt. In the oscillation of a pun, or a rhyming return, i sensed a narrative that wasn't only mine, though i participated in its telling & was thereby told. Caught up in it, connected, in the body of language where we also live.[19]

To live within "the body of language." The effect of words, as being felt — what a beautifully concentrated and irresolvably ambiguous phrase. Being: verb and noun. Words, being felt. And the condition of being, as felt, through words. Here, as in her poetry, ambiguity struts and stutters with more substance than mere coherence could possibly muster.

Marlatt, Bowering and Kroetsch all write to make words things, as-being-felt. But Marlatt, especially, also insists that words on the page are things in themselves, discrete objects, fully two-dimensional in the two-dimensional world of print. Not as the concrete poet, who builds flat sculptures out of the alphabet; but like Mallarmé, to control, break from the linear tyranny of syntax and logical meaning, to make of the unyielding word an act of initiation, leading into a vision at once private and liberating. While Bowering and Kroetsch also attend to the impact of print on the reader's eye, their poetry shows more concern for what Christopher Fry has called "the intervening landscape between me and you," poet and reader.[20] The word as object is, in their poetry, to continue with Fry, "a coil spring of energy within an architectural shape," released within the reader's consciousness, while reading.

In Kroetsch's poetry, the Husserlian principle to which all three implicitly subscribe, of word and object interpenetrating, intertwined within consciousness, finds its purest and most playful expression. But Kroetsch differentiates between the fusion of word and thing, and the equation of word with thing in practical usage. The latter denies the possibility of poetry, the existence of the poet. In the following passages from the delightful and unsettling sequence of poems called "Seed Catalogue," he rather sardonically puts forth the case against himself, what he as a growing young poet was up against in the illusory practical world where the landscape was presumed to be shaped by a few measures of wire, and words were a distraction from the real work at hand, subduing the land, making it yield. But, as with everything Kroetsch writes, things are not quite what they seem. Seemingly in spite of itself this passage shows, by a brilliant deployment of unadorned language, how the poet ultimately prevails. Despite the equation by his father, separating word from thing ("Son, this is a crowbar"), the poem itself insists, not this is a crowbar, but crowbar, the thing, is crowbar; as fencepost is fencepost.

While identifying the problem, in words which apparently deny imaginative presence, Kroetsch offers its resolution — for the words he uses insist on their own substantiality, word-things which admit the poet as a real presence among them. And us, too.

> Son, this is a crowbar.
>
> This is a willow fencepost.
>
> This is a sledge.
>
> This is a roll of barbed wire.
>
> This is a bag of staples.
>
> This is a claw hammer.
>
> We give form to this land by running
>
> a series of posts and three strands
>
> of barbed wire around a quarter-section.
>
> > First off I want you to take that
> >
> > crowbar and drive 1,156 holes
> >
> > into that gumbo,

> And the next time you want to
> write a poem
> we'll start the haying.
>
> How do you grow a poet?²¹

In this country of Kroetsch's childhood, with difficulty. But after the haying is done, after there's no-one left to do the haying, the poem remains, the story, the song. After the fenceposts have rotted away, and the claw hammer has been lost, perhaps for a poet to find, the words remain, connecting the mind that made them right and the mind that reads, connecting both with a whole list of things and with the people who used them, connecting people to the land. Even in denial there is affirmation, if the words are right. As Bowering says, in a sentence that is a poem on its own:

> To name is
> to begin
> to admit.²²

II

As a prelude to what follows, which is less argument than demonstration, a marvellously conflated line by Irving Layton might serve as a pivotal conceit: "Whatever else poetry is freedom."²³ The precondition of freedom is to be, and Layton in his poetry speaks with honesty and absolute passion from the depths of his being. But it is a persona we read, in his poems — the lover, the rabbi, the clown — an intriguing, appealing, obstreperous, sensitive, joyful, outrageous, and angry poetic device. He comes alive for us through language, not within it. A poet of his own generation, his poetry expresses himself, exposes himself, but refines the living consciousness of the poet, himself, as Joyce might have said, right out of existence. He was the source or, perhaps, catalyst — but to find a poet at the centre, *being within words*, one must look to the aggressive post-modernism of writers such as Bowering and Kroetsch and Marlatt, whose poetry makes of absence a presence, of lack a plenitude, whose words in poetry are more substantial than anything they might be interpreted to mean.

Influenced by American poets more than most of their contemporaries (open to an English which Americans since Whitman and Melville have steadfastly determined to be their own); apparently far more responsive than younger poets in Canada to the philosophical bases of postmodernist thought and aesthetic theory; these three are at the centre, alive in their poems, within words, among words. Sometimes with infuriating disregard for coherence, sometimes with delightful candour, they tempt or invite or demand their reader's presence there as well.

The essence of their anti-romantic exploitation of self is both argued and illuminated in a stanza from the poem 'Farewell', by Frank Davey:

> The only process
> is moving now onward. Causing breath
> to follow breathing. I walk naked
> within my clothes, within
> this hostile air. I write these words
> that someone, will remember me,
> or at least finding me here
> poisoned, burned, loved, unloved, will see words
> moving.[24]

As the reader is made conscious of reading by the poem's art, the words in effect become conscious of being read. They move. And in their movement the reader and the process of reading, the writer and the process of writing, are merged, as lively as atoms in a renegade molecule — the reader reading the reader reading writing the writer writing wrote the reader reading.

The following passages are given with little reference to context. Where whole brief poems are quoted, form and meaning are disregarded except specifically in relation to individual words on the page. Interpretation, explication, *explication de text*, reduces such poetry to an aesthetic arrangement of signs — of no more significance than speculations on where the nude descending Marcel Duchamp's' staircase might have left her clothes, or why. Dance is more than a body in motion to music.

George Bowering might easily be the invention of his own writing. He seems perpetually to be drawing himself into splendid existence through the sheer force of words on paper, sharing with boundless generosity the experience of being with his readers. sharing experience and being with readers. Being together, in words.

Especially in his poetry, Bowering comes alive, not so much through words as among them, sly and vivacious among words — not personality but a vital presence, which the reader shares. His poetry is never about himself, but about being. Consider the following poem, "The Frost":

> But the morning
>
> hoar frost
>
> the breath of cold birds
>
> on trees
>
> the metal of January
>
> in this place.
>
> The crystals, white
>
> hanging from the iron handrail
>
> cold to fingers sweet to taste.[25]

At first it seems the reader has stumbled into a winter scene by William Carlos Williams. So solid do things appear things, they might be Paterson, New Jersey. But this is a landscape alive with more than the breath of cold birds. It is alive with the shifting values of language and the literal presence of the poet's mind. This is no scene, but a drama. The words are precise, specific. No verbs in the poem (unless you count "hanging," a participle with adjectival value). The nouns are things (except January, which is adjectival). An arrangement of things made exact by concrete adjectives. The nouns and adjectives are reciprocal, qualifying each other in tight solid clusters, each pair hinting at narrative. In the first three couplets, personality is elusive, implied by attitude and perspective. In the last two, crystals, the handrail, are cold, sweet, conditions of being, to fingers, to taste. Being is a definite presence, not individuated but sentient and dynamic. Cold and sweet become verbal: that is what crystals and metal do, in this place, in January.

In an excerpt from another winter poem, "The Snow," Bowering transforms words into perceived experience. Despite the syntactical simplicity of the passage, the simple precision of the words taken separately, he goes beyond evoking response to the poem, he brings the reader to life within the scene, the scene and words inseparable in the reader's experience from perception itself:

> The snow
> does not clasp
>
> it falls away
> from foot steps
>
> a light spray
> of energy, soundless
>
> as the crackling
> of the sun.[26]

This poem rises from passivity into palpable action. The observing consciousness which notes the snow "does not clasp/ it falls away," is represented in the poem only by an adjectival foot, an absence, the shape of imprints. And yet, out of this an image gathers force, then overwhelms. Each word means in itself, and the clear syntax draws them forward in a sequence, the music building, towards completion. But with a slight shift, suddenly the image surges out of control — it transforms from an image of the landscape, the external world, into one of perception, of the senses fused:

> a light spray
> of energy, soundless
> as the crackling
> of the sun

A brilliant dazzling witty image: not of sight or sound but an implosion of the senses through words, an experience of oneself experiencing, beyond the capacity of words to describe. Bowering exploits a created tension between conventional and contextual meaning, turning words upon themselves, to re-create in the reader's mind an instantaneous and inarticulable experience as if it were happening as read (and it is); the reader alive in the poem's world (rather than in the poet's world, as with Layton).

In the following poem from *Between the Sheets*, Bowering attends explicitly to the capacity for words to reduce "personality" to inconsequence, while simultaneously rendering things real and the self, substantial.

> Against Description
> I went to the blackberries
> on the vine
>
> They were blackberries
> on the vine

> They were
>
> Blackberries
>
> Black berries.[27]

To begin: a rather simple lyric, beginning with "I"; a singular action of no significance. I went to. But "they," they had substance, they were blackberries. And they were alive. This is their distinguishing characteristic: they were "on the vine." They "were" what they were, blackberries being blackberries. Past tense. Past tense, at least, until the irrepressible poet sneaks in; asserts himself. "Black/ berries." A perception; insight. Black. Berries. As things change in the poem from objects of description to word-objects, being-in-words, the poet is transformed from an ephemeral "I," a pronoun, into the very act of perceiving, a verbal presence. As much there, in the final couplet, as black/ berries themselves.

Robert Kroetsch writes poetry, it seems, to be free of words. In a good-natured way, his poetry follows the austere architectural dictum of Mies van der Rohe that "less is more." The fewest words, placed perfectly, reach farther, touch more, probe deeper, transcend language, become experience, more so than a flood of words enhanced by the most fluent orchestration. As we are contained by language, to be most truly ourselves we must struggle to be free of the limitations it imposes upon us, upon our consciousness of self and the world, self in the world. This, the poet might achieve by shaping words on the page, the way sculpture shapes air. Through the space among words, freedom from the tyranny of their limitations.

It is as much by the spatial arrangement of words as things, as by their temporal flow, that we and the poet are freed, to become real. If words remain words, they are only words. But Kroetsch demands that poet and reader and poem are one, fused for the time of the poem in a unity of being. The poem frees us from words, as words, to be. Being there, in-the-world. *Dasein*.

Consider: the entire fourth stanza in a poem from the sequence "The Criminal Intensities of Love as Paradise." (Surely there is a complete and vast poem in that title alone.) The poem is called "Standing Near a Waterfall":

> bent & the break
> and then comes
> after after
> the reaching sea.[28]

Forcefully, and rarely done in such a panache of vital obscurity, Kroetsch acknowledges that we the readers are alive in the world. We are not creatures of the poet's imagination as Eliot or Layton implicitly would have it. We have seen waterfalls. We exist. Listen: words, and a waterfall.

> bent & the break
> and then comes
> after after
> the reaching sea.

The water is bent. We know that from our own experience with waterfalls. The flat surface arcs away from the horizontal; heavy, inexorable. It doesn't drop or plummet, it is bent — "& the break," smoothness shatters. Between bent and the break, not even an "and." Only an ampersand. Break is not a consequence of bent, in our perception of the scene, to be aligned in a sequence of causality by a co-ordinating conjunction. Bent and break are visually part of the same action, inseparable. The visual ampersand, a non-word, confounds the linearity of syntax, allows for the simultaneity of events. But the second line of the stanza begins with "and." Now, from the waterfall, "then comes" — and Kroetsch's readers have all seen for themselves the water roiling in heaving pools below, and in consequence of, a waterfall. Water gathering power and form, moving away. And suddenly, in the refusal of image our minds fill with images — as "after after" gathers divers landscape into simultaneous presence: after, after, until the water joins "the reaching sea." The sea reaching in, beyond the landscape of after and after, to the water breaking from the fall; the sea reaching out, the broad reach of the sea bent over the surface of the earth.

In reading such lines, one becomes aware that most poetry describes landscape as if readers were blind. Kroetsch assumes we have seen, and uses our experience in the world to play with us among the words, to affirm that we are as real as the words and the world they contain.

The following is from the same sequence, a four-line stanza from the poem "And dreamers, Even Then, if Dreaming."

>   eerie & enter
>   if
>   & the pale garden
>   chill as white.[29]

George Bowering has described literature as "telling the story as it happens." The immediacy of these lines as process, virtually committing the reader to creation as the words struggle towards coherence, the poem not in the words but in the struggle — literature is, here, reading the story as it happens. The story is happening not just while, but because, it is being read. In the haunting narrative born of these four lines, the reader's dream and the poet's, merge:

>   eerie.

Without a capital, "eerie," vulnerable to the margin; isolated by blank space and an ampersand; a story on its own, a word trembling with stories. The sound alone, a story;

>   & enter

The soft e drawn out to an abrupt halt. A command: enter. The inexorability of action in a dream. Or an invitation: the eerie draws inwards; enter —

    if

on a line alone. Unadorned with cap or punctuation. Following hard on the previous line, followed by space. "If" becomes verbal, the beginning and the centre of a maelstrom of possibilities. If …

    & the pale garden.

No matter what, at the end of if, a garden. Paradise regained? Pale! Death. Pale garden; spectral, frozen,

    chill as white.

The refusal of "chill" to be a part of speech! Insistence on "white" as a noun, a thing!

Words, forcing confrontation with the dream-horror they cannot express. Words, making the story happen, within us. Our story; the poem as story. Consciousness struggling towards coherence while paradoxically the words move towards disturbing ambiguity and the extinction of personality. An anomaly within a dream, "if dreaming."

Kroetsch also picks up on the poetic possibilities of blackberries, crediting his interest to the French poet, Francis Ponge (on whose work Marlatt did an M.A. dissertation).

    … If blackberries can be
    blackberries, I reasoned, by a kind of analogy,
    lemons can, I would suppose, be lemons.

    Such was not the case.[30]

With characteristically self-deprecating good humour, Kroetsch is apparently overwhelmed by words, reduced to inanity, a casualty of thought, of thinking.

"Blackberries." Things and word. Inseparable. Blackberries are blackberries are blackberries. Echoes of Gertrude Stein. Real language. But the reasoning "I," witty, speculating, intrudes. Lemons, objects of speculation, separate from the word, the tentative poet between. "Lemons" is only a word and the poet, now, is lost in the emptiness of such/was/not/the/case. Yet the creating consciousness which shaped all the words upon the page and plays among them, especially among the empty ones, is undeniably a presence in the poem, as are we, who share his sport.

In a beautiful poem called "Daphne Marlatt," George Bowering suggests development in the impact of Marlatt's poetry. He is driven to metaphor:

> I always thought the words snapt from
> her one by one, twigs the birds rested
> on & when they flew someone snapt them
> off.
> ...
> how could you follow them without breaking
> your tongue.
> Even then no one knew she was pisst off,
> she didnt know because women didnt really
> know & she made poems that were questions
> stretcht out in space, ready to be snapt off.
> Now you should hear her shout. It
> is as if a stick had come alive in your hand.[31]

Hearing some of Marlatt's short-line poems aloud is like reading the script for a mime-show. The experience may be interesting, but it

68   Finding the Right Words

is incomplete. To know really what is going on, we must see the words played out on the page. Marlatt insists that words are literally spatial — not merely a visual cue as to how they might be heard (as by convention poetry generally appears in written form; pause, breathe, stress; the music of meaning), but spatial, things upon paper. And the words sometimes skitter about, among the commas and slashes and dashes. And sometimes they remain utterly enigmatic, objects on a stage around which the action takes place, shapers of the action by their presence but as bereft of singular meaning as an unexplained column of stone or of silk reaching from the stage high into the flies.

This does not mean Marlatt is unaware of the music. As she explained to Bowering in an interview published in *Open Letter*:

> Any word is a physical body. Its body is sound, so
> it has that absolute literal quality that sound has,
> which connects it up with sounds around it. And
> then, it has that other aspect, which is meaning ...
> You move out from the word to a shape, which is
> the whole poem.[32]

You move out from the word. It is the sound of words, as the eye hears, that gives them a third dimension, a physical body, in the reader's mind.

Consider: the stanza opening her poem called "ardour's":

> fire light
> livd in from
> within.[33]

The arrangement of words does not confute their sequential meaning, but it draws each word out of context in its turn, lets it be an object, almost a poem in itself. The weight of each word is felt. Normally, the weight of words is severely modified by syntax and contextual meaning: firelight/lived in/from within. But here, Marlatt

John Moss 69

separates "fire" and "light" on the first line, giving them equal value. Instead of one word qualifying and limiting the other, she allows each to stand for a variety of possibilities limited only by the reader's experience and imagination. Fire. Light. Two phenomena, forced into a relationship by their isolation following the poem's title (which, however, in different print and elevated, keeps drawing at the poem, drawing the word "fire" away from literal meaning into a syntactical context: ardour's fire [is] light lived in from within. Fire as metaphor. But arranged as it is in the poem, the fire is real, a burning.).

The second line curiously gives each word, livd/in/from, equal weight and value. Dropping the e from 'livd', Marlatt allows a hint of the word 'livid' to enter, but of far more consequence she forces attention onto the ascending I-v-d, soft-to-hardness, presence of the word, and separates it decisively from "in." Sense, in turn, demands caesura after "in" and before "from." Being on a line of its own, despite following the word "from," "within" is forced to maintain a prepositional value. From within, where "within" takes on the value of a noun, suggests merely a location, more or less anatomical. But "from/within, paired prepositions, opens towards opposing possibilities. And in/from/within, which by the spatial arrangement we are forced to read separately, each word a presence on its own, suggests experience without limit. Again:

>   ardour's
>   fire light
>   livd in from
>   within

Marlatt demands our presence within the poem. She shapes the world; we enter and take on substance the way we might, enthralled with a Miro sculpture.

In the following few lines from the poem called "largely sea," the words clash at first in a dissonance of meaning, syntax and sound, then settle into a strange and haunting coherence before breaking again into discord:

> at, eye
>
> cloud your
>
> silence casts
>
> a light
>
> spray sea
>
> islands us
>
> out of the waves'
>
> crash we stand
>
> stranded.[34]

Following the title words, "largely sea," the first six words in the first three lines seem to dart about in a manic rush in a search for meaning generated by the proximity of the words, shrewdly shattered by their syntactical discontinuity:

> at, eye
>
> cloud your
>
> silence casts.

The words try to mean but they cannot quite connect. Then suddenly, "a light." The mind circles — "your/ silence casts/ a light." "At": direction/-place. "Eye": perception, a mood received. But a light in the poem also leads, anticipates: "a light/spray." The spray, the "sea" it "islands us," we stand "out of the waves' reach, "crash we stand / stranded."

Coherence is only an illusion. Yet listen to the music of this second part as it builds towards substance:

> a light
>
> spray sea
>
> islands us
>
> out of the waves'
>
> crash we stand
>
> stranded.

The near-rhyme solidifies: islands, stand, stranded. The consonants harden; and the sibilants harden too, from the long sigh of spray and sea, through the dying hiss of waves'/ crash, they gather into the stark complaint, stand/ stranded. But the music is also due to syntactical distortion: "islands us," for example; both words have different sound values here than grammatical convention would normally grant them. And to the eye — poems within the poem. The eye makes a poem of the isolated elusive enigmatic title; and a poem from the spatial pairing of "a light/… stranded".

What at first might seem self-indulgent in Marlatt's poetry, so fiercely does it sometimes resist our efforts to penetrate the surface, will eventually be felt as we enter the poem, become the poem, with all our senses working, to be the result of her determination to create a theatre of words on the deep white spaces of the page.

Berry-picking must seem a Canadian obsession, when you think of how often it appears in Canadian poems — the best-known example is probably Irving Layton's, on himself as the victim of poetry while his beloved picks on, real in the world, her lips "redder than the raspberries." Marlatt's contribution to the genre, the first lines of a poem she names "to, carry thru," is characteristically more difficult to paraphrase. The poem begins:

> to/
>
> go pick black
>
> berries & raz
>
> berries,

>   she sd the
>
> contact high in
>
> vites rambles well. [35]

"To/" Everything follows as a consequence of "to." A directional preposition, or, more likely, the first half of an open infinitive. "Go.". The completion of the infinitive, or an imperative, or even a plea for sharing. Then: words spaced as objects tumble forward in a sequence of animation and meaning — briefly. Movement is halted abruptly with the drop in a line and the disintegration of sense. Each word in the last two lines is a sound-rune, separate from the others, an object on its own — relating only through inference, through conjecture; the way objects in a field relate to one another only in the consciousness which perceives them. A tree, a stone, a road.

And then there is space (the end of a stanza?), and the eye leaps back for reference, something to root the mind in, a structure of simultaneous meanings that will yield coherence. Instead, syntax breaks apart and the word-objects lie scattered on their own, each as real in the field of consciousness as the others: "black" as real and substantial as "pick" or "berries."

In her long-line poems, Marlatt creates an illusion of greater coherence, but the same austere integrity is at work. The poem is not a text of meaning, nor convoluted metaphor. It is an arrangement of possibilities. It must be entered, experienced from within, as we, reading, become the poem that she was, writing it. Marlatt makes poems in which to lose and find yourself, reading them.

>   Words, vacuous as
>
> kites. Race the air currents tug at strings for opening
>
> mouths, gulp, air tails are laid in. As i'm jealous of her,
>
> she-fish, her ease. Myself divest of aches, pain, Rain's

a festival the way it gentles us now. We bend in to see
the sky's immense racks of rainwear,

Naked our skins swim
this element, those kites, paper, shouting the wet air.[36]

III

Bowering, Kroetsch, Marlatt share the common influence of certain American poets, but even more they share a concern for the reader as a participating presence within their poetry, which lends to their work an air of distinctively Canadian postmodernism. William Carlos Williams has taught them all a literal precision, through words unobscured by metaphor or metaphysics, through which things occupy space in imagination. The three of them as a matter of course accept in their poetry Charles Olson's ideas of composition by field, where word/objects on the page shape in the mind a landscape as real as the world around us. More real. But they also write directly out of their experience of themselves in the world as Canadians. They make it possible to live within the Canadian landscape, "in a language so precise ... there could be no translation." To be, in the world; to be Canadian.

WORKS CITED

1. Margaret Atwood, "Two-Headed Poems," in *Two-Headed Poems* (Toronto: Oxford
2. University Press, 1978); iv, p 64; ix, p 70.
3. Archibald Lampman in *Canadian Anthology*, ed. Carl F Klinck and Reginald E. Watters (Toronto: Gage Educational Publishing, 1974, Third edition); "Winter Uplands," p 133; 'Winter Evening', p 132.

4. A.M. Klein, "Portrait of the Poet as Landscape," in *Canadian Anthology*, vi, pp 347–8.
5. Margaret Avison, "Butterfly Bones; or Sonnet Against Sonnets," in *Canadian Anthology*, p 449.
6. Jay Macpherson, "The Fisherman," in *Canadian Anthology*, p 518.
7. David Helwig, "The Bugbear," in *Canadian Anthology*, p 557.
8. "Progressive Insanities of a Pioneer," in *The Animals in That Country*, Margaret Atwood, (Toronto, Oxford University Press, 1968), p 39.
9. "Two-Headed Poems," vi, p 67.
10. Konrad Fiedler, quoted by Sheila Watson in "Gertrude Stein: The Style Is the Machine," in *Sheila Watson: A Collection, Open Letter*, Third Series, No (Winter, 1974–75), p 170.
11. A. J. M. Smith, "To Hold in a Poem," in *Canadian Anthology*, p 273.
12. John Newlove, "The Pride," in *Canadian Anthology*, vi, vii, p 562.
13. Gwendolyn MacEwen, "Poems in Braille," in *Canadian Anthology*, i, v, p 572.
14. "The Pride," p 563.
15. Margaret Atwood, "This Is a Photograph of Me," in *Canadian Anthology*, pp 364–5.
16. Earle Birney, "Anglosaxon Street," in *Canadian Anthology*, p 296.
17. James Reaney, "The Bicycle," in *Canadian Anthology*, p 499.
18. "Two-Headed Poems," v, pos.
19. "Two-Headed Poems," xi, p 75.
20. Daphne Marlatt, *What Matters: Writing 1968–70* (Toronto: Coach House Press, 1980), prefatory note.
21. Christopher Fry, "Looking for a Language," address at Great St Mary's Church, Cambridge, UK, 20 November 1983.
22. "Robert Kroetsch, "Seed Catalogue," in *Field Notes* (Don Mills: General Publishing, 1981), p 58.
23. I credit Bowering with the phrasing, but the arrangement is mine, a sort of found poem, lifted from I'm not sure where.

24. Irving Layton, "Whatever Else Poetry Is Freedom," in *Canadian Anthology*, p 394.
25. Frank Davey, "Farewell," in *Selected Poems: The Arches* (Vancouver: Talonbooks, 1980),
26. George Bowering, 'The Frost', in *Touch/selected poems 1960-70* (Toronto: McClelland and Stewart, 1971), p 44.
27. George Bowering, 'The Snow', in *Touch*, p 32.
28. George Bowering, 'Against Description', in *West Window* (Toronto: General Publishing, 1982) p. 135.
29. Robert Kroetsch, "Standing Near a Waterfall", in the sequence, "The Criminal Intensities of Love as Paradise', in *Field Notes*, p 135.
30. Robert Kroetsch, "And Dreamers, Even Then, if Dreaming", in "Criminal Intensities."
31. Robert Kroetsch, "Sketches of a Lemon," in *Field Notes*, p 124.
32. George Bowering, "Daphne Marlatt," in *West Window*, p 43-
33. Daphne Marlatt, interviewed by George Bowering in "Given This Body,", in *Open Letter*, Fourth Series, No. 3 (Spring, 1979), pp 69-70.
34. Daphne Marlatt, "ardours," in *Net Work Selected Writings* (Vancouver: Talonbooks, 1980), p. 85.
35. Daphne Marlatt, 'largely sea," in *Net Work*, p 79.
36. Daphne Marlatt, "to, carry thru," in *Net Work*, p 32.
37. Daphne Marlatt, "Getting there," in *Net Work*, p 81.

HAUNTING OURSELVES:
ATWOOD AND THE OPEN EYE

In the spring of 2005, with doctoral student Tobi Kozakewich, I organized a conference on Margaret Atwood at the University of Ottawa. When we put out the call for papers, we were flooded with proposals, many of which were accepted and subsequently went into a voluminous book called Margaret Atwood: The Open Eye. *(University of Ottawa Press, 2006). Tobi and I both contributed essays, as did my daughter Laura who was and is a professor at the University of British Columbia. My piece, here, has been edited, amended, and altered to include most of my introductory essay. In the same year, I was invited by Christine Evain and Reena Khandpur to write an introduction to their remarkably detailed and insightful interview with Margaret Atwood, published in a series called* Canadensis *by the Université de Nantes. It, also, has been included, and likewise has been edited, amended, and altered, I hope for the better.*

I

It is inconceivable to imagine a collection of short stories in English without Margaret Atwood's representation. It is highly unlikely a poetry anthology would exclude her work, whether it's of Canadian poetry or a survey from Beowulf to the present. Any canon of the novels of our time, in genres as diverse as speculative fiction, parody, social realism, and historical metafiction, would include an Atwood title or two. There can be no consideration of Canadian literary criticism without allusion or deference to Atwood's commentaries. There could be no discussion of Canadian cultural politics during the past fifty years that did not centre on the contributions of Margaret Atwood and her partner, Graeme Gibson. In any discourse on Canadian identity, she provides key terms of reference, maps and mirrors, reassurance and reproach. She has iconic status in Canada and is our greatest emissary abroad, not because she is characteristically Canadian but because as a Canadian, she is wholly herself, her work and her vision impossible to ignore. She shows in turn of phrase, delineation of character, twist of plot, subversion of generic conventions, how we connect, all of us to each other, if sometimes through the differences that define us.

For all that, how little we know her. Behind the authorial voice and the public persona, behind the cultural edifice is a woman of singular talent and drive and achievement. Perhaps it is the commodification of her celebrity that protects her. We know the name, Margaret Atwood, but the person, when she writes, writes alone — I imagine in a room teeming with voices and ghosts. We hear these voices as they filter through, the voices of literature, voices of the past, memories of bubble gum and great events; we see the ghosts of our literary forebears, the ghosts of our human trek through the ages, ghosts of our childhood, of our future, of our dreams.

We could become lost trying to know Margaret Atwood. She lives like the rest of us in a labyrinth of libraries that interconnect, her mind a treasury of infinite possibilities. Unlike the rest of us, she walks through those libraries, along those corridors, plucking books from the shelves, shaping their contents for others to share. She has the gift to be everywoman and to be unique, to give us access to universal particularities through her words, shaped on paper in startling and memorable design. We know all about her, for she shares what she hears, what she reads, what she imagines and schemes; and we do not know her at all.

II

In the twenties, Robert McAlmon gave his memoir of Paris the perfect title *Being Geniuses Together*. Margaret Atwood gave her most recent novel the unwieldy title *Oryx and Crake*. Interestingly, *Oryx and Crake*, after a while, seemed inevitable. As the novel embedded itself in the reader's consciousness and in the public mind, it became wonderfully allusive. McAlmon's title was the best part of his book. Atwood's book has now made her title seem perfect.

Margaret Atwood does this; she says things that, once said, seem inevitable. Her fiction, as well as her poetry and essays, displays that peculiar kind of originality that seems to coalesce our fragmented experience into coherent patterns that resonate inside the skull. Critics as critics are sometimes unnerved by her familiarity. Readers, including critics, find in even her most ominous and sinister writing something reassuring. For example, take "A Women's Issue" (listed portentously in the table of contents of her *Selected Poems 1966–1984* as "A woman's issue"). The images are gut-wrenchingly horrific; they are of abuses to women "we" all know about and try not to. In their rendering as poetry, we are forced to confront them directly, but there is something profoundly positive in how she invites us, forces us, to share in the poem's outrage, to recognize the absurdity of moral relativism, that sometimes culturally sanctioned things are inherently evil. Although our recognition of this means we're not evil, it still means that we're complicit. It is familiar territory: an unnerving blend of ambivalence and certainty.

III

> You fit into me
>
> like a hook into an eye
>
> a fish hook an open eye (Atwood, *Power Politics* 1)

Quite possibly, Margaret Atwood dreads the thrill of three decades past, finding her open eye poem transcribed from raw nerves onto paper — it must haunt her like Earle Birney's "David," which became so much a signature epic that readers forgave him for murder, while the smashed and implacable David lurched through the years in pursuit, until Birney died. Who says it's by our lack of ghosts we're haunted? Birney said it, of course, in a poem, but he was wrong. We live in a world teeming with ghosts; however, we don't always see them. Margaret Atwood apparently does. Reading her, we find ourselves haunting ourselves in her words.

Much has been said and will be said about Margaret Atwood's writing, about her themes and motifs and their ramifications; much has been and will be implied about the woman herself, based on research and gossip and perhaps on intimate insights through astral projection, but I would like to talk briefly about words. Most work on Atwood is concerned with what Saussure called *langue*; I would like to speak on *parole*. A brief sentence will do to suggest how language in Atwood's jurisdiction may incarcerate the reader and still set us free. On the front cover of a book by Alice Munro is a terse statement, credited to Margaret Atwood, that declares, "These stories are real as kitchens." Now, when I read that, a generation ago, I felt I was in the presence of genius, perhaps more than one. And the interesting thing about "These stories are real as kitchens" is that I have no idea what it means.

Well, I do and I don't. I've been in kitchens and I've read stories, and I can appreciate the copula that binds them together. I am also aware of the differences on a literal level: phenomenologically, stories and kitchens are mutually exclusive. The terms of the equation are arbitrary, their connection both self-evident and absurd — but that's their impossible alliance, that's the hook. And we know about the startling efficacy of Atwood and hooks — how, when you think you've caught the glory, you've also fished up something unexpected, like a drowned walleye with a ring in its gut, or an old rubber boot with the remains of a foot inside.

The refusal of her brief description to settle into meaning excites the mind on a visceral plane. Of course, you know what the words mean; these stories are as real as kitchens, it's as simple as that. You just do not know how to put what she means into words; you end up repeating her words. They are your words, their meaning inside you assimilated as a quality of the things she is talking about — kitchens and stories by Alice Munro.

Atwood has invented the postmodern analogue: her statement is neither metaphor nor metonym; Munro's stories are not like kitchens, nor are they kitchen-like. It is not a statement redolent with symbolic possibilities; it is not a trope of any sort. It does not invite interpretation. It is placidly hostile to what used to be called explication and is now euphemistically described as close reading. I have no more idea what her sentence means on a figurative level than on the literal. But the ineluctable rightness of her analogue — its dazzling subversive resistance to rational explanation — is wondrously generous.

IV

I have been acquainted with Margaret Atwood for almost five decades, the first one from a distance, as I listened to her read, back when we were young and geniuses together. I think I remember her reading at the Bohemian Embassy in the early sixties, in Toronto, back when I was falling in love twice a month, and, enthralled with her words, I wrote bad poetry in weak imitation. She might deny having read at the Bohemian Embassy. It doesn't matter; my memory is not about to collapse from an excess of truth. Over the years our lives intersected now and then. I grew to admire this woman who has become strangely iconic, strange because she remains one of us, the slightly eccentric neighbour in the apartment next door who might be clairvoyant or simply is able to see through adjoining walls. And yet she is a formidable high-flier, totally at ease in the grand circus of international literature.

As years turned into eras, I came to realize was her remarkable generosity, not only to readers but to causes, to friends, and to fellow writers. I discovered in Margaret Atwood's contributions to the Writer's Union of Canada and to Pen International, as well as in other public causes whose sympathies I share, the stunning bounty of her sometimes obstreperous spirit. But what has been most exciting as her peer, in age, if nothing else, is having been able to follow the wondrously subversive and irrepressible social conscience in her writing as each new work appeared, and to recognize as I gained the soul and wit to appreciate such things, the evolving aesthetic of her creative vision. She has grown marvellously and yet, as Eliot observed about literature in general, this has not been a matter of improvement, for who would presume to improve on *Surfacing* or *The Journals of Susanna Moodie*? It has been a matter of shifting, refining, and developing, of keeping pace with her own and outpacing her readers' maturing sensibilities.

Teaching her work at the university level, I have watched as her name has become a rubric for what she has written, in the same way that Shakespeare and Austen stand for their canons more than for the man or woman behind them. "Atwood" means the novels and poems and essays, as well as the deftly deployed persona in the midst of public controversy, but it is also a label for feisty attitudes, a clear moral vision, devastating wit, and a genius for making words mean more than they say. She has not fallen into the Hemingway trap, reprised by Leonard Cohen, in which the persona displaces the person, nor into the Virginia Woolf trap, reprised by Michael Ondaatje, in which the person appears as her achievement's creation. The personality of Margaret Atwood is forthright and steadfast, while Atwood, the work, is a creation of remarkable and diverse complexity.

I have taught Atwood to university students since the late sixties, sometimes in a context of Canadian literature and sometimes in courses on genre, courses shaped by critical theory, courses on themes in world literature, courses on Arctic narrative, courses on authorial subversions. I have never taught a course solely on Atwood, but she has a way of dominating the courses in which she appears. This is because she has a knack for making the ineffable effable, for wringing the most astonishing meaning from words, for conspiring with readers to share a moral perspective on even the most arcane or unimaginable issues (imagined, of course); she has the capacity to be succinct about the wondrously complex and to expose complexity in the apparently simple. She creates memorable lines and memorable images, she creates memorable characters, she creates memorable visions of our world as it might have been, might be, and might possibly become. And perhaps the most telling aspect of Margaret Atwood's writing, from a pedagogical point of view: people love to talk about it. There is no other writer who connects to the reader on such a personal basis, on so many planes. She makes us more aware of ourselves.

V

I once said to Margaret Atwood that there is a strong postmodern tendency in her writing. She told me I was wrong. Being an academic I assumed she therefore did not understand my point. I now suspect she did. I have often been disconcerted to discover that she has my ideas before I think of them. Her denial of postmodernity was very postmodern. The crux of the postmodern analogue is not meaning but sense. It is this that resonates through much of her poetry, this refusal to explain that allows us to know, and it is in much of her fiction. Words are arranged; images, characters, and events are articulated in ways that refuse interpretation, invite speculation, and affirm the brilliance of her narrative and poetic imagination. They open, in the tension between various terms, the doors of perception, avenues in a private garden which fork and converge like Borges' fiction, and shift like a staircase at Hogwarts.

VI

In a country where, at Tim Hortons, customers vie with each other to hold doors open for other customers who are laden with hot coffee and doughnuts, and courtesy is considered a defining national characteristic, which translates to an international reputation for being terminally decent, Margaret Atwood reminds readers that Canada has put forward the most ferocious and committed military forces in two world wars, that we play hockey with brute panache, that we are a primary refuge for the misbegotten and dispossessed of the world, and she does this without writing of war, sport, or sanctuary, or of valour, vigour, or virtue. Atwood is the quintessentially Canadian writer because she takes Canada for granted. Much like the rest of the world. And yet she writes so precisely of human being, massaging and excoriating the human heart, that Canada as the usual backdrop, in all its historic, social, and cultural complexity, becomes as "real as kitchens." It is too easy as Canadians to ignore Canada; it is too easy for the rest to confuse the quiet, determined, and sometimes righteous Canadian for merely a citizen of the world. What may seem transparent and of little consequence, she etches with diamond motifs.

Margaret Atwood is the most Canadian of writers, and yet among the most accessible to others (in Canada, we avoid the American habit of describing "others" as aliens or foreigners). In terms of Canadian literature and culture, Atwood changed everything. She chose to play on the world's stage, when other Canadians were content doing summer stock. Or disguising themselves as Americans (Mary Pickford, Morley Callaghan, Leonard Cohen, Joni Mitchell, Saul Bellow), or misplaced Brits (Raymond Massey, Mazo de la Roche, Robertson Davies). Or being appropriated (Alice Munro by New York; Elizabeth Smart by London; Mavis Gallant by Paris). Or insisting on non-

Canadian status, residents resisting citizenship (Malcolm Lowry, John Irving). Canadians are traditionally diffident, not lacking in confidence but reticent about being noticed. This is the way our colonial past plays out against a backdrop of forests and rivers, the orchestra at our feet burbling with revolutionary cant; much different from Australia, where settlement rings a desiccated continent, or New Zealand. where people of the ocean never fully relinquished their grip on the land. We are American enough to be bold, and New World enough to be quiet about it. (We export comedians to the States, where their chief attribute is disengaged candour.)

Our earliest writers were British, because we were. Several, most notably Frances Brooke and Rosanna Leprohon, observed worlds colliding, French and English, Old World and New. A few, like Major John Richardson, tried to form bridges between Walter Scott and James Fenimore Cooper, British historical and American frontier romance. Others wrote back to the centre: women such as the Strickland sisters, men such as Hearne and Galt. A few, like Thomas Haliburton, rode success back to the ancestral homeland, or like Charles Roberts and Bliss Carman, used it as a vehicle to escape south of the border. For the most part, those who played at home stayed at home. Early twentieth century Canadian writing was of little interest outside Canada; perhaps less, within. Summer stock; straw-hat players. Stephen Leacock was the exception that proved the rule.

In the post-war period (WW Il), when the Empire was reduced to an island and the United States seemed on the rim of a vortex, swirling first around McCarthy and then Malcolm X, writers like Hugh MacLennan, and, with more conviction, Margaret Laurence, declared Canada was enough. Some fine writing made its way into the public consciousness: writers including Sheila Watson, Ethel Wilson, Sinclair Ross, Ernest Buckler, Al Purdy, Graeme Gibson, Marian Engel, wrote for a Canadian readership, or at least defined their readers in Canadian terms. A few, like Mordecai Richler, Mavis Gallant, and W.P. Kinsella wrote as if Canada were a beloved embarrassment, even slightly ridiculous.

Out of this insular confidence, signified by the founding of the House of Anansi and the establishment of The New Canadian

Library, a new kind of writer emerged in whom Canada was an intrinsic condition of being, yet for whom the larger world held illimitable possibilities of access. Writers such as Margaret Atwood, Carol Shields, Jane Urquhart, Robert Kroetsch, Michael Ondaatje, Rohinton Mistry, Yann Martel, swarmed the bookshelves of Dublin and Tokyo, London, Berlin, Paris, and Melbourne. Particularities of experience from a Canadian perspective assumed universal significance, while peculiarities of human experience attained astonishing illumination from a Canadian perspective.

Chief among these deconstructing postcolonial cosmopolitans was Margaret Atwood; this, in good part, because she has shown the Canadian perspective to be multivariate, polyphonous, and wondrously unstable. No one else shifts with such facility from poetry to prose, gothic to historical fiction, romance to realism, nightmare dystopias to chilling evocations of childhood, strident polemics to diffident manifestoes of collective identity. No one else displays such rage, nor such wit and affection; no one else moves so casually from the depths to the surface, back and forth, as if the divine comedy were, indeed, an appalling joke, to be endured only if we get the punchline.

There may be writers more courageous than Atwood. Amnesty International, PEN International, would bear that out. Dissidents in jail, diarists in bedlam, might face more terrifying moments than she could imagine. But her writing, that messy art form that above all others connects minds and the world, is singular in its commitment to the ineluctable sanctity of human consciousness and the human spirit, no matter how silly or depraved or ignorant or frightened we are. Writing from the comforts of middle-class Canadian privilege, fully aware that what might seem a majority perspective is in actuality a dangerously narrow and limiting point of view, she writes of matters and in ways that emphasize the differences we so casually erase in our impositions of cultural imperialism, our assumptions of connected experience. Her writing challenges the snares and delusions of social equality. It takes great courage to be an empowered subversive, and great wit, and a prodigious facility with language and a wicked imagination.

Atwood upsets her readers. She disturbs our social equilibrium, wreaks havoc with our sense of ourselves, invokes moral vertigo, makes us laugh in all the wrong places, makes us weep without pity, often at the same time. It is easy to write pathos or irony, the residual echoes of tragedy and comedy. It is very difficult to bring them to the front simultaneously. Samuel Beckett did it and knew he did it but did not know how he did it or whether he did it by accident or design. Margaret Atwood does it and she does it by design and she knows exactly how she does it and she does it well. She engages us to enrage us, to change us, and to make us smile.

Perhaps no other writer could be so amusing while invoking the end of the world. From her earliest poetry to *Oryx and Crake*, she plays reason and emotion against each other with Miltonic intensity, she defies the rules of genre, she strikes up supratextual alliances between writer and reader. She once told me defiantly she is no postmodernist. She was so wrong. She is, of course, the consummate postmodernist, but like Leonard Cohen turning down the Governor General's Award, Canada's highest literary honour, or Winston Churchill, surely with an ear for posterity, spurning a peerage, she resists titles that bind. Nor is she a feminist, a postcolonialist, a realist, a visionary, because she is all of them. Some writers tell funny stories, create comic poems; she subverts pathos and confounds irony with devastating wit. Some writers tell sad tales, with their poetry move us to tears; she adds the manic glint, the cosmic jest, that make terror and chaos familiar. If literature is a frenetic mixture of sideshow, three-ring circus, and the Circus Maximus, she is the Cirque de Soleil.

She speaks as a Canadian, as if that were not vaguely embarrassing, and writes to the world. She has given voice to people mute not through tyranny but as the legacy of imperial condescension, colonial struggle, and postcolonial privilege. She makes a lifelong engagement with poetry of vital concern, the engaged autonomy of the artist a matter of public record. She is fiercely clever, sometimes cranky, exceptionally generous; she is perennially precocious, prescient, wise. There is no writer, living or dead, who turns a phrase with such ironic precision and wit. She is us; we, her.

LABYRINTHS AND JIG-SAW PUZZLES

This piece brings together writings from several sources, the principal one being a paper delivered to a conference, Canada Ieri e Oggi, *held near Brindisi in April 1990 and subsequently published by the Associazione Italiana di Studi Canadesi. It was called "The Feminization of Narrative Form." I also draw heavily on an essay published in* The Paradox of Meaning, Turnstone, Winnipeg 1999 *as "Mrs. Bentley's Gender"; and on an essay published in* The Journal of Canadian Studies, *"Gender Notes: Wilderness Unfinished," Summer 1998. Delving into the depths of Canadian literature, from the earliest to what was at the time of writing the most contemporary, I explore and try to illuminate a continuing concern, how men and women seem impelled to tell their stories in fundamentally different ways. For a more recent and quite exhaustive exposition of such differences cross-culturally see* The Shrinking Goddess: Power, Myth and the Female Body *by Mineke Schipper, Westbourne Press, 2024.*

It was set in holy writ and learned text that humankind is, in essence, male, and, in substance, female. (Take care in saying the word "mankind" means all of us — the concept embedded at the base of our entire civilization says it does not). Through scientific method and visionary speculation, the complementarity between man and woman was taken to preclude equality, for the male is spirit, vision, vital force, while females are the very stuff of mortal flesh. This is not a notion peculiar to the Western world. The first two trigrams of the *I Ching*, which are called Ch'ien and K'un, are yang and yin, male and female, heaven and earth: ostensibly reflections of one another, one is active and one is passive, one creative and the other receptive. And so on.

To spawn and nurture flesh is woman's lot, while man is given to create on the higher levels of art and science, religion and the law. Woman is stranded within each generation, isolated from one generation to another by her function as the material source of life, the embodiment of earth. She *is* her function. By law, man isolates her from her daughters and her mothers. With science, man founds authority for his privileged state in the activity of molecules and stars. Through religion, man sanctions his ascendancy, sanctifies his own apotheosis. And through art he explores and celebrates his continuity with all mankind.

Understand this; in such reality — which, until recently and with few exceptions, we have taken to be categorical — life has no meaning in itself. Sustained in the Western mind, no less than in the East, is a profound discrepancy between the lived-in world and what it signifies. Everything must be named and explained in terms of something else. All our institutions, our religious, civil, and aesthetic laws, our science, our philosophies, function on this basis.

The artist, no less than any other, exists in such a world to invest it with meaning — with significance, relevance, and continuity. To connect, that is the artist's great desire; to create analogues, correlatives, fields in text, to devise allusions, archetypes, hermeneutic encounters, to arouse, to illuminate, to affirm the presence and validity of a higher hidden self. To connect, give life meaning and meaning life. To make of life, in short, a metaphor.

To act otherwise, it would seem, to collapse metaphor, to found reality in the immediate, is feminist subversion. To say that life is not a metaphor would be the usurpation of male dominance. To evade meaning, to refuse the quest for connectedness and significance is to valorise the real, to deny art, and to deconstruct all masculine imperatives of control. To create narrative in dissociative patterns which must resolve in memory and by intuition, is to insist that art is not a medium but reality itself. To affirm that human experience is not a signifier but the signified, is a declaration of female power.

***

Who determined that men and women, male and female, are opposites, as black and white, day and night, hot and cold, north and south, substance or essence, energy and stasis, instead of complementarities, like east and west, whose differences are determined by direction faced, by point of view — not colours on a wheel, each implying its antithesis, but colours on a spectrum radiant from a common source?

***

Bronwen Wallace, who died last summer of cancer at forty-four (1989), entitled her last book of poetry, *The Stubborn Particulars of Grace*. There is no rhetorical structure to the poems gathered, yet in their denial of form, there is tremendous power. Some of her poems are dramatic, some exquisitely lyrical, some touching, and funny, and sad, and all are so filled with the miracle of ordinary living that they take the breath away. The structure of each poem and the movement among them is discursive. They are poems which insist on the reality of women's experience, which insist on reality; poems which insist we are surrounded in the world by unyielding details that in arrangements with other details become important. In the accumulation of particulars, articulated with intensity and compassion, Wallace shares the beauty of her vision and the courage to endure. Her title is a poem itself, a brief narrative about female reality: *The Stubborn Particulars of Grace*.

***

In 1954, Ethel Wilson published *Swamp Angel*. It is a very engaging novel to read and, at the same time, unsettling. It is not a great novel. Ethel Wilson is not a great writer. But it is a good novel, good in the sense of being well-written, and good, also, as an affirmation of the good life, a fragmented life made whole and lived well.

There is something curious about the narrative form of *Swamp Angel* that is the source of its strength but is also a weakness. Maggie Vardoe deserts her husband (there is no word in English for a woman leaving marriage that does not imply negative responsibility). She leaves Vancouver and travels by taxi and bus into the Interior of British Columbia. At the town of Hope she intentionally veers away from her route to fish along the Similkameen River. After three days, she returns to Hope and continues her flight or quest towards Kamloops and Three Loon Lake, where she settles in, for the rest of the novel. A lot happens in the first third of her story, then it seems that not much happens, and then her story is over.

Swamp Angel is the modest manifesto of a woman's will to prevail over the divisive forces against her. On her journey, Maggie Vardoe reverts to the name of her first husband and becomes Maggie Lloyd, preferring that to Maggie Macdonald, the name of her father, and then she becomes Maggie, alone. In the last two thirds of her narrative, she learns, in the rich imagery of the novel, to reconcile the seal and the angel, swimming and soaring, substance and essence, the present with the past and future. She becomes complete in herself, a whole woman — although a woman whose self-reliance depends on the nurturing of others.

Swamp Angel relates two stories, and there is occasional friction between them. One is on the level of meaning, in which themes, motifs, symbols, and images relay to the reader a progression in Maggie's life towards self-possession. The other, through a discordant narrative structure which arrives at the same end, on the level of being, allows Maggie, finally, to be herself. Within time and space determined by the vision of the novel as a whole, the temporal narrative coheres in a sequential and rational continuum, and is radically subsumed by the spatial narrative, which is analogic, synthetic, holistic, and for Maggie, as well as the reader, immensely satisfying. Structural uncertainty leads in the end to narrative closure.

＊＊

The short stories of Bronwen Wallace were published as a collection shortly after her death. As with the apparently random arrangement of her poetry, their title itself holds them together, frames them as a single narrative. The collection is called *People You'd Trust Your Life To*. The reader shares in those words a grave responsibility with her characters, though one easily sustained.

Wallace's stories have something of the same easy familiarity and impact as her best poetry, which seems due as much to their exuberant form as to specific content. Her stories explode gently and settle as memory in the reader's mind. She literally writes the female body into fiction, writes an entirely female perspective on the world, but what gives her narrative such authority are the insistent discontinuities in her presentation of women's experience, of female reality. Each story develops in layers, and by indirection, implication, and apparently free association, until even the most intimate acts of joy and madness seem inevitable.

＊＊

There are two extremes in narrative structure. The model for one is the labyrinth. The model for the other is the jigsaw puzzle. Think of a labyrinth. At the heart or centre of the labyrinth is meaning; to arrive at the centre of a labyrinth is the only means of escape. At the centre is the outside. A well-constructed labyrinth is a maze; that is, the walls of every corridor are walls of adjoining corridors as well. There is no waste space. To arrive at the heart, you must experience every wall and corridor in your journey. You could lay a string behind you or breadcrumbs, or film where you have been, but you don't know where to go until you get there. When you reach the centre, you are on the outside looking in. The labyrinth is contained within you; what you see there is a projection of your own desire.

This is a paradigm of reading, as well as of narrative structure. But it is only one approach to reading, one kind of structure. There is also the jigsaw puzzle. It, too, is a paradigm of reading; the model for another, perhaps subversive, form of narrative.

Consider the puzzle. Like the labyrinth, it is arbitrary, an intrusion on the silence of time and space, an ordering in the chaos of experience. It, too, has its edges. But the edges of a jig-saw puzzle are determined by the integrity of each separate piece. Each piece is its own centre. You can place the pieces on a plane according to intuition, to your general knowledge of the world. A light blue piece goes high; it is the sky. A deep blue piece goes low; it is water. And light comes from one direction, and shadows fall away from it. But after a while, you realize that a particular piece of sky is reflection and lies within the water, while the shadow of a rock is in fact a tree, and what you took to be a tree is part of a cart. You begin outside the puzzle, to put everything in its place, but as the puzzle-pieces fit together, you enter the picture more and more, until your perspective is in the end among its many parts. You are contained by the puzzle, and its reality is inseparable from your own. Your location is in a constant state of flux; as you set the pieces down, each new piece alters the alignment of those already there. You can't go back the way you came.

***

Read *Blown Figures* by Audrey Thomas, or read it again. You cannot move forward through it with any certainty. You keep sliding off the page. The picture keeps changing; you move through its changes. In the end you read with rapt attention a series of blank pages. She is so successful at engaging you in sorting out the narrative chaos, in finding form, and the hell with meaning, in holding everything together long enough to see it whole, that the printless pages of her puzzle are a narrative delight.

***

The labyrinth is a two-dimensional text, although it gives the impression of being three. The walls have height, but the maze itself is on a single plane. You move through it sequentially and no matter how disorderly your progress may seem, it still follows one thing from another. It is experienced as a temporal construct. The picture puzzle, by contrast, insists on its own two-dimensionality. It is, in fact, a three-dimensional experience, a spatial construct, for its resolution depends on cumulative shifts in perspective as you enter with each new piece into the picture and withdraw to review the whole before entering again. You, as reader, provide the third dimension. If this suggests a more readerly text, it would be best to shelve Roland Barthes, for the moment. The corridors of a labyrinth can be as surely demanding as the separate-centred pieces of a puzzle.

***

In his 1975 novel, *Badlands*, Robert Kroetsch develops separate narratives: an existential male quest for meaning and a discontinuous female account which contains and, ultimately, discards it. Margaret Atwood's novel, *The Handmaid's Tale*, published in 1985, chronicles a woman's displacement within what has been officially legislated as a man's world, only to have the female story rendered ephemeral by male academics in pursuit of historical significance. Both novels isolate modes of narrative according to gender; both place the male and female modes in opposition, articulate them as mutually exclusive, and allow one to override the other. Yet the over-all narrative strategy of each novel depends on the interaction of these modes. Reality in Kroetsch's vision lies in ultimate complementarity between the sexes and in Atwood's, in perpetual conflict between them.

In *Badlands*, William Dawe travels down the Red Deer River in pursuit of dinosaur bones which will bring him fame and immortalize his name. He is on an archetypal quest for meaning through experience. Anna Yellowbird watches from the riverbank. Occasionally and in a random pattern she connects with the different males on Dawe's expedition, and then withdraws to watch again. Some fifty-six years later, with Dawe's daughter, who is also called Anna, she travels to the river's source while the Dawe account is re-enacted as their common dream.

The female narrative, both structurally and thematically, is spatial, not temporal, embodying not progression but transformation. The two Anna's provide the necessary witness to bring Dawe's field-notes to life. But in the end, with a bear suspended from a helicopter passing overhead, its testicles dangling stupidly through the net, they are moved by male absurdity and copious quantities of gin to tear up the notes, the photographs, the artifacts of the Heideggerian adventure. Both are set free from Dawe's story, from the impositions of male reality to be, at last, themselves.

Offred's story in *The Handmaid's Tale* opens to us through a series of discontinuous revelations about her delimited experience in the future-world of Gilead, without the author either defining that world beyond her protagonist or drawing the injured Offred through it in a linear series of episodes towards completion or defeat. In the dystopian vision of the novel, Offred is a handmaid, a woman whose sole function is to bear children as a surrogate womb. The primary activity of Offred's narrative, however, is in the reader's mind. The reader extrapolates a coherent if terrible world from Offred's pathetically narrowed vision, projects beyond the severe emotional constraints of her conditioning, and literally shares with Offred, and with Atwood who is a separate presence in the text, the dilemma of how to construct a woman's narrative within a misogynist nightmare.

The Handmaid's Tale closes with a section entitled "Historical Notes," which is a transcript of a symposium on Gileadean studies held at the University of Denay, Nunavut, in the year 2195. This is nearly two centuries after Offred's narrative. Her identity, even her existence, is called into question. The academic inquisitors, in pursuit of history, in deference to data, in their quest for meaning, historical relevance, and objective truth, virtually deny this woman's reality.

After we shared in Offred's struggle to write herself into being, we are appalled as her account is reduced by a male set of mind to documentary artifact, as her existence is reduced to merely an historical possibility.

***

Think about the short stories of Alice Munro. Each is a jigsaw puzzle. As you read, you encounter pieces which you hold simultaneously in mind until the story is complete. Each piece seems arbitrary in design, each is an episode, or a thought, a feeling, an image, a discrete and separable entity. As you read, patterns take shape, perimeters fall into place; the patterns shift, perimeters expand. Munro leaves out just enough pieces that, when you tilt her narrative to the light, in the end, to admire your readerly craft, it collapses. The elusive genius of a Munro story lies in its refusal to be still, to convey meaning. It is not a delivery system. In the end, it is itself. For most readers, that is more than enough.

Think about the design of a jigsaw piece. It has narrative significance, enough to be recognized as a part of something else. But its shape is arbitrary. Its shape is jigged by a saw to fit adjoining pieces without reference to content. It is forced by its shape to be its own centre of interest. Yet, when it is aligned to fit another, both the content and the cut of its edges hold it in place, and another centre of interest comes into being. And so it goes, until the end, when all the centres become one. Read an Alice Munro story and think about the pieces in a puzzle. When the puzzle disappears, the story is complete.

In *Lives of Girls and Women* and in *Who do You Think You Are?* Munro links her stories into sequences determined more by chronology than anything else. The main characters in each, Del and Rose, get older. Their lives change, they learn more about themselves, and they become tentatively reconciled to who they are. The structure of each book is based on the model of the labyrinth, even though the separate stories so beautifully exemplify the narrative as puzzle. In reaching for continuity, Munro writes in response to the dominant mode in our culture, which is an existential quest for meaning. Yet the separate stories in these two books are intricately shaped in narrative patterns which reflect the subversion of meaning, the importance of being. They are disguised, but each stands on its own.

***

There is pathos in reading Gwendolyn MacEwen, who died by suicide in 1987, when she writes in "The Tao of Physics" of her own reckless vulnerability. This is a woman's story of defiance and defeat, for even as she hurls her poems against death and change, she accepts their primacy, submits to the terrible beauty of her lord. Male over female, time over space, might over matter; in such reality the grace of her poems gives tragic assent to her own demise.

> In the vast spaces of the subatomic world where
> Matter has a tendency to exist
> The lord of Life is breathing in and out,
> Creating and destroying the universe
>
> With each wave of his breath.
> And my lord Siva dances in the city streets,
> His body a fierce illusion of flesh, of energy,
> The particles of light cast off from his hair
> Invade the mighty night, the relative night, this dream.
> Here where events have a tendency to occur
> My chair and all its myriad inner worlds
> Whirl around in the carousel of space; I hurl
> Breathless poems against my lord Death, send these
> Words, these words
> Careening into the beautiful darkness.

***

The notion that narrative modes are intrinsically bound to gender acknowledges polarities that have been sustained in our culture though millennia. The male and female of our species have arrived through social evolution at a curious symbiosis, based not on intrinsic difference or biological function but on the politics of power. Aristotle codified an evolving concept wherein men are the source of human energy and achievement, while women provide the base materials, body substance, which is stimulated into life by the male through copulation. In *Genesis*, God charges the first man to name the world and thereby gain ascendancy above all earthly things. With language comes control, but also consciousness of the self as other. The post-Freudian fabulations of Jacques Lacan do not appreciably differ from this paradigm. God's elevation of man led to the necessity of creating woman as a vital link for Adam to his earthy origin. In *Feminine Sexuality*, Lacan likewise struggles to provide a viable reality for woman that his pre-emptive speculations have casually denied. So much for the divinity of our beginnings.

***

Di Brandt says in a poem:

>   the meaning i say through clenched teeth is relate to
>   the structure
>   of the sentence for godsake anybody can see that you
>   can't just take
>   some old crackpot idea & say you found it in these
>   words even the
>   Bible has to make some sense the Bible my father says

***

Catherine Parr Traill wrote *The Backwoods of Canada* and *A Canadian Settlers Guide*. Her sister, Susanna Moodie, wrote *Roughing It in the Bush* and *Life in the Clearings*. Anna Jameson wrote *Winter Studies and Summer Rambles*. Traill instructs her reader on the etiquette as well as the techniques of survival in the wilderness. She does not write about conquest but about accommodation. Following a crazy-quilt pattern, she leads her reader among the discontinuous procedures of establishing her place, as a woman, in the world. These books were all published before the Confederation of Canada. Traill is sedentary; Jameson is itinerant, an aristocratic tourist. Moodie is somewhere between. There is little narrative progression in any of these books, despite change of setting, especially in Jameson. Yet each woman, in her own way, has written herself into the landscape of Canada.

The journals of Samuel Hearne, of David Thompson, of Alexander Mackenzie, describe harrowing tales of exploration and adventure along a labyrinthine maze of lakes and rivers. Each man is the hero of his own story; each writes his name across the North American continent and into history. Hearne is an exciting writer, Thompson an interesting writer, and Mackenzie a pedestrian writer, but each is responsible for stringing lines of direction, distance, and authority across terrain that recognizes alien sovereignty as the expression of power, not common will. Their journals attest to the struggle of putting, not people in the world, but the world in its place.

The male accounts are about the conquest of geography over landscape, historiographic gridlock as an expression of both corporate and personal power. The women write to share their experience of the wilderness, the men to be admired for surviving theirs. The men write to achieve meaning, the women as witness. Men, passing; women, presence.

***

It is interesting that in a novel so urgently concerned as Daphne Marlatt's *Ana Historic* with the marginalization of women's reality through language, the story is narrated in an intricately devised linear mode which accedes to the male dominance it is attempting to overthrow. Marlatt urges the creative reunion of language and the female body. Words that pre-empt female reality occupy narrative interest throughout the text, yet the novel's narrative structure reinforces notions of historical progression and rhetorical coherence through which male language sustains authority. It is chilling to realize that the word "vagina," with its regal sound in Canadian parlance, rhyming as it does with the city of "Regina," which itself echoes colonialism of another sort, in French is masculine: "le vagin, there must be some mistake, I thought, not knowing its history, a word for sheath, the cover of a sword." But for the reader to discover this in an essentially conventional story pattern isolates the linguistic denial of women's reality as an aberration, when it is in fact embedded deep in the structures of literature as well as language.

***

Molly Bloom's story of herself in *Ulysses* goes nowhere. Contained in a single sentence, which is the syntactical denial of progression or change, Joyce creates a puzzle of magnificent complexity, and Molly Bloom lies at its centre. Her husband Leopold and Stephen Daedalus are moved about in the first parts of the novel with great deliberation, as Joyce scours the streets of Dublin for meaning. Maundering male sexual desire becomes a constituent part of female desire, as Molly's yearning towards sensual completion subsumes their pedestrian quest. The tyrannies of religious and racial, aesthetic, and masculine meaning are put in their proper place.

***

In her book, *Drawing on the Right Side of the Brain,* Betty Edwards applies current knowledge about the asymmetrical functioning of the human cerebral hemispheres to the enhancement of artist skills and appreciation. Her books bear the same relationship to an instructional manual as *Zen and the Art of Motorcycle Maintenance* does to a Honda owner's guide, or *A Hitchhiker's Guide to the Galaxy*, to a backpacker's *Baedeker*. Edward's intent is to liberate the intuitive, synthesizing, analogical, spatial, nonrational, holistic functioning of the right side of the brain from the suffocating dominance of the logical, analyzing, abstract, temporal, rational, linear functioning of the left side. Only then, when imagination and the unconscious are freed from intellectual constraints, when consciousness finds access to unfettered perception, will the mind rise in the act of creation to its fullest potential.

The vocabulary and syntax of language in service to the left hemisphere impose linear coherence on such linguistic emanations from the right as analogues and tropes. The left, which is associated with right-handedness, corresponds to what through human social evolution we have taken to be masculine side of things. The right, and left-handedness, have been deemed the feminine side. The left, or male, hemisphere long ago seized control; reason over discord, order over anarchy. But discord and anarchy from the right are freedoms, the freedoms to be different and the freedom to create. These, our human cultures have deemed to be subversive, to be female, and to be discredited or ignored.

Literary precedent brings imagination, the tropes and analogues, symbols and images, rhythms and patterns, into line. Literally, into line. The female, in this model, provides the materials of art, but the male arranges them in sequence. Guided by intellectual awareness of tradition and the conventions of genre, as well as society, he arranges them to yield meaning. She may be the muse, but he is the artist. In Blake's model, she is Enitharmon, who combines with disembodied male rages, the Spectre of Urthona, to drive and draw poor Los to make great art.

Betty Edwards argues that you can learn access to the suppressed right hemisphere and restore its proper functioning through discipline. Whatever led us in the distant past to give authority to reason, we can usurp such power by an act of will. Whatever led to acceptance of meaning over being, of memory and dream over present desire, of the existential quest over existence itself, we can deny its continuance through creative anarchy. That we can do so, is evident in works of great and original art which combine the so-called male and female principles. *Ulysses*, for instance. It is also evident in the birth of every human child.

***

There is sadness in reading the opening stanza of Gwendolyn MacEwen's poem, "Breakfast at Midnight," as the speaker opens herself with such urgency to the tyrannies of language and of time, to male authority and power:

> There are times I look at you with such shock and surprise
> I cannot breathe. Who are you? Why do I hear
> Speech of your seed, languages, voices of your
> Million unborn children?

***

The narrator in Margaret Atwood's *Surfacing* begins her story in a quest for her absent father that would seem the very expression of Lacanian doctrine. Fortunately, Atwood seems guided more by the psychoanalytics of R.D. Laing than Jacques Lacan. Granted, there are many replications of the primal mirror crisis in the motival patterns of *Surfacing*, but the narrator's search for her father is not at all motivated by Oedipal considerations or the need to recover the law, enforced by his absence, which sustains the split in her experience of herself. Atwood rejects the dissociation of self as an absolute and found its reintegration in the gifts of her mother.

If you will remember, after seeing random souvenirs left by her mother and piecing together the remnants of her father's scholarly research in an effort to resolve the mystery of his disappearance, the unnamed narrator dives into the depths of a lake, where she comes face to face with death. In a rush of horrific images, she surfaces. She has seen human monsters, her drowned brother, dead frogs, an aborted foetus, and herself.

When she hears that her father's drowned body has been recovered at that exact place, where it was weighed down by the camera he was using to record Indian pictographs, a victim of rational technology in confrontation with the bestial side of natural man, she breeds with her lover and then retreats into the utter solitude of primeval, prenatal, preternatural consciousness. She is transformed into the beast she has been forced to recognize within herself. She is an animal waiting for the fur to grow on her skin. She is beyond reason, beyond language, but she is aware. When she comes across the picture she drew as a girl, which her mother saved, suddenly the ordeal is over. The picture shows an unborn infant looking out from its mother's womb. The narrator sleeps, sure now that she is pregnant, wakes up, and prepares herself for the surface world of language, men, and provisional surrender to the realities into which her child will be born.

While much of *Surfacing* follows a linear pattern through the labyrinth of a deeply troubled mind, envisioning reality from the narrator's increasingly dissociated perspective, it resolves in a brilliant splash of images that, once given, swirl through the text towards wholeness and completion. It is a little as if the walls of a maze in which we found ourselves reading were suddenly tossed into the air and they fall in the form of a picture puzzle which only depicts a maze. The temporal pattern has become a spatial design.

Structurally, the transformation of narrative shape in *Surfacing* reflects the radical change in the narrator's understanding of herself. Her long and rapid descent into the generic past, from acquiescence to male power, willing victim in the intellectual games that separate her from the animal within, to the asexual condition of animate awareness, collapses suddenly with her recognition of maternal continuity. Structurally and thematically, *Surfacing* is a feminist *tour de force*.

***

bp nichol published the novel, *Still*, with Pulp Press in 1983. It is very obscure, in both senses of the world. It is largely unknown and as a text it is difficult, teasing the reader at the edge of incomprehension. Red Deer College Press published *The Prowler*, by Kristjana Gunnars, in 1989. Despite a structure that could best be described as chaotic, it is a narrative of exquisite clarity and coherence.

Each novel is a labyrinth; each is a puzzle. Few people have read either. Perhaps few ever will. But they are very important for a number of reasons. *Still* will remain a major work in the minor tradition of avant-garde writing in Canada. *The Prowler* may yet find a larger readership. Certainly, it offers splendid rewards to those who seek it out. Among the discord and the anarchy of its discontinuities, the quiet voice of a solitary woman achieves the echoed resonance of multitudes.

With *Still,* think of a film camera moving across the planes of a still photograph, recording the architectural patterns of its journey as it passes. And at the same time, think of a conversation of the most terse dialogue possible, laid over the accumulating images like a soundtrack. There are two people talking. They are unseen. One is a woman. One is a man. We know this by the way they talk. By syntactical nuance. By subtle assumptions and prerogatives in their discourse. Tensions and momentum build around him more than around her. In the beginning they discuss their end. In the end they agree to go on exactly as they have been. Somehow this seems, for him, a triumph. For her, it is an acceptable compromise.

That is the story. They talk. And interspersed between the discontinuous moments of their conversation are beautifully detailed descriptions of a house, inside and out. Overlapping visions of the grounds gradually give way to a room-by-room tour of the interior. Words are a camera: nichol moves with meticulous care through his scene, sometimes zooming in for a close-up, sometimes panning across a wall, sometimes angling a shot for intentional distortion, sometimes withdrawing to a neutral distance and at other times forcing an intimacy on the reader by such proximity to artifact that you feel implicated in a violation of some sort. This is a lived-in place, yet never do we encounter there a living soul. All motion is in our shifting perceptions; all duration, in the time we take to read. Occasionally the scene takes in whole seasons, and at other times we see a table set, a toilet roll half gone; and we are haunted in this place by the apparent absence of its inhabitants. They are voices only. Only the text as context, the text as an extension of the reader's mind, brings characters and setting onto common ground.

I wrote about this elsewhere: my conclusion was simply to celebrate what I took at the time to be a variation of Robbe-Grillet's *La Jalousie*. I realize now that the endless return in Robbe-Grillet to the image of a woman brushing her hair is structurally the laying down of a thread, a sequence of crumbs from the same loaf, to get you through the text. Nichol is doing something more radical. While coaxing the reader with vague intimations of continuity, he simultaneously denies the reader's progress with convolutions of fragmented imagery. You get to the end of Nichol's labyrinth but you don't get out.

In *The Prowler*, Kristjana Gunnars refuses the linear authority of time. She prowls among the random jig-saw pieces of her narrator's life; her narrator is a prowler in her own life, and you, as reader, prowl the text as well, among discrete passage which seem to slide elliptically across the narrative plane. There is something delightfully sinister about your progress through the text. You share in the conspiracy of re-creation as you piece the narrator's life together without reference to continuity or duration. Almost by stealth, you encounter, capture, and sustain the fragments of her story. Even the text is a prowler, slipping with furtive deliberation among the fragments of the narrator's story held within the reader's mind.

Gunnars' novel claims modesty to the point of self-effacement. Never trust the obvious. When the writing-narrator claims, "It is a relief not to be writing a story"; when she echoes Joyce by saying, "Perhaps it is not a good book ... but it is the only book I am able to write"; when she says, "I do not want to be clever," and "It is a book marked by its ordinariness. That knows there can be nothing extraordinary in a life, in a language," she is giving fair warning of her radical intent. Each denial is an invitation to participate in the novel's narrative complexity. A story is, after all, being written. It seems as if it is being written while you read. It violates the linear conventions of storytelling, which dictate that the story knows where it is going, even if the reader doesn't. It is many stories, each with its own centre, some only a few words, none more than a few pages, each one numbered — the novel's only and ironic concession to continuity. All are written as surely out of the writing-narrator's own life as Joyce wrote from his, but in her refusal to be clever, to be portentous, she accedes to the function of art as an expression not of the intellect but of intuition, not of the body politic or the body aesthetic, religious or otherwise transcendent, but of the body itself, her own presence in the world.

Do we know the narrator's name? We are told that as a girl growing up in Iceland she is "owned" by her father, Gunnar Bodvarsson. This gives her the right to speak on certain rare occasions. Kinship with her mother gives her no such right. She is somehow less related to her mother. We learn this, and about her anorexic sister. About Iceland, about children's work. Children's silence. Growing up as a white-Inuit. School in Denmark. School in California. Libraries and words. Versions of the same story. We come to know the narrator as intimately as she knows herself — even if we can't remember whether we know her name. Naming is an expression of ownership and while we may become familiar with the narrator's life, she is in no way our possession or under our control. "The project was to clarify the picture. To make the patterns emerge out of a random set."

***

Di Brandt writes of women:

> i have subscribed to endless circulars
> proclaiming us blood kin in these rooms

> i have rolled and unrolled with the rest
> wordless sheets announcing the damp odour
> of our common text …

***

Men and women have learned to tell the stories of their reality in different ways. Woman's story has been violated or expunged from the myriad records of our progress towards eternity. But subversively her story has been inscribed upon the landscape of our consciousness, to be shared among the over-lapping generations which converge with each collapsing moment and renders the notion of eternity irrelevant. Woman's story turns her confinement in immediate experience to advantage. She explodes time in fragments across the narrative plane. Spatial tension displaces the temporal continuum.

Being female does not make the writer's writing "feminine" any more than being male makes it "masculine." Consider *Badlands*; consider *Still*. Consider the stories of Alice Munro. For a moment consider the stories of Margaret Laurence. Laurence's stories follow the male pattern; there is no change but through progression. They unfold in a sequence of transitional episodes towards illumination and epiphany. Munro's, despite the influence of Joyce, develop seemingly at random through a succession of transformations. Following the model of the female story, each instance stands on its own, yet depends on every other for its final place in the design. One layer of narrative reality lies upon another and another, each containing the ones preceding it, until the picture is complete. There is no progression, but through change.

There is a correspondence between the evolution and impact of feminist ideology and the opening of art in all its forms to structural anarchy and creative discord, to the subversion of meaning, to grace as the alternative to transcendence, and to the worth of life itself. In the last century, men and especially women have learned to revel in the freedom from meaning, the freedom to be. Without the rise of feminism to foster violations in the patrilineality of narrative syntax and crumble the authority of patriarchal structures, perhaps Joyce might never have completed *Ulysses*, nor Chagall defied the gape of gravity, nor Balanchine made ecstasy a dance. Nor would we have *Swamp Angel* by Ethel Wilson or *The Prowler* by Kristjana Gunnars, and Bronwen Wallace might never have recorded the stubborn particulars of grace.

WORKS CITED

Atwood, Margaret. *Surfacing*. Toronto: McClelland and Stewart, 1972.

Atwood, Margaret. *The Handmaid's Tale*. Toronto: McClelland and Stewart, 1985.

Brandt, Di. *Questions I Asked My Mother*. Winnipeg: Turnstone Press, 1987.

Edwards, Betty. *Drawing on the Right side of the Brain*. Revised. Los Angeles: Tarcher, 1989.

Geddes, Gary. Editor. *15 Canadian Poets X 2*. Toronto: Oxford, 1988.

Gunnars, Kristjana. *The Prowler*. Red Deer: Red Deer College Press, 1989.

Joyce, James. *Ulysses*. Paris: Odyssey, 1932.

Kroetsch, Robert. *Badlands*. Toronto: New Press, 1975.

MacEwen, Gwendolyn. *Afterworlds*. Toronto: McClelland and Stewart, 1987.

Marlatt, Daphne. *Ana Historic*. Toronto: Coach House, 1988.

Moss, John. *A Reader's Guide to the Canadian Novel. Second Edition*. Toronto: McClelland and Stewart, 1987.

Munro, Alice. *Lives of Girls and Women*. Toronto: McGraw-Hill Ryerson, 1971.

Munro, Alice. *Who Do You Think You Are?* Toronto: Macmillan, 1978.

Nichol, bp. *Still.* Vancouver: Pulp Press, 1983.

Thomas, Audrey. *Blown Figures.* Vancouver: Talonbooks, 1974.

Traill, Catherine Parr. *The Canadian Settler's Guide.* Toronto, Canada West: Old Countryman Office, 1855.

Wallace, Bronwen. *The Stubborn Particulars of Grace.* Toronto: McClelland and Stewart, 1987.

Wallace, Bronwen. *People You'd Trust Your Life To.* Toronto: McClelland and Stewart, 1990.

Wilson, Ethel. *Swamp Angel.* Toronto: Macmillan, 1954.

HIMMLER'S GOT THE KING

What is it in the coming together of language and consciousness as we apprehend narrative that permits us to suspend disbelief? This essay examines how narrative strategies work in relation to language, and how language works within narrative, while exploring distinctions between modernist conventions of realism, born out of humanism, and the vital extravagance of postmodernism. The discontinuities in the essay suggest a struggle against linear constraints. Perhaps influenced by Kroetsch and Bowering, I was finding expositional formalism more and more suffocating in my desire to articulate creative as well as critical responses to language, experience, and particular texts. This was written while I was Visiting Professor of Commonwealth Literature at the University of Leeds in the fall of 1983 and delivered at a conference there on April 27, 1984, the proceedings of which were published in 1985 by the University of Leeds Press in a book called Re-Visions of Canadian Literature, *edited by Shirley Chew. Variants also appeared in* Present Tense, *published by NC Press in 1985, and* The Paradox of Meaning, *Turnstone Press, 1999.*

"'Himmler's got the King locked up in the Tower of London,' said Harry Woods." (SS-GB. Len Deighton. St. Albans: Triad Panther, 1980.) The opening sentence of Deighton's novel says everything he has to say. The rest is anti-climax, the explication of a premise.

In the mode of existential realism adopted by most writers of male adventure from Dashiell Hammett to John Le Carré, by most novelists in fact of the twentieth century, Len Deighton exploits the actuality of language, the factuality of words. His writing assumes that he can say virtually anything he wants in print, so long as he says it with reasonable decorum. Words on the page are more reliable, and even more real, than the time-tossed moment of our separate lives. Insofar as the reader reads, there is no reality but what is being read. That is the illusion, the fallacy, and the largesse of literary modernism.

"'Himmler's got the King locked up in the Tower of London,' said Harry Woods." How is it possible, not merely to arouse the willing suspension of disbelief, but to inspire reader complicity in the suppression of contrary knowledge? For Deighton's statement to work at all, the reader must be aware of the historical implications which render it absurd. However, in written narrative, words are the only facts, logic is the logic of grammatical structure, limits in all respects are determined by language. Within a declaration sanctioned by Harry's apparent disinterest, everything connects. Each naming word is a nexus of historical possibilities; the verbal phrase suggests plausible action among them. Harry, whose statement in the present tense contains the historical and therefore establishes priority over it, speaks in the narrative past, as the action is happening. This, then, is the truth that counts because it is immediate, past, and irrefutable. Anything else is hearsay, an extratextual rumour. History is re-made, as always, in order to make the present instance inevitable.

Grammar is absolute. Even when it sustains enigma or anomaly, as is often the case in a poem, it is the precision by which the terms of the contraries are arranged that allows articulation beyond words, which is the genius of poetry. Verb tense and grammatical alliance in Deighton's sentence are open neither to ambiguity nor paradox. Meaning is no more irrelevant here than in poetry; it follows the dictates of grammar; it does not determine them. Each part of speech relates to all the others in a relationship that ultimately is shaped into coherence as a clause, subordinate to the fact-in-action, Harry Woods speaking, or having spoken. There is nothing to refute. In the closed world of Deighton's opening sentence, and sustained throughout his novel, a separate reality prevails. Himmler's got the King.

Possibly because print occupies space in order to give language a temporal presence, it fosters the illusion that time and place are subject to the rules of grammar. Syntax, like gravity, apparently governs all. It has no substance and no duration, but time and the substantial world are utterly at its disposal. In ideogrammatic languages, syntax is relative, governed by proximity and implication: grammar is determined by meaning. But in phonetic print, the rules precede meaning. Perhaps the cumulative dynamics of syntax follow from alphabetical necessity (the word "alphabet" itself declares sequence). Perhaps the exacting structure of syntax derives from a print form in which the letters bear no intrinsic relationship to the words they articulate. Without words, syntax has no relevance, yet paradoxically a phonetic word only exists as a potential of meaning, without syntax to place it in relation to time and space. The smallest self-contained phonetic unit is a sentence. The ideogram for "chair" is a spatial concept, a thing in itself. But the word "chair" in phonetic print awaits the linear context of a coherent grammatical construct to have meaning. Otherwise, it is simply a familiar arrangement of letters, waiting.

Reading in a narrative world where the limits of consciousness and of knowledge and experience are established by the principles of grammar, the reader enlivens a reality more coherent, more sound, than his or her own — and probably more exciting, since anything can happen there, if it is said right. It seems we are alive, reading realistic fiction, the way many of us never are in living life. God's word-whirled creation is apparently no match for Len Deighton's world of words.

But, of course, the success of such reading depends on the denial of self. The syntactically structured world only works at the expense of personality. A confrontation between reader and text or the critic and himself or herself, a violation of absolute distance between the writer and text, threaten to collapse the illusion of narrative reality. If one approaches the fiction sufficiently informed, then nothing of matter will matter, least of all personal being. The highest achievement of art, and this is the essence of modernism, is to make life irrelevant. Syntactical realism refines both the real world and the reader right out of existence.

Fiction in the realistic mode is the ultimate solipsism. There is no life beyond art. Therefore, to be is to be fiction, a figure in the narrative ground, a word. As George Bowering's ironic conception of his namesake, George Vancouver, is described in *Burning Water*: "He wanted to be a famous story very much. And so, '"he wrote all over the globe?"' His cartographical expedition was a "fact factory," writing the world down on maps to make it real. To make no-where into something, a text, and to place himself within it, Vancouver is obliged to name the world and then become "the name they thought of first," to become, in short, a word. Bowering's Vancouver is simultaneously an example and a parody of the ironic questing hero in search of himself. Dawe, in Robert Kroetsch's *Badlands,* likewise yearns to be a word, to have his name pinned to a rumple of bones, the *Daweosaurus*. Not the man but his desire is what Kroetsch burlesques. William Dawe struggles towards immortality and when he discovers that it is not conditional on his personal presence, he lets himself die.

Both Kroetsch and Bowering confound heirs to the New Critics who take the illusions of realism for reality itself. The existential quest of the protagonist in these two fictions is conveyed in language and a context that insists such a venture is arbitrary and of dubious significance, either inside the narrative or without. The conventions of realism prove to be their own undoing. The more we doubt the verity of Bowering's ridiculous Vancouver, the more engaging he becomes. And Kroetsch's Dawe, his story told is declared, like the view of life his life embodies, radically incomplete.

It seems more inevitable than peculiar that characters in modern fiction should quest for meaning to their lives through language, meaning which experience of the world increasingly denied. Even Sartre, ever suspicious of the word, called his autobiography *Words*; and Barthes wrote *Barthes par Barthes*. Both of them tried to make the phenomenon of personal being comprehensible; not to liberate or re-create it, but literally to make it real, the subject as object. Perhaps language all along has only been a metaphor. Perhaps it offers nothing more than illusory compensation for our bereaved condition; or only a distraction from it.

In this sudden age of ours, which we sometimes call postmodern, it is equally as inevitable, perhaps, that the desire to be, through language, should be contained in a narrative design which not so much refutes or ridicules the existential quest as incorporates it into a more elastic and exacting vision. Kroetsch and Bowering often in quite different ways demand their readers *be*, but don't make being easy. Kroetsch reconstructs the deconstructed universe, with us inside. In Bowering, time and again, the word-world wobbles on its written axis, gravity for an instant dissipates, and we are flung back into reality for brief and disconcerting encounters with ourselves, reading.

Badlands does not insist there is reality beyond the text, except by implication; Bowering's world, however, sometimes quite aggressively, interpenetrates with our own. The differences between the closed world, re-conceived, and the defiantly open are evident in the different use of language to expose the arbitrary and limiting nature of conventional narrative. Bowering, for instance, delights in using proper syntax to convey the sheerest nonsense, in forcing the reader to accept as narrative reality what is patently absurd. He is adroit at deflating or violating expectations with a turn of phrase that makes the solemn suddenly obscene, or the bizarre tenderly affecting, or the outrageously fake for an instant real. One whole chapter, devoted in lurid detail to a sexual encounter, careens away from us when in the last line we discover the intimacies were experienced not by whom we had assumed but by another couple entirely, the incorporeal word-name Banks and his incorporeal wife. It is for the reader a jarring moment — stuck with trying to assimilate not only a retroactively extraneous incident but what, on a word, has become a disconcertingly extraneous response.

Kroetsch in a more subtle violation of expectations, consistent with the narrative illusion that must be sustained if he is in the end to declare it null, if not quite void, uses words to play response against meaning. The following allusion to a murder is effectively contrary:

> And Web's innocence would light the room. As it lit the dark that night, years before, when he burned his own father's shack to the ground. And used the light of that burning to make his way.

Web's father was inside the shack at the time! One is exhilarated by the image, however, not horrified by the action. The word "innocence" is turned inside out and brilliantly illuminated. Kroetsch's language not only distracts from a conventional response to the event but evokes its opposite.

Not that Kroetsch is always subtle in matters of language, especially where Web is concerned. Web probably swears better, with more verve and obscene affectation, than most readers are likely to have encountered before, in print or on the street. But his innovative use of words draws attention to elements within the narrative and not away from it. Essential to Kroetsch's novel, the illusion of narrative reality must remain intact. While quirks of language in *Burning Water* reach with frequency beyond the text, intentionally violating narrative perimeters, Kroetsch's shore them up.

In the structure of *Badlands*, wherein Dawe makes field notes which through his daughter blossom into narrative, while Anna tells a story of herself with another Anna, in which her father's notes are something of a talisman and ultimately as ephemeral, two distinctly separate versions of reality are held simultaneously present. They must be equally convincing if each is to prove the undoing of the other. As the novel draws towards completion, the woman's structural vision which contains the male linear quest, transformational reality nurturing the existential, proves as incomplete as the contrived experience of the man. But the closed system which contains and nurtures both, which is the novel itself, insists they are complementary and, together, form a whole. The two Annas at the end, resolutely free of time, walk off arm in arm singing a lusty song which commits them to its flow, in spite of themselves. We the readers walk between them.

The tremendous vitality Kroetsch gives to Dawe's world and to his daughter Anna's, and the intriguing tension he sustains between them, comes ironically in good part from the extent to which he taunts credulity. Just as the misdirections and excesses of language lead not away from the fiction but deeper into it, so too with the plethora of ironies, conceits, motifs and thematic contrivances. The reader is repeatedly confronted in Dawe's narrative with such improbabilities as Grimich's perpetual toiling beneath Drumheller, with such incongruities as Sinnott's car parked in the middle of the river, with such absurdities as Web's mid-air encounter with Anna Yellowbird and their subsequent discovery of the *Daweosaurus*. What is amazing is that the narrative sustains it all: it is all part of the story, episodes and adventures in the meaningful quest. Anna's world, though different, is no less a strain on the reader's imaginative benevolence. There are two Annas, many Billys, lots of gin, a reversal of the river quest, ending at the source, and a defecating bear suspended overhead, its genitals exposed. Yet the reader accedes without, even realizing it. The patterns and transitions seem appropriate, even inevitable, in context.

Each version of reality works, yet they would seem to cancel each other out. If the male quest for meaning has narrative legitimacy, then the female remains Penelope on the side-lines. If the female transformation is convincing, then the male has properly been discarded. The reader, who has conspired to make each version work, is caught in the middle, caught reading. The novel, of course, subsumes both into a single vision, one reality. The reader then is inside, looking out.

Bowering's *Burning Water* more directly involves the reader, not as a result of reading, but in the process. In a brilliant series of deflations, Bowering uses the reader's vulnerability to the realist mode to highlight its fallacies. Many of his premises and postulations are more outlandish than anything Len Deighton could muster, but whereas Deighton's creation is deadly earnest, as realism essentially must be, even the gothic, romantic, and comic varieties, Bowering demands that his readers have fun, extra-textually as well as within the narrative. He insists there is a world beyond the text at every turn, and adroitly makes it, too, a part of the fiction, as fiction is a part of it. And each time we, or one, or you and I, catch a glimpse of ourselves in the shards of interpenetrating realities that are strewn along the way, the possibility of the objective reader, the reliability of the dispassionate critic, both dissipate. There is no place for the bloodless, except in the boneyard of yesterday's prose (a macabre conceit, but one that Bowering makes plausible).

Bowering is as determined to expose the illusion of narrative reality as Kroetsch in *Badlands* is to maintain it — both for much the same ends, to break down the artificial and the arbitrary barriers between life and the printed word, to break through the walls of the labyrinth which language has built around us and in which we too readily find ourselves lost. Not surprisingly, Bowering's principal tool in the constructive demolition he undertakes is language itself. This he mercilessly deploys to flaunt our apparently obsessive will to accept the unacceptable. Words, phrases, clauses, sentences, paragraphs, in *Burning Water,* all fall into place according to grammatical convention. And if they baffle, mislead, or confuse, if they amuse, infuriate, or impress, so much the better. Instead of rejecting narrative reality when forced into confrontation with ourselves, responding to it, we make allowances for its idiosyncrasies. If a passage with Vancouver vomiting, after trying to quell his desire for a taste of the remnants of Captain Cook's flesh that have been retrieved from the cannibals, concludes on the entirely irrelevant note by Mr. Menzies that the sea "is also a garden" (p 126), well, why not. That is what happens to be on Menzies' mind. The breach of linearity makes him more real, not less. And if Vancouver occasionally contemplates the "reassembled body of his old teacher" (p 18g), that too is possible. Vancouver and Menzies are real inventions, after all, and if their behaviour is anachronistic or bizarre, or the focus on them is somewhat oblique, that in no way discredits their narrative validity. It only means that we must work at a more frenzied pace to suppress our disbelief, drawn to do so by the irresistible pull of imagination at the mercy of syntactical coherence.

On one occasion, with dazzling silly irony, syntax itself becomes the joke. Captain Vancouver interrogates some "Indians":

> "You have been a great distance inland?" asked the stout sailor of all the world's seas.
>
> 'It is a relative question,' said the first Indian ...
>
> Vancouver couldn't wait for the interpreter now. He leaned forward, his short wig slipping a little on his head. He addressed the young barbarian directly, in a rough estimation of the Nootka tongue.
>
> "How through forest it days with canoes many is?"

Years later Benjamin Wharf would be built where this aching query was put. Even here, Bowering cannot resist the historical follow-through which, in context, is a jarring *non-sequitur*. To continue for a moment in Latin, however, *post hoc ergo propter hoc*. Everything connects; perhaps not always because print is a linear medium.

Grammatical convention in *Burning Water* sustains the illusions of narrative logic and progress, even when the language itself, what it says, denies both. Consider the following, in which the language struts and preens like a lexical Mick Jagger — patently fake, ingenuous, aggressively trite. As narrative, it works, while simultaneously declaring itself absurd:

> ... one evening, just when the orange and red sun was falling into the edge of the ocean like a polychrome postcard, an alarm went up from the gallery, and a dark-visaged man raced by the guard and dived with less grace than dispatch into

the darkening brine. He just missed two canoes on entry and was halfway to shore on egress from the water.

"That thief has five of our best *coltelli*," hollered Mr. Gransell, who was under the impression that he had uttered a French plural, and thought that the occasional such borrowing gave class to his galley.

"Hang it, the Old Man will be hotter than last night's fireworks," said the watchman.

"I am already heated fair to well," said Captain Vancouver, who had hied himself to the position upon first hearing the cook's shouts. He had been a bundle of nerves all day, and now he was glad that some action seemed called for.

"You'll be wanting the cutter, sir?" suggested the sailor, anxious to deflect attention from his inevitable failure.

"Of course, we shall employ our one cutter to retrieve our other five," said Vancouver, flushing with excitement and anger in the red light.

"Droll," said Menzies.

Droll, and much else besides.

It is interesting to speculate on the relationship between print and time.

To what extent does the predilection of our culture with linear time and with causality derive from the sequential nature of phonetic construction? One of a finite number of letters must follow another, and they, another, in what may be an infinite progression, as letters become words and the words, sentences, and the pattern of sentences, a text. Could there be a determining relationship between the linearity of phonetic print and our various mythologies of origin and ultimate ends? Or between the reduction of world to a sequence of letters and the abiding cult of progress in Western civilization, which presently goes by the name of Science, but has been in the past called Reason, Faith, and Destiny? Could the structure of the printed word itself bear responsibility for our obsessive conception of history as a forward flow or as the lengthening shadow at our feet? What is not recorded as history, we call pre-history; that which happened before the text. Perhaps time begins with the printed word; and all that we conceive as cultural absolutes are the consequence of phonetic design.

Human consciousness has been determined not only what was thought but how we thought about it, as we willingly, even wilfully, submitted to the tyranny of syntax and the printed word. Bowering and Kroetsch, however, demand we free ourselves of the modernist fallacy (the fallacy of existential realism), wherein we accept words as facts and syntax as sense, where we think of reality as text and text, reality. Both Kroetsch and Bowering are determined, it would seem, to break us free of linear time and our obsession with the present moment as the culmination of an historical sequence.

Bowering's ambition in *Burning Water* obviously extends beyond a revisionist history of Captain George Vancouver, although it may well include a revision of what history is. To force the collapse of time as an ordered sequence in the reader's mind, Bowering does nothing so crude as to violate chronology — that would merely replace one questionable structure with another. Rather, through word-games of occasionally outrageous proportion but sometimes with the subtlety of needles, he makes the very notion of historical time both arbitrary and irrelevant. By fusing variants of a present-day idiom with blatant fakery of an idiom of the past, his prose insists that time has no dimension at all, that everything is now. So wary does the reader become of language which even hints at historicity that excerpts from the real Vancouver's journals seem a sham, a narrative trick (if indeed the note of acknowledgement can be trusted, and they are Vancouver's words). It is as likely that Vancouver and Captain Quadra have interludes in one another's arms, as that Vancouver is shot by his Scots botanist, the one with the "glittering eye" who also bags an albatross which in this version skids into the deck on its chin, virtually at the same moment that Coleridge half way around the globe is envisioning his poem "The Ancient Mariner" on a like motif, and Blake is being put upon by philistines for confounding the linearity of print and carving picture poems (but of course is bound thereby even more to linearity as each line is painstakingly etched upon a copper plate); or that coastal "Indians" of the late eighteenth century debate middle-class values in the talk-show idiom of the educated modern masses ("There you go, speaking out of some habitual framework of guilt, says one to another"); or that Vancouver's men survive on sauerkraut (and perhaps they do: it is impossible to know where imagination has given way to fancy, but it is a curious culinary oddity that Bowering has them cook the sauerkraut and soak it down with vinegar rather than ferment it); or that Vancouver shares with Quadra, as well as tender moments, the occasional cup of Blue Mountain brand coffee. All this is as likely as not.

Historical linearity is an illusion which Bowering's zany sense of the absurd finds most accommodating. To be violated, conventions must be effectively present. The conventions of historical time, of sequence, coherence, and causality, are so thoroughly ingrained in the reader's consciousness that nothing is too bizarre, if placed in the proper context; nothing is too silly if surrounded by the pomp and circumstance of history. Language used against sense, words that violate authenticity, these do not impede the narrative flow. Events are related in the past tense, after they have happened, so no quirk of language, farce of words, will alter them. They exist prior to the immediacy of text, which is present experience in the reader's mind. History is what we make of it; whatever we will.

Kroetsch's demolition of historical time is performed less through ridicule than Bowering's. Kroetsch does not play grammatical inevitability against absurd language and incidents. Consistent with the closed form of *Badlands*, time is not collapsed through reader response, but rather its nature is re-invented as an integral part of the narrative and the novel's structural form.

Kroetsch attacks conceptions of time in the Western world with an abundance of irony. The form of his novel is ironic. The journey in search of immortality, the quest to defeat time, to become a word, is linear, a river journey. But the story comes to us through Anna —

she does not so much tell it as mediates between it and our world outside the text. The words are not hers — - they are a separate domain, the narrative world of existential reality. Anna's own story, which is not linear but transformational, as she moves through phases of drunken illumination towards an independent and separate self, contains her father's. The ironic tension between the two is sustained through the novel. Historical time is merely the expression of one man's fear and desire; it is related by courtesy of a woman's loneliness, which is its legacy. It is finally dismissed as irrelevant; but in letting her father's story snap like an elastic into another perspective, Anna implicitly acknowledges it as a source. She is not the son Dawe yearns for. With Tune's death even the chance for surrogate immortality expires (ironically, beneath the very clay that contains the bones on which Dawe rests his bid for fame). Anna is not his son: but he is her father (she, being the result of one of his forays East). And she, in the end, displaces him.

Irony runs deep, through the Dawe narrative especially. The ironies of Anna's world are primarily in relation to what we know of her father's. But everything about Dawe is couched in irony. He is the questing hunchbacked shaman on a journey into dead land, in pursuit of forever. While a world war rages in the background, he searches among bones for lasting life for himself. He digs among prehistoric remnants, the detritus of an era discarded by time, for a place in history. His search to defeat the linear flow of his life is sequential, an episodic narrative. Dawe is the ironic embodiment of Western man; he searches in death for meaning. He mounts history as if it were an aging whore and rides it into oblivion. He dies of his own success.

In his important essay on Noam Chomsky's theories of generative and transformational grammar, originally published in *The New Yorker*, and reprinted in *Extraterritoriality* in 1971 with footnote responses by Chomsky, George Steiner argues that a universal grammar and innate deep structures as determinants of language acquisition and usage would lead to only one or a few languages whereas, he declares, there are over four thousand in current use and these are likely the remnants of an even larger number. Chomsky argues that multiplicity of language is the result of specific adjustments necessary for cooperative survival among inseparable groups. Steiner insists that such diversity is contrary to the Darwinian principles of competitive progress.

They are, of course, speaking of the spoken word — language as an oral medium. They are speaking of an epoch preceding rapid travel of the masses, when language was a garrison to protect the interests of an enclosed and participating segment of the species. Steiner is rhetorical and Chomsky didactic, but both argue that language is the expression of a people, defines them, provides the limits of their consciousness, and is the repository of their collective experience with the world. Whatever the implications as to origin and evolution, the relationship between syntactical arrangements of the spoken word and man's enduring presence on the planet has undeniably been intimate. And the relationship between separate languages and sub-sections of the species seems, in terms of anthropology, an absolute bond.

Perhaps print changed everything, but so subtly we hardly realised. The garrison became a weapon, the weapon a vehicle, the vehicle a prison; and the prison has become the labyrinth of our present lives.

In the beginning, before the word was written, reality could be conceived, perhaps, as female. Language, and the consciousness it sustained, occurred in the perpetual present, each word a timeless moment, each sentence an expression of the speaker's presence in the world. Continuity was through repetition, through re-birth, and language was magic. But after print, when the word became substance, language came to be the mediator between consciousness and the world, and reality became male. Magic gave way to reason; circles to lines; rebirth to renewal; timelessness to chronology; patterns to fact; the pool to the river. History began.

Now we live among atomic particles and micro-chips, on the edge of an absolute night; and time means nothing again.

Perhaps language is only a metaphor. Perhaps another reality, integrated or even androgynous, is in the offing, and history, finally and mercifully, has come to an end.

Kroetsch and Bowering both use language and the narrative text in efforts to effect a change between consciousness and the nature of reality. In their small immodest ways, they aspire to alter not only how we perceive reality through print, but our conception of what it is. These are not mean ambitions, and if only partially realised it is perhaps because their objective is inseparable from the medium they are bound to use to achieve it.

Bowering's concern in *Burning Water* is primarily with perception; with how we read the world to be. With a lovely sense of paradox, the collapse of historical time is related through incidents which affirm the primacy of language to historical process. Languages that once held diverse peoples separate, at some point turned into the implement of collective aggrandisement. Captain George Vancouver sails "sixty-five thousand English miles" across the surface of the earth on behalf of the British Crown. He uses language to turn the unknown world (from a British perspective) into historical and geographical facts, in the service of national interest. The blood red of an English tongue spreads over half the globe: Empire is founded and sustained on the written word.

But with even greater irony, George Vancouver inhabits a world written for him by a fictional George Bowering. The world he claims for England, and for the sake of his immortal name, is just a fiction within another fiction. His story and all the facts that it contains are only the made-up project of a writer in search of himself in a story. Poor George. The poor Georges. One is merely an historical remnant, a word re-invented, and the other is an author who travels the globe in pursuit of the words that are already inside him. It is essential to note that the Vancouver written by the fictional George Bowering is intended as an authentic historical reconstruction. The benighted author of the dustjacket copy apparently mistook this for the novel's intent. But the George outside the text, in control of the Georges within, of course insists that Vancouver is absurd, and history unreal; and insists that the quest of the textual Bowering for meaning and completion through narrative patterns is equally as absurd.

The two Georges are locked to a common destiny by patterns and affinities that derive in fact from accidents of language — Vancouver, a place and person; George, a word both characters inhabit. The connections are not spatial (the fictional author flits about the globe with little reference to the subject at hand); and not temporal (the fictional author is convinced of the time that stands between them); and certainly not in deference to logic. Yet their lives eventually merge. When Vancouver at last weeps for himself "utterly and perfectly ... alone," he transcends words to become a fiction inseparable from his fictional author. He dies, and that version of Bowering disappears into the words of his death.

The character, Bowering, has been the reader's persona as well, the reader inside of the text, for whom the narrative worked, likewise, as a real created world. But, for the writer writing and the reader reading outside the text, that same reality is impossible, an illusion of words sustained by the most arbitrary of patterns, derived solely from language itself. *Burning Water* reduces the word-world to words and restores to the reader a sense of the real beyond text, of reality as a context in which all time may be present, all places here, a context in which even books may be real.

In *Badlands*, the conception of reality rather than its perception is the object of the narrative's implicit discourse. Kroetsch establishes within the text two distinct versions of reality: one is linear, an existential adventure, which Kroetsch associates with the male quest for continuity and significance, a quest for renewal which is ultimately bound to failure; the other is transformational, a structuralist reality of patterned repetition, associated with the female, with re-birth. Dawe's whole existence is contained within the story nurtured by his daughter into being, transliterated from his field notes into narrative simply by virtue of her being aware of them. But the female yearning for completion is no less illusory than the male's, for continuity. Had there been no Dawe, there would be no-one to tell his story.

The triumph that Kroetsch allows the two Annas at the end is not destruction of linearity and the existential conception of reality — merely its deflation. Reality, the text insists, is a story told in two ways, each of which may deny the other, but which are mutually dependent on the other's presence. The concept of reality as a text has been reduced to metaphor.

In her novel, *Surfacing*, Margaret Atwood displaces the existential quest of the female narrator with a transformational descent into the primal source of human being. The image of her mother guides the narrator back through all the selves that have preceded her, but the image of her father snaps her into time again, and leaves her there. In *Green Water, Green Sky*, Mavis Gallant breaks narrative linearity by boxing a vapid central character within four largely discontinuous accounts and draws a sad and squandered soul into substantial presence as the heir to familial patterns that make her ultimate demise inevitable. This is a narrative world informed not by Heidegger and Sartre but by Lévi-Strauss. In *Badlands*, Kroetsch insists that reality, despite the narrative flow, is not an existential treatise; nor, despite narrative displacement, is it a structuralist design. It simply is; and therefore so are we.

Criticism has long been the diversion of a colonised mind. For consciousness governed by the printed word, the world of experience is derivative and ephemeral. But the conception of reality as a text, the conviction that text is reality, no longer hold. Novels like Badlands and Burning Water challenge the logical structures of conventional inquiry, which deny the uncertainties born of the text or from prior knowledge. For myself, I would opt at this point to be guided by Wittgenstein's fragmentary and cumulative model, or McLuhan's field approach, in which the tension between antinomies might well convey more than their resolution. How much that we mean, I wonder, has been lost in trying to be understood.

WORKS CITED

1. George Bowering, Burning Water (Don Mills, 1980), pp 62, 63, 186, 100.
   Subsequent page references are to this edition and are included in the text.

2. Robert Kroetsch, Badlands (Toronto: 1975), p 103. Subsequent page references are to this edition and are included in the text.

BEING/FICTION

This foray to the edge of critical coherence was first published by Essays on Canadian Writing *in 1989 as "Life/Story: The Fictions of George Bowering." I wanted to include it not only to illuminate Bowering's renegade achievement but also to offer a context for my own developing sensibility. Rereading the essay now, I'm not at all certain I know what I'm talking about. Rereading it now, I thrill to rise above or beyond the limitations of rational discourse.*

Talking about George Bowering's fiction is a tall order, if the intent is to make any sense out of it or resolve the anomalies. You could get lost in a single story and after two or ten thousand words still not be out in the open again. Or ever.

That's the beauty of it. Once into a Bowering fiction, one of the good ones, you never really get out. It's not like reading Conrad, where you and the work are separable entities and as it is read to completion it is assimilated, becomes a part of you and you contain it. When you read Bowering, you and the text exist by mutual consent; you affirm its presence and it, yours, but, and this is where a story such as "Four California Deaths" works so brilliantly in its refusal to submit to the criteria of logical causality or narrative convention, your place in the rational world is subverted. You as reader are effectively contained by the fiction. You cannot think your way out. Contained, yes; affirmed and shaped by this and all the myriad other encounters you have had that make you who you are. You contain Conrad, but being contained, being brought quite literally to consciousness of yourself within a given text such as those of Bowering at his best, is another story. You are shaped and haunted by a Bowering fiction — haunted not by demons from within it but by the mirrored walls surrounding you. You see yourself at play among the image fragments and these, too, become a part of you.

What Bowering does is to counter George Steiner's argument that art bears no responsibility for being. The symphony at Auschwitz resounds no less than in a concert hall. Suffering and moral outrage might render listeners deaf, but not the music mute. To say there can be no poetry after Auschwitz is to miss the point. Words and language are still there, so long as consciousness survives. But can they again be used or heard when a) they have been reduced to vile servitude, and b) their most splendid sound has risen unperturbed through human smoke? The answer must be yes. But only through a radical change in the relationship between art and life, through the demolition of barriers between the two — so that the experience of art and the experience of life are not somehow discrete and different, but interpenetrating aspects of individual consciousness. It is necessary now, I think, that art affirm our presence in the world as individuals, separable from the collective. As individuals we survive and perish. It is when art and language gather us in groups, deny our individual presence, that we make concentration camps and die in them.

To bring art and life together, and here we move a long way from the thoughts of Northrop Frye, involves a radical change in the nature of art itself (and not merely in our perception of it). To be adequate as other than cultural and aesthetic artifact, art must command presence. Knowledge and appreciation are no longer enough. Participation is the only way out of the silence that threatens to close around us.

Two things come immediately to mind from this, neither of which has to do directly with George Bowering. The first is that most contemporary writers of fiction, especially in Canada, are utterly unaware of this change in necessity. Most of them write nineteenth-century narrative with a patina of modernity; and some do it exceptionally well — Robertson Davies, for instance, and Alice Munro (hardly peas in a pod). A few respond intuitively with occasionally grotesque experimentalism (Godfrey), or displaced historicity (Wiebe), or domesticity (Shields), or myopic specificity (Richards). And a few have been rendered silent (Laurence), or nearly so (Gibson, Wiseman, Watson), and others, perhaps, should have been.

The second thing is the opportunity that participatory fiction offers for "the excitation of moral response" — I use that cumbersome phrase on purpose, in an effort to circumvent a discussion of the moral dimension or moral intention of art, which has little to do, as Steiner indicates, with morality itself. Rather than sustaining a particular moral vision as a sort of subtext throughout, or culminating in a specific moral conclusion which might be extrapolated for critical analysis, or ignored, such fiction as now seems adequate involves the reader directly in moral experience. Not, as in Dostoevsky, to complement an aesthetic effect. Nor, as in Shakespeare. Moral experience is, rather, inseparable from aesthetic effect, from the experience of the work itself.

The moral confusion of Margaret Atwood's latest novel, *The Handmaid's Tale*, is exactly what I mean. There is not a moral dimension to the novel, or structure, or conclusion. Yet it involves the reader with explosive force in the moral complexity of its world. Reading *The Handmaid's* Tale is in itself a moral experience. We do not learn through the novel that morality can be confusing. We are genuinely confused. What Atwood gives the reader to think about is often at odds with what the narrative demands we feel. We find ourselves within the text, unable to sort out the contraries. And outside the text we find ourselves reading. The relationship between reading, morality, and individual presence in the world is a major concern of the novel and, obviously, of the author whose personality informs the work, inhabits the text, and shares with us her deepest and most whimsical fears.

Bowering avoids morality. As with many of his postmodern peers, there is a higher and more common purpose to his art. He wants nothing less than to give his reader life, and himself in the process. The ambiguity stands. This is what his fiction says: the barriers between life and art must fall; let's meet in the text for a while, free among words to become ourselves. It was inevitable, perhaps, following Husserl, following Saussure, Wittgenstein, Hitler, Goebbels, following Barthes, following Derrida, inevitable that realities beyond the text and within would eventually merge, that writers like Bowering would conceive fiction as the interpenetration of personalities.

***

"Four California Deaths" is a narrative labyrinth turned inside out. We cannot find our way in, yet we cannot escape. A seemly paradox in the contemporary world.

"Four California Deaths" is a wonderful story — the narrator in the frame story is right, though; his story is not properly a story at all. Nor is the story he occupies; nor are the two of them together, the frame and the narrative quartet it contains; not stories, not properly. And yet, "Four California Deaths" is quite wonderful.

The story, properly, occurs inside the reader's head, where, in the act of reading, we give Bowering room to play. It must be understood this is not a quaint description of imaginative response to aesthetic stimuli, not description by analogy of what happens when we read, in normal circumstances, the more conventional narratives of writers up till now, from Renaissance to Holocaust, who have dreamed to create alternative realities whole, in which to become lost. It is a literal account. The text is only the beginning. The story, properly, is what occurs to us within the text, while we are there. In mind, we complete the narrative; with personality, our own personalities, we participate to make it whole.

Recreation becomes re-creation. Reading "Four California Deaths," I make the story happen not by merely being the perceiving consciousness; I make it happen by actively participating as an individual human being holding all the disparate parts in mind and building from them a coherent experience of my own which may or may not have anything to do with someone else's story.

Let's consider what Bowering gives us: a frame story related by a Bowering persona, and four brief accounts of death by misadventure. The reason I describe the narrating persona as Bowering is that a whole network of connections is established between the person speaking in the text and a person, more complex and enigmatic, outside the text. Whether or not the prior originating personality is truly Bowering is, of course, relevant only to Bowering. What is important to us is the extent to which the frame is an expression of consciousness. The narrator is there as he tells it, and what he tells is this: he has made love with the woman who will be, and, as the frame closes, has been his reader. His own behaviour he finds mildly ridiculous — as lover, as writer asking to be read, as writer read. He banters with her about themes and purpose, about sex and death, mystery and puzzle. He thinks, while with her, about writing and nakedness and the time it will take her, and does take her, to read what he has written. She, his reader-lover, whom he has promised a salad afterwards, has "gorgeous long legs as important," he says, "to me as the air now filling my lungs." Now; even now, the reader counts.

But leave the frame, with all its whimsicality and high seriousness, its inconclusive affirmation of life, art, sex, and salads, its canny celebration of this writer's relations with the reader, this writer who won't just leave off, "turn over and go to sleep, like a normal man," and refine himself out of existence, as it were, but insists in the end on asking if the reader-lover "got it" — even when, especially when, we did not (though she, our representative, says *she* does). Look to his four brief narratives linked by an absurd web of incidentals and a network of common themes. Each tells of the death of a celebrated personage: Jean Harlow, Babe Ruth, Albert Einstein, and Tom Mix. Each celebrity is a fixture in the popular imagination; each has become an archetype. Their deaths here are absurd — there is no connection in fact with the actual demise of the person behind the personage. The accounts are presented in clinical detail or, perhaps "with reportorial dispatch" would be a more appropriate turn of phrase. And each death is a joke, relative to the world outside the text.

Harlow dies naked in a tattoo parlour; the Sultan of Swat dies in the minor leagues; Einstein suffocates in a high-school chemistry lab; and Tom Mix is squashed to death by Tony, the Wonder Horse, who has been bowled over by a 1937 De Soto. All die within the jurisdiction of the San Diego Police Department. A quotation from Joseph Conrad looms over each death scene; ambiguous evidence, suggesting foul play of more than somewhat elusive significance. A character in one account becomes a street name in another. Details from one account recur in others. Names connect; facts connect. Conspiracy is confounded, however, as the solid facts of one account become evanescent or peripheral in another, absent from a third, transformed entirely in the fourth.

The importance given to facts within each segment would seem to preclude personality, and yet the narrator's presence is virtually unavoidable — in every smart-ass turn of phrase, in each manipulative revelation of detail to suggest mystery and significance, in the insistent disinterestedness, the aggressive objectivity of voice, reminiscent of documentary journalism on the CBC.

The corpse of each ensconced in a bed of quasi-facts, conveyed to us with an air of urgent realism, these for us are the "real" Harlow, Ruth, Einstein, and Mix. Bowering brilliantly exploits the fallacy of realistic fiction: words displace sense, syntax is the only logic essential to narrative conviction. (Himmler's got the King locked up in the Tower of London). Even knowing the absurdity of these accounts, we struggle towards conspiracy, towards a conclusion which will resolve the contradictions on some coherent plane or another. The quartet is a puzzle — it must be. It can be unlocked, if only we find the key; solved, if we can discover the proper equation. That's what narrative is all about. Why tell a story otherwise? On some level, the metaphysical, the psychological, the epistemological, the facts, the design, the voice will cohere. We expect that of fiction, of narrative art (though, interestingly, not of visual art, not anymore). Why read a story otherwise?

Then, in the closing frame, the reader says yes, she got it. That's what makes her his reader; not reading but *getting it*. But what does she get? We don't know, for despite our best efforts to retrieve the story from absurdity, to make it cohere on a rational plane. And yet, paradoxically, when she gets it, we get it too. She says: " the only thing that puzzled me was why you decided to use my initials." Since there is no possible answer to this, either within the text or outside, puzzle, for us, gives way to mystery. Puzzles can be resolved. Mysteries cannot. Puzzles, in the story, have been associated with death, mysteries with life. This is a mystery, this story. It amuses, it entertains, it arouses, disturbs, stimulates, intrigues, but it does not answer. It is. Reading, we get it! Not what it is about, but the story itself. Our experience is the story. We enter the text and are contained by it; we enter the fiction and contain it. Our presence completes it. This is a wonderful story of we the readers, wrapped in mystery, containing the puzzle, becoming ourselves.

"Four California Deaths" is a mystery story in the true sense. It cannot be resolved; it remains a mystery. And it is not an upbeat version of interactive fiction, like those whodunits of the thirties which involved the reader in choosing among a cluster of options in order to shape the final story (the precursor to the game Clue, or the controlled-option story making a comeback on home video). Like a Borgesian garden of forking paths, such stories will ultimately coalesce on a rational plane. But in this story Bowering deploys conventional devices of realism and manipulates the readers' conditioned responses to realism, to create a dynamic narrative that goes nowhere, to involve us in a puzzle that cannot be resolved. In the end, the mystery remains — surrounding us.

Bowering displays a tremendous sense of fun in demolishing the barriers between his own life and the art he makes out of it. With personality, as the expression in language of individual consciousness, he prods and pries and scoops and shifts within the text. By being there in words, he opens up the narrative for us to be there too. I'm not talking about prose style. The distinction is important. Style is integral, inseparable from narrative. The story is the telling. The presence of personality, however, is a matter of words confounding narrative, subverting narrative design and undermining the apparent intent of the narrative in what appears to be the free exercise of being, in a contained or finite context. Style is the reduction or transliteration of personality to aesthetic effect and this other, its celebration.

To the extent that one is words — and it has been argued long before this, of course, that words and consciousness are coextensive, that language and personality are codeterminant — one may enter into a text and be there; be, there. It is not the possibility of doing this that is a radical innovation; it is the need and will to do it. That is what is new and different. Conrad worked with exquisite care to render personality, to transform it, into prose style. Hemingway reduced himself, his private being, to a variety of personae within accommodating verbal contexts. Closer to home, Sheila Watson recreated whole regions of her private being in a stylistic *tour de force* which utterly disguises who she is. In contrast, in *A Short Sad Book*, George Bowering celebrates his presence in the text and invites us to share the pleasures opened to us of being there with him.

In this novel, *A Short Sad book*, Bowering writes of writing, of his novel, of being written as he writes. This is not subject matter so much as it is a revelation of process, whereby the reader is invited to share in the novel's creation — for otherwise the narrative threatens to falter. We will not let it, though. We are conditioned, perhaps only by the force of syntax on procedures of thought, to perceive linear coherence even where there is none. We make narrative, as we read, out of grammatical construction. If a text audaciously defies conventional expectations, we impose coherence, nonetheless. If Bowering says, let's see where this will go, we go with him. The narrative writes us, and him, into being within the text.

Amid quips and gibes and jokes and various asides, the textual Bowering tells the reader what his novel would be about, if it were a novel at all — which it isn't until we join him there and complete the narrative design. From our own experiences and personalities, we provide continuity, coherence, shape, and significance to the narrative his text implies. So, amid a riotous display of images and allusions we make a novel together, Bowering and I. Surrounded by references to staking peonies, to pursuit of the Pretty Good Canadian Novel, to rootless cosmopolytes, baseball, the West Coast Experience, Evangeline, postmodernism, and the "*Tercentenary History of Canada*, Volume III, From Laurier to King," Bowering expresses himself — literally, he squeezes, pours himself onto the page. I, as reader, we, surrounded by the same detritus of a manic mind, we, to find order, impose our separate selves upon the page — again, quite literally. To make narrative out of this, we must see ourselves there, watch ourselves at play within the text, making sense. Even, perhaps especially, where there is none.

A Short Sad Book is the most successful antinovel novel of my acquaintance. One of my favourite books. One of the few books in which I am a featured participant, though unnamed, and co-creator, both within the text, where my presence is a narrative necessity, and outside it, where I revel in the pleasures of lending narrative completion to Bowering's experiment in being. As I open to the novel, the barriers between life and art disintegrate. And the novel opens to me. We coexist, by mutual consent. Mutual affirmation. Bowering too. He's there as well. Here and there.

By making sense, I do not mean sensible or even logical or rational. We make sense within the text by bridging opposites and anomalies in ways that neither art alone nor actuality would (seem to) sustain. Sense, then, in the sense of presence. By being there, within the text, we provide coherence. Or, to turn it around: by asserting contraries, the text commands our presence. Demands our involvement; not response, but participation. Demands we be, affirms our being.

Postmodernism flies in the face of sailing to Byzantium (what a lovely mélange of allusions!). It does not refute Yeats, for what argument could be mounted against the argument that places art above life? You do not reason against fascism, even when expressed by the most beautiful of poets. You provide an alternative. Life and art, you insist, can be interpenetrating and inseparable. I have seen

Ben Bulben from the churchyard near Sligo and thought poetry. But I would rather Yeats had shared the experience with me, than lie buried there beneath a modest stone and the finest of words.

The point of postmodernism is not to achieve immortality through self-exposure, nor to make the text a vehicle for self-expression. Rather, it is a refusal to fade, to do a Yeats and yield being to art.

Postmodernism thrives on paradox and anomaly. When we are brought to an awareness, simultaneously, of opposing realities, when we accommodate within consciousness the contraries of a particular text, then our experience of life and of art becomes equally the experience of ourselves. Yeats left behind a marvellous legacy, but nothing of Yeats.

In the novel *Burning Water,* there is a character called George Bowering. There is a character called George Vancouver. If you know enough of the world to find your way into the text, you know that both Georges are based on, or somehow related to, actual people in historical time. You also know that, at the time of writing, George Vancouver had achieved historical completion — that is, he was dead. And George Bowering was not. But the textual Vancouver is very much alive, while the Bowering persona moves through the narrative towards annihilation. The fictional Vancouver becomes inseparable from his fictional author, and as Vancouver dies into textual immortality, the fictional Bowering disappears into the words of his character's death. The reader is not left, though, with absence, a vacuum. Another George Bowering, the personality surviving the text who has been at play with you throughout the narrative, is still very much a presence. While the textual Bowering, the fictional Bowering, has kept you at a distance from the text he claims to be his own, the fiction he says is his — the living George, alive within the text, at play within the fiction, has subverted the distancing effect with weird and dazzling word games, games of paradox and contrariety, that demand awareness on your part of both yourself and the author together creating a narrative of marvellous design.

Reading *Burning Water*, you repeatedly bump into yourself reading. The narrative does not thereby collapse, the illusion somehow shattered. Rather, you exhilarate in finding yourself alive among the words.

How does Bowering do it? The real George Bowering, whose personality you encounter line by line, if only in an ampersand, does it by playing thought and feeling off against each other, rational response against emotional. We are moved, when reason says there is nothing here to move us, only nonsense and the bizarre; we are made to think, when feelings render thought absurd. George Vancouver is a ridiculous character, utterly improbable, yet we care for him. His penchant for Blue Mountain brand coffee, his comfort in the arms of Captain Quadra, his inept anachronistic utterances, his bombast and spleen, all these make him historically unlikely, rather unlikable, yet textually so real that we know him as an extension of ourselves.

In this field of play between intellectual and emotional response, we find ourselves. Such fields the postmodern writer cultivates assiduously in pursuit of art as an act, not work, of imagination. An avant-garde modernist, such as Graeme Gibson in his rigorously experimental novel, *Five Legs*, commits to print his finished work. We, the readers, immerse ourselves amidst the brilliant flashes of fractured syntax, thought shifts, voice-mood distortion, and other such devices by which Gibson attempts to transform conditions of consciousness into art. Gibson — just as Faulkner does in the opening phase of *The Sound and the Fury*, where the reader is caught up in Benjy's crippled mind, or as Joyce does in the closing of *Ulysses*, where the reader is surrounded by the injured mind of Molly Bloom — deploys elements of style quite radically to fix in print the procedures of a particular imagined consciousness. These models, paradigms, or artifacts do not evoke conditions of mind within the reader but rather arouse our variegated response to those conditions.

By comparison, a Bowering fiction is often radically incomplete. Perhaps in a story like "Arbre de décision" it is only grammar that urges the reader towards completion; conventional narrative design displaced by syntactical coherence. Not displaced in the sense of being pushed aside, but rather as in "taking the place of." Only grammar in certain Bowering fictions offers sense. The text in such a fiction becomes an open field or "context" in which the dynamics of the reader's response quite literally bring the narrative into being.

Sentence by sentence, scene by scene, events occur in the reader's mind. They do not logically follow, one from another, and are, in the sequence offered, often contradictory, often mutually exclusive. Yet, as read, they exist with equal probability. They have clearly happened. Narrative use of the past tense is affirmation of this — although the act of reading, of entering these events into consciousness, would suffice as evidence of their having already occurred.

In the normal course of things, our minds, conditioned by several thousand years in service to the doctrine of logical causality, would sift through the conflicting possibilities in a story like "Arbre de décision" and select the most likely combination as the dominant reality. Everything else would then be accounted aberrations due to character imagination, altered states of consciousness, or authorial ineptitude. But what of a story which refuses intentional coherence, which makes sense, paragraph by paragraph (although occasionally one paragraph does spill into another), but will not submit to rational inquiry; a story which proceeds with casual eloquence towards completion but yields upon analysis no structure, only pattern, no architectural form at all, but only a fine and intricate design?

"Arbre de décision" is Byzantine. From the possible or possibly imagined ringing of a telephone, a number of bizarre narratives emerge. None would be especially bizarre on its own, but each precludes the possibility of the others. They are related, usually paragraphed to keep them apart, with equal verisimilitude and in much the same jaunty third-person voice. There is a certain sequential and chronological development as attention shifts from one account to another, but this is periodically violated. Arthur Cuff inhabits all of them, although, as I said, each precludes the others. Passages of fear, bewilderment, erotica, and pedantry follow one after, but not from, another. Darlene in bed, Judy on the phone or in the bathroom, Valerie in the office, Elena in the taxi. Or not. Oral, anal, inverted, sado-masochistic, and ordinary acts of sex. Or not. Propositions, threats, queries, conjecture, and discussion. Murder, torture, grammatical dysfunction. White slacks, blue slacks, bathrobes, and towels, covering, revealing, disguising nakedness/ fear/loathing/ lust. There is so much, to this story, and it is all possible, all there.

It is not given to us, the readers, to resolve the narrative complexity of "Arbre de décision." Bowering has not created a puzzle in which, if we are smart enough, we will perceive the narrative intent, what he was up to, what the "real" story is. That, ultimately, is a trivial activity. We may be driven or drawn through the story by an innate desire for coherence. That's what motivates us to fill spare corners of our lives doing crosswords and playing bridge. But this story is more like Scrabble. Intersecting clusters of meaning bear no relevance to one another yet exist at each other's pleasure. As the reader-players, our purpose is not to make connections on a rational plane, to sort out the story line. It is, rather, to discover within ourselves the knowledge and the tolerance that will lead to closure, to completion of the game. By tolerance I mean our ability to accept the syntactical confusion of Scrabble, the narrative confusion of "Arbre de décision." Neither, ultimately, admits analysis. We accept all word/realities as possible. It is in exploiting our capacity for doing this that both text and game demand a reassuring intensity of consciousness. But from beyond the text, within our separate lives, we gather more of ourselves and give more, when reading, than when we play a game of Scrabble. We are amused and changed by Bowering, amused by Scrabble — and perhaps a little edified by the discovery of a word or two previously hidden from us; but not changed. Knowledge does not change us. Only experience does, even when it is the experience of knowledge.

"Arbre de décision" is puzzling, but it is not a puzzle. The various erotic, psychotic, confused, and distracting events surrounding Arthur Cuff are not offered as options from which either he, or we, must choose in order to make sense of his life/story. As readers, everything we read is equally valid. We can hold many narratives simultaneously in mind. We are used to doing so in conventional fictions, where plots and subplots are woven together in complex structural patterns. We can hold opposing responses simultaneously in mind: it is on this basis that irony has evolved as the voice of modernism. But here, Bowering confounds sense — the narrative fragments will not cohere. They are for the most part mutually exclusive, yet they are equally possible. The responses they demand are not ironically modulated but often utterly in opposition, and quite irreconcilable on a logical plane. It is not Arthur who imagines the diverse lives each fragment of the narrative implies. We are used to that. But here, each possibility for Arthur is as real as every other, as it happens. And as it happened.

It is not Arthur but the author who imagines Arthur's multifoliate presence in the text. It is the author, being there, who makes Arthur plausible, despite logic. It is the author as text who invites the reader to participate in the mélange of narrative realities adhering to the personality of Arthur Cuff. And we do. With reason and emotional response thrown thoroughly askew, we hold all that happens possible and respond without reference to logic and the outside world. We are, in other words, contained within the text, though not the narrative, and of necessity become a presence there — for otherwise there would be only an agglomeration of contraries. Our presence is integral to the narrative design.

And in seeing ourselves caught up among the contraries, the cementing seams in this Byzantine mosaic, and in seeing Bowering there, inseparable from the mosaic itself, we are brought to a deeper understanding not of grammar, sex, and mayhem, or alternative realities, but of ourselves within and, as readers in the living world, outside the text.

The principle thrust of postmodern fiction such as Bowering writes is the revelation of being. I'm not talking here about epiphany, where variations of Stephen Dedalus expose themselves in a glare of intersecting narrative beacons. Nor about propriocentrism: that's a matter of subject matter, ultimately, a lyric concept, what poetry can be about. No, not revelations about, but of, being. (One almost wants to bring in a discussion of *dasein*, but Heidegger leads away from text, not deeper into it.) What I mean to say is that, in these words, this text, in Bowering fictions, consciousness is intensified and the self revealed — the individual personalities of writer and reader both.

In "Four California Deaths" and "Arbre de décision," the impress of personality is flamboyant and yet in the lovely melancholy tale, "The Clam-Digger," the Bowering presence is exquisitely subtle and the reader achieves the revelation of self only by implication. There are many ways to the same end. The purpose of all such fictions is to be life affirming. The content of each of these three stories wears the tattered shroud of death, yet each celebrates life, proclaims the author's presence and evokes the reader's consciousness of being. I know of few new-written tales to match "The Clam-Digger" for its poignancy and beauty. It calls to mind Antoine de Saint-Exupéry, or even Hans Christian Andersen. And yet (and this is the third use of a qualifying conjunction in this short paragraph), it is West Coast contemporary; upbeat, laid-back, and lots of fun.

Woodruff, the poor and lonely clam digger, is recognizable from the pages of fairy-tale romance, and from a passing encounter perhaps on Wreck Beach the last time you were in Vancouver, someone you saw on the streets of Winnipeg, or in a pub in Halifax. Woodruff rides the back of a giant turtle into the depths of the ocean where he lives in languid splendour as Prince Woodruff, marries, has children, and is adored by all in his realm. But he longs to visit one more time the world he left behind. Once back, he is suddenly aged beyond recognition; he is stranded there, in the real world of barber shops and city streets, and another young man prepares to take his place. As you read of Woodruff, you find yourself tumbling forward through the lovely prose, wonderfully anxious to know the come. And even on your third or seventh reading, as with all good fairy tales, you still yearn towards the end, towards completion, so that what will happen can happen.

Each telling of it, each reading, plays on the delicious certainty that it will be the same. And yet, it never is. In the course of telling Woodruff's story in such a way that it seems to tell itself, Bowering occasionally and whimsically intrudes, riding a twist of phrase, an unruly word, or a lovely inappropriate image such as the one of ocean layers as the shifting colours on an old-fashioned jukebox. Look, he says, this enchanted world, it comes from somewhere, comes from me, I'm here. And for the reader, his presence adds poignancy; the enchanted world is accessible, and yet isn't ours. As it contains the writer writing, so too does it contain us reading — but paradoxically, it will not let us in. There is a timeless quality about any fairy tale that bittersweetly affirms our presence outside of it, in time.

If one wanted to, one could offer up a reading of "The Clam-Digger" in which exactly what I've said above about time and timelessness, the illusions of parallel realities, the relativity of stasis and change, is shaped as fiction.

But why, when the fiction itself says it better? It is enough to note that, as with the rest of Bowering's work, "The Clam-Digger" is an exemplar of its own inherent argument.

Nowhere is this more evident than in the novel, *Burning Water* —

Or in such rough and brilliant fictions as "Looking for Ebbe," "Carter Fell," and "A Short Story."

Only by watching the birds fly do we know there is sky between the trees.

EXPLODING SLOWLY

For those unfamiliar with postmodern discourse, think of this as a poem. Following essays on form in fiction, it seems appropriate to share what I hope is the effectiveness of deconstructing rhetorical structure. "Exploding Slowly" is meant to accumulate in the mind and then, in retrospect, reveal what it has to say. In that sense it is a poem. Or, if you prefer, think of it as postmodern dialectics: discontinuous, contradictory, esoteric, and. more than the sum of its parts. It was created for a conference entitled "Under Fire: The Canadian Imagination and War," held at the Royal Military College in Kingston in February, 2000, and intended to draw a mostly military audience into reconsiderations of John McCrae's iconic poem, "In Flanders Fields." The proceedings were published in Under Fire *(Blue Heron Press, 2003). The full title of my contribution was "Exploding Slowly. The Mutability of Meaning:* Buffy, *'In Flanders Fields,' and* The Faerie Queene."

When I turned fifty, I swore I would never write another footnote, and when I turned sixty, I vowed to abjure irony and speak only from the heart. After a lifetime wandering through the undergrowth of academe, I have found myself emerging from Dante's dark wood into a tangled luxuriant undisciplined wilderness of actual experience, and as Martha Stewart would say, it is a very good thing.

Why the confessional opening? Because what I have to say about war in a Canadian context represents the confluence of culture and memory, perception and thought, at a particular point in a particular life. All knowledge is personal. Every discourse is a confession, and if I were to tell you that John McCrae's "In Flanders Fields" can be positioned as a mediating phenomenon at the moral interface between two extended allegories, one Elizabethan and the other California chic, you would need to give your own personality free rein to follow the metaphysical conceit of my argument.

Edmund Spenser's very long poem, *The Faerie Queene*, is not something you may be intimate with, and the television saga, *Buffy the Vampire Slayer*, might be alien to many who know all six books of *The Faerie Queene*. Despite four hundred years between them, the difference in medium, the leap from high romance to wrought irony, *Buffy* speaks to and for our age as indirectly, perversely, and effectively, as Spenser's visionary epic did his. Knowledge of one does not preclude familiarity with the other; quite possibly the educated imagination is familiar with neither. But everyone knows the accidental allegory, "In Flanders Fields." It is from that premise I would like to talk about all three, in an effort to say something important about the instability of absolutes.

John McCrae's poem is so inextricably a part of you, of us, it is impossible to read as a text, or even to re-read it, as T.S. Eliot said was a requirement for the appreciation of all good poetry. "In Flanders Fields" is embedded in our brains, encoded among neurons, encrypted in impulses of electrical energy and chemical interactivity. It is a part of our personalities, a component of character, not a poem at all but the memory of a poem. Not a remembered poem, but an inextricable element of our individuality and our collective identity, a memory as important as the day Kennedy died, or Elvis, or Princess Diana. Part history, part myth, intensely private and very public, shared and guarded, misquoted with embarrassment, treasured like an old tennis racket or an ancestral wedding band.

In a discussion of "In Flanders Fields," you need to be aware of yourself thinking.

Before I go on, in what appears to be an essay of asides, and at the risk of sounding cantankerous, I need to suggest there is no such thing as *the* Canadian imagination. To think otherwise raises an impediment between us that must at the least be acknowledged if it is either to be scaled or demolished. A common or shared polyphonous or multicorporate imagination is a notion, although questioned by cultural theorists, often employed by well-meaning critics, pollsters, and hysterical politicians. It is a phrase intended to articulate a collective personality that can be contained within national boundaries, one both familiar to its constituents and recognizable to outsiders. "The Canadian imagination" as a concept is a flag of convenience. I live within the English language, but I do not think as an Englishman. I am surrounded by the clutter of American consumerism, but I do not spend like an American. I am a Canadian, and fiercely so, but my imagination has been pummelled and refined by forces of language and culture that leap national boundaries with the alacrity of Superman who, as we know from a Canadian Heritage Moment, originated in Toronto.

You cannot think of cultures as continents. If — Donne to the contrary — we are each of us islands, locked into a personal journey from conception to death, we share the world from our separate perspectives. Culture is a disciplinary construct for the convenience of study, but there is no such entity, only an infinite array of interpenetrating experiences. The holy books of George Bush and Osama bin Laden overlap, their foundational stories and values are not complementary but identical. The music that thrilled Winston Churchill in the bath was the same that filled the house of Rodolph Hesse while each morning the doomed scraped off the grease of human smoke from the windows of his home in Auschwitz. The poetry of Li Po, transliterated from Chinese of the fourteenth century Ming Dynasty finds its way into Pepsi commercials. Homer's Odysseus, the Roman's Ulysses, becomes an Irish expatriate's novel and informs the existential angst of gangsta rap. We are all separate, we are all in this together. We are a collectivity by imperial fiat, the limits of geography, cultural memory, academic convenience, and the aesthetic presumption of common experience.

"In Flanders Fields" has evolved into a defining moment in the Canadian collective, and yet it is a subversive poem. It was written by a doctor at war — surely a necessary oxymoron, only exceeded in contrariety by the notion of a battlefield chaplain. It was originally published in 1915, in *Punch*, a British humour magazine that occasionally used wit as a weapon against the imperious Germans and more rarely published caustic commentary on the British Imperial Project, of which the Great War was both the culmination and the terminus. Not only is John McCrae's poem subversive, but it has ironically been misread by nearly a century of readers as the subversion of what it subverted. It is a poem against war, against the values it is used to celebrate, the virtues it is felt to proclaim.

Such a reading of the poem etched in the minds and hearts of generations nurtured in the blood-drenched memory of Flanders might seem to be heretical, or worse, in bad taste. So, before we consider the implications of aesthetic revisionism, let us address the poem itself. I do not believe it is necessary to rehearse the words for your benefit since everyone within range of my critical rant will know it by rote. Instead, I ask you to scan the lines in your mind, search out the sentiments for which the poem is best known. Isolate, if you can, the images pertaining to patriotism, to service, to God.

Meanwhile, I wonder, have you seen the movie, *The Four Feathers*? The recent remake — I am old enough to remember a black and white version. The present variant appeared on the market after 9/11, and it is racist, sexist, and morally simplistic, but then it is about the racist, sexist, morally simplistic Victorian English, as exemplified by British military adventures in the Muslim Sudan. The contemporary twist at the end of the movie, which is a gripping good yarn, has a wounded soldier declaring that when it comes down to it, on the battlefield there is only one fight and that is the fight for survival — but, curiously, not of oneself. You fight and you die for your comrades, for the soldiers to your left and your right, not against the enemy ahead, not for the generals behind, nor the society they serve.

By now you will have subvocally reiterated McCrae's poem while attending on another level to my distracting peroration on popular culture, and you will have been met by frustration, and the dawning excitement of familiarity as you recognize that the message of the film, delivered quite literally as a sermon, is the same as the meaning of the poem. McCrae's dirge is the anthem of the universal soldier. There is no lofty cause expressed, no corner of a foreign field that on the soldier's sacrifice will be forever Canada. This is no creed to pious thought, nor grim devotional to the values of a home and native land. Heroic virtues are not held as consolation for the misery of ignominious death. On the darkling plains where ignorant armies clash by night, the only honour is the honour among comrades whose veins in the crucible of war flow with common blood.

My older brother flew with the Blackhawks out of Malta in World War II. My cousin Molly was a CWAC. My great uncle, Lynne Pattinson, was an officer who led his troops into death at Givenchy. My father's flight boots were big enough, there was a time I could stand inside either one of them. When he died his casket was draped in the Canadian flag. Fifty feet away, there was a plaque below a stained-glass window in St. John's Anglican Church in Preston, Ontario, commemorating the sacrifice of his uncle Lynne.

My brother was eight when the war ended. The Blackhawks were a comic book creation. I suppose they were American. Uncle Lynne was inexplicably a private. My cousin Molly moved to the States. When I was asked by the funeral director if "father" would want a flag over his coffin, I said in a cranky response, he's my father, not yours. And I said no. I could not imagine why there should be a flag. My father never spoke of the war as a personal experience. He talked about Rommel and about Montgomery, and he read Blackhawk comics with my older brother. My mother insisted I call the funeral home and tell them he would definitely have wanted a flag. I was five when the war ended, my father was three when Lynne Pattinson went off to the wars, and five when he died. My father remembered his uncle's death but not his life. My father's war was singular, not plural, the War, not The Wars.

My mother's mother lost a son in World War I and another in World War Il, although both came home and died years later. She remembered the day the Black Donnellys died, she remembered when Poundmaker lost the plains war and when Big Bear signed a treaty. My daughter's husband is from Malta. His grandfather was an aide to Lord Mountbatten. She lives in the United States. In 1814, the Americans were our enemy. Italy was on our side in the First World War, their side in the Second. I used to read Blackhawk comics, that was before I could read. My other daughter lives in Vancouver. She would be annoyed if I left her out. She was in the navy one summer, aboard HMCS Cataraqui.

And that is how history is made. It is a weaving. War is a cultural event, where the personal and public converge.

"In Flanders Fields" reverberated through my brain as a child, while I fell asleep dreaming of blowing Japanese Zeroes to smithereens and pulverizing Nazis who were German, but not at all like my German grandfather. John McCrae's poem vied in my mind with images of Charlie Chaplin as the Great Dictator and Bugs Bunny doing a *seig hiel* dance with Elmer Fudd. When I was fifteen, in real life, I could strip a Bren Gun, blindfolded. I do not know if we were actually blindfolded, but that's how I remember it. I learned how to toss the plumber's nightmare, a Sten Gun, into a roomful of Nazis so that it landed on its butt end and bounced about, killing the lot of them. I learned how to scream like a banshee while I stuck my bayonet into some poor bugger who was trying to stick his bayonet into me but was disarmed by my blood-curdling rhetoric. This is what I was taught in high school. And how to throw hand grenades, exactly when to pull the pin and when to throw. My teachers were mostly veterans. I also learned to recite "In Flanders Fields" as a mantra.

Listen, I am trying to tell you something important. For me, in the wake of World War II, the words "We are the Dead" echoed with a visceral thrill: Come! Be with us! Lay down your life to honour your comrades — there is nothing here of God or country or transcendent values. It is a celebration of the kingdom of death and the values that provide access to the fellowship of the dead. Not maimed and mutilated, but slumbering in eternal restlessness. This was a restlessness I connected with as an adolescent that was not assuaged by playing football or committing the periodic table to memory or drive-in movie dates. It was a restlessness informed by the conflicts between being and meaning, although I would have recognized it only as longing; a diffuse anxiety at having nothing in a secular age to admire. "In Flanders Fields" made war a dreadful fantasy, a sort of performance. And it continues to do so, if only on Armistice Day, when Dying affirms the virtue of sacrifice, and Death is a judgement.

This I understood: War is not good but it is right, or else we would not engage in it. War is not evil but it is wrong, or else we would wage it perpetually.

Edmund Spenser wrote *The Faerie Queene* in the 1590s, about the same time Shakespeare was writing the history plays. It is interesting how much better Shakespeare has fared than Spenser. Perhaps it is because Spenser was pretty boring as a stylist and repetitive in his various thinly disguised supplications to the Queen; or perhaps it is because Shakespeare used language in ways that shaped how we still relate to each other through words — not just at the Stratford Festival but in ordinary conversation. In any case, both poets wrote about war. For Shakespeare, war was an expression of character and the manifestation of destiny. He knew the outcome from the beginning and portrayed kings and tyrants accordingly, to make their ends inevitable. Spenser reduced warfare to allegory, the battles, to jousting among knights. The winner was determined by virtue. In neither are soldiers of intrinsic importance. For Shakespeare they are machinery to work the will of their leaders. They are indistinguishable from scenery. For Spenser, they are an implied absence. In the rarefied world of symbolic existence, those not engaged in the romantic enactment of moral conflict are no more than shadows. Spenser's allegorical *zeitgeist* is a quest for the meaning of grace in human affairs; an exploration of how right, which is a relative measure, relates to goodness, which is transcendent and absolute.

"In Flanders Fields" is about forgetfulness. Unlike Spenser's poem, it is a narrative related from the perspective of the dead, for whom love as the defining characteristic of their lives is an absence. There are no adventures left to pursue, no virtues to be enacted amidst dramatic pageantry. Only sleep, deep within the earth, that is all that remains, all that is wished for. But it shares with Spenser a profound desire to tell a story that is laden with meaning. The meaning, however, is not what it appears to be. This is not surprising with allegory, which is a form given to misdirection, but it is quite disconcerting in an elegy, a truncated epic of thoughtless sacrifice.

Poppies are the colour of blood, the poppy bloom looks like exploded human flesh, perforated with a bullet in the black gaping hole at its centre. And the poppy is an opiate. McCrae as a doctor knew opium was an extract from the unripe seed pods of the poppy and must have felt the bitter irony to see these flowers of forgetfulness blowing in the breeze among crosses marking the graves of the unnaturally dead.

When you were a child, did you have trouble recalling whether the poppies *blew* or *grew* above the fallen soldiers in the earth below? As the poem opens, the poppies blow; there is an immediate scene played out for the eye of the listener, the flowers are alive within the sound of booming fusillades as artillery and small arms interminably shatter the air. At the poem's close, the epic's end, the poppies grow, deep-rooted in the earth, the opiate of forgetfulness, beneath which the restless dead shall not sleep, if you, their cohort, do not close ranks and sustain their unarticulated cause.

Buffy the Vampire Slayer is allegorical. Buffy is a knight errant of the modern era. She wanders about Sunnydale in search of adventure and romance with no purposeful pattern of motion, driven only by the motive to destroy evil whenever it happens to find her. Edmund Spenser in *The Faerie Queene* was revolutionary in his rejection of a simplistic divide between good and evil, the Manichean chasm that dominated moral and ethical thought in his time. He would have found George W. Bush a moral primitive, unable to recognize the ambiguity informing human affairs, or perhaps an ethical pragmatist, in response to the universal comfort in knowing friend from enemy. Joss Whedon, the creator of *Buffy*, has no problem identifying the enemy or distinguishing between good and evil. Buffy and the Scoobies are attractive and good; the forces of darkness are grotesque, their malevolence often marked by the instability of their physical being, or in their misshapen flesh. Even Spike, the vampire with a soul, is only handsome when he is behaving himself or having sex with the slayer.

The genius of *Buffy* as an allegory is not in the intricate analysis of the relations between virtue and vice found in *The Faerie Queene*, amidst tales of heroes and heroines, knights and their ladies, laden with symbolism and metaphor. There is not even the moral ambivalence in *Buffy* to be found in *Xena: Warrior Princess*, with its truly bizarre wrenching of history and myth into a parallel world of homoerotic insignificance. What Joss Whedon has done is post-Freudian; characters are not driven by their sexuality; their sexuality is driven by their characters. What he has done is postmodern. Characters do not fight evil because it is right and good to do so, but because they have been conscripted by fate, and their enemies do not enact evil, scheming to bring about the end of the world, because that would provide fulfillment, but because that is what evil things do. Only the irrepressible Spike recognizes that the end of the world would be a bad thing, even for bad people — while he personally might survive the apocalypse, since as a vampire he is already undead, but there would be an extreme shortage of blood.

What Joss Whedon has done in *Buffy the Vampire Slayer* is to develop through a series of allegorical episodes a champion for an ordinary world threatened by the absurdity of evil, constantly in danger from arcane forces buried deep within our collective psyche. This unlikely champion began in book one, the first season, as a diminutive Lolita in a tight sweater and a mini-skirt, exploding vampires and extinguishing demons as she struggled to pass algebra and maybe make the cheerleading squad. After seven seasons, she is a brooding avenger. Her breasts are smaller, her legs are sheathed in slacks, and she is a guidance counsellor with all the problems of premature responsibility as she hovers above the Hell Mouth, saving the world. She is isolated from her friends, understood only by the lover she despises. Consistently, she occupies her author's moral vision wearing the armour of worldliness and wielding the sword of irony, as she brings the bad guys down.

In the Buffy-verse, as in the allegorical world of *The Faerie Queene*, written four centuries earlier, there is good and there is evil. There is right and there is wrong. In Spenser, unreal characters live in a courtly fantasy; in Joss Whedon, the wondrous is ironically ordinary — realism in a world where the fantastical is as probable as a bathroom sink. Sunnydale is Pleasantville, Smallville, Mariposa, with contemporary values, contemporary problems. And to complicate matters, it is a strategic centre for bad things to happen, emanating from the lower world, where even the most monstrous entities have reassuringly human flaws. Good and evil are clearly distinguishable. But right and wrong are not. And that is the genius of *Buffy*. Right and wrong are related to intention and consequence, but good and evil are unequivocal, immutable, absolute. Those who cross over, Angel and Spike, do not move from evil to good but from evil to right and that, of course, is wrong, since evil remains their defining characteristic, no matter how good they become.

"In Flanders Fields" offers the opposite. Right and wrong are clearly defined. It is right to fight on and to keep the faith with fallen comrades. It is wrong to stand down. Within the poem, the dead press the living to stand firm beside them, and for the reader, encountering the poem in *Punch* in 1915, as the war raged just beyond the eastern horizon, there is a powerfully brooding exhortation to sustain their quarrel with the foe. It would be wrong to do otherwise. But these are social values, behavioural imperatives. Nothing is said of good and evil. The narrative voice shifts in the final stanza from the clarion wail of the ghostly Dead to an admonition by soldiers hovering on the brink, for whom death is an ongoing act. It is no longer the dead speaking to the living, but "us" who are dying, who speak for the dead. Even in that terrible shift, there is no movement towards consolation or clarity. McCrae's poem is about dying in vain, for nothing is offered to make the unnatural death of a soldier worthwhile.

Armistice changed everything. Imperial Germany was humbled. The killing fields of Europe congealed. War's end declared war obsolete. The better part of a generation gathered what was let of itself and went home. "In Flanders Fields," a poem which took no sides, as the greatest of war novels take no sides, novels such as *The Red Badge of Courage, All Quiet on the Western Front, Generals Die in Bed, The Naked and the Dead, Slaughterhouse-Five, The Wars*, the poem that took no sides became a record of the cost of victory. What had been a threnody or dirge took on epic proportions after the war, for the numbers who had died to achieve that victory were imponderable. And the poem was cast in a new light, exploding slowly through time. A moving plea against breaking ranks became an allegory of national purpose. Our quarrel with the foe became, implicitly, the unarticulated declaration of good over evil, peace over war, the moral justification for the slaughter of innocence.

I use the word "innocence" advisedly, for one of the great ironies of war is the notion that only civilians are innocent, while soldiers fall outside the perimeters of morality, fallen already, before hostilities begin. It is these, the fallen, marching smartly off to yet another conflict, for whom the allegory is a necessary fiction — not the poem itself, which gives them fellowship with the dead, but the expansive simulacrum of the poem that has entered into our cultural makeup as a memorial for the triumph of good over evil. That, their innocence stripped away, is cloak and shroud for fallen soldiers still unborn.

We cannot know to what extent art reflects our sensibilities at the times of its creation and to what extent it shapes our future. Consider the monumental statuary by which we memorialize war. In ancient Rome there were arches and obelisks raised to commemorate victories. Some of these still stand amidst the traffic congestion of modernity. Rising over Trafalgar Square in London is the modest statue of Lord Nelson atop a vast column of stone, and in Washington the Washington Monument excoriates an urban sky, both in celebration of national heroes. But the art that moves us most is the art that marks not victory but the sacrifice of lives. Descend into the cool shadows of the Vietnam Memorial in Washington, gaze into the voluptuous austerity of the monument at Vimy Ridge, so passionately illuminated by Jane Urquhart in her novel, *The Stone Carvers*, and quite literally your life will change. But does the vast and terrible beauty of these monuments to military losses, which in the wars of the preceding century were the collateral damage of conflicting ideologies, and in many conflicts fewer by far than civilian casualties, does their austere beauty offer an adequate measure of posterity's regard for the sacrifice, or are they messages to the future, messages read in the hearts of the children of the fallen as they march to wars of their own? At Vimy, heroic stone stands proudly grieving, vast, too large for any man; and soldiers like my father went to war believing in heroic causes. He made a pilgrimage to Vimy just before hostilities began. The Vietnam Memorial marks the end of righteous romance, as it quietly grieves the wasted lives of men and women whose defeat was moral censure, and it articulates an American commitment to protect all their future soldiers within a garrison of technology, a fortress of rhetoric.

"In Flanders Fields" is a minor poem, with greatness thrust upon it, and it is a great poem, whose allegorical presence has shaped our sensibilities, however limited its moral vision. That's what aesthetics is, the meeting of rage and inspiration, meaning and significance. In his own time, Edmund Spenser captured the *episteme*, as Foucault calls the moral personality of an age, in a tale that exposes the complexity of evil, the necessity for right to prevail. In *Buffy*, Joss Whedon mirrors Spenser's paradigm with an obverse vision, in which evil is simple, while doing right is fraught with moral and psychological complexity. McCrae's poem, by confounding what it says with what it has become, mirrors both, catching us amidst the refracted imagery, thinking both of sacrifice and the necessity of moral purpose. In a Martha Stewart world, where morality is an illusion, subject to social absolutes, it is a good thing to think of McCrae's poem, and to remember the mutability of meaning — and here we are talking of peace and war. It is good to remember, this is a world not of books and allegory and aesthetic composition, but of actual experience, that evil and good are polarities, and any axis between them will ultimately be measured by what is deemed right, and what turns out to be wrong.

INVISIBLE AMONG THE RUINS

While living in Ireland late in the last century as the Craig Dobbin Chair in Canadian Studies at University College Dublin, I became aware of the possibilities of making stuff up in the service of exposition, while deconstructing rhetorical privilege to set thoughts free of an arbitrarily limiting context. In past writings about Canada and the Arctic, I had increasingly broken protocol by using poetics to convey intent. Enduring Dreams: An Exploration of Arctic Landscape *(Anansi, 1994) mixes lyrical contemplation and rhetorical metaphysics with abandon. In Ireland, postmodern metafiction rose to the fore. Where better to contemplate the impositions and limitations of English as an alien tongue. As I progressed through a year-long project that was ultimately published as* Invisible among the Ruins *by Cormorant Press in Dunvegan, Ontario, and University College Press in Dublin (2000), I found myself reaching deeper and deeper into fiction to explore my experience as a Canadian in Ireland. The following is from the first section of that book, each section having been delivered as a lecture somewhere in Ireland (this one at University College Cork). By the final section, it all becomes fantasy as I analyze the poetics of Declan Fitzwilliam, an Irish writer who never existed. On hearing this in a lecture in England, graduate students laughed at my temerity, if not my wit; more senior academics blushed to think there was a poet they knew so little about.*

There is a part of Dublin where children ride wild horses through the streets, but outsiders dare not go, even in daylight, for fear of their lives. Along the Liffey there is stonework a thousand years old revealed by the crumbling of newer façades, and new buildings in their decorative finework invoking an Ireland more ancient than God. There are diverse levels to the city; some parallel others without ever touching. There is a Dublin familiar to many, intent on itself as invention, a literary artifact labelled with plaques and playful conceits — Molly Bloom's, a florist, and the hair stylist, Finnegan's Wave. Joyce is the first you might notice but the others are there. Take Swift, for example. In half an hour you can walk from the gates of Trinity College to St. Patrick's Cathedral, where Jonathan Swift is interred, patient beside Stella, in the grounds where he laboured as dean. Almost anywhere among the Georgian residue of Dublin, you can feel the presence of Yeats and Synge and Fitzwilliam and Wilde reaching out from their homes on Merrion Square, and of a dozen others from their various times. You walk down Dame Street, turn one way and meet George Bernard Shaw strutting like a foreigner, turn the other and encounter Brendan Behan, with an angular lisp to his stride, and turn yet another, look lengthwise towards the oncoming traffic in time to see Samuel Beckett looking away, and turn to the last and see coming right at you a crowd of poets, playwrights, novelists, surging forward, like the thronging underworld rising to meet the incoming dead.

November 27, 1997. Bev and I sit quietly in the Reading Room of the National Library as late arrivals search out the last remaining seats. Several times we huddle closer and whisper to draw attention to details of the plaster cherubs overhead, hovering between the symmetrical eloquence of the dome with its rising bands of green and the numbered cubicles of darkened wood against the walls, open-faced confessionals sequestering matched book-sets with muted bindings. Although there is nothing yet to disturb, we are hesitant to violate the ritual hush of anticipation. Eventually the speaker, an unprepossessing man, has begun his lecture and we discover ourselves resisting the room's soporific atmosphere, intent on listening. Terry Eagleton has come from Oxford to tell us about Yeats, but it is impossible to hear his words, to gather any sort of syntactical coherence from the falling sounds, especially when he quotes the poet's lines. I have read enough of Eagleton to know his cadence and have read Yeats enough to recognize from any fragment the entire poem, but the self-absorbing grandeur of the Reading Room conspires to stifle meaning, dissemble music, and distract the ear towards inner harmonies entirely out of keeping with the lecture being sacrificed before us.

Behind masks of rapt inscrutability, the Irish audience pursue their separate thoughts, as Bev and I do ours. My own take me, carried on the wings of muffled dissonance, to the Canadian Arctic, where wind sweeps horizontally in lines of snow across the landscape, and I am most at home.

We dwell among ruins on the planetary surface, pinioned by perspective between the infinite and the absolute. Language in itself is an archaeology of consciousness; in speaking we articulate our presence on the uppermost storey of an ancient edifice, words buried beneath us like a Borgesian library with infinite rooms. We rehearse the anthropology of landscape each time we co-opt the natural world to our advantage, building aesthetic response to the environment on the crumbling foundations of previous desire. Future antiquarians will sift through the rubble of our lives and construct elegant cultural designs which they will superimpose upon the receding past in an endless sequence of palimpsests, making the ruins of their own time inevitable.

Driving by the iron gates of Wicklow, painted black and faded gold, closed across avenues of unexplained history, shielding from casual interrogation shoddy grandeur, I wonder at the strangeness of Ireland; and me, a Canadian living among steep hills in the often-rain, on the grounds of Glamore Castle at Devil's Glen, in the shelter of Ballymaghroe, I wonder what I will do here so far from Arctic tundra and glacial Arctic streams as real to me as any memory, more real than the flesh on bone that seems an ageing constant in my life, being always me, as I survey my naked self discreetly stepping from a shower, or catch myself in a mirrored glance, looking away, a familiar form yet strange to awaken into out of dream, even though I was born in the Canadian south, a three-day walk from the American border, and took decades to work my way north through suburbs and cottage country, bushland, scrub, and taiga, walking and hiking, canoeing, trekking, until the whole of Canada became my body, not the state nor the history but the landscape itself; yet here I am now in a place where the land drowns in a maelstrom of history, a culture of religion and politics, and hidden estates behind gates by the public roadways articulate privilege.

If you are born into a world where untamed nature is regarded as reproach, untrammelled wilderness as moral approbation, and the walls of your garrison, your farm, your civil community, or the walls of your mind, form the boundaries of your replica of Eden, then you might not comprehend that outside Eden there are others quite unlike yourself, except by the superficialities of primeval genetic design, who are content to be there and appalled at acquiescence to such arbitrary limitations on vision and experience as your philosophies engender. The edifice of Western thought collapses in the winter gale that seals the igloo warm. Explorers to the Arctic huddled against coal fires in the clammy holds of wooden ships and, when they ventured out to survey their adversary, froze to death in their leathers and woollens, starved to death or died of terrible deficiencies, and the Inuit around them, in no rush to claim posterity, stood by the breathing holes of seals for hours on end, honoured those they killed, ate raw flesh, clothed themselves in fur, and slept naked on benches carved from snow inside their houses, piled warm with the coats of creatures with whom they shared a common destiny. Time for the Inuit was a place to live, not a passage to be hurried through on the way to somewhere else. To some extent it is still so among the northern people whom from time to time I visit, travelling in Canada.

By the fresh waters of Ireland, I have talked among anglers and they have said that to snag the shimmering light in a twist from the shallows, turn trout as it leaps on the line, you must think like the river. I have spoken to Inuit hunters in the great open bays of east

Baffin who say seals that sound the depths in small rings of silence, while still out of range, will surface in reach of your sights, in the direction you travel, if you think like a seal.

I have heard that Prince Charles talks to his garden and occasionally addresses a flower by name. Myself, I have favourite trees and in crisis have pressed their bark so firmly my hands have come away blood. I have heard of a novelist Out West who grows orchids, and whispers erotic entendres among recalcitrant tendrils until they rise from the soil, splayed to perfection, shaped the colour of wind in the greenhouse night. I have camped in the liquid hush on a great river's banks and slept through the roar of a stream's crashing. To be at home on the earth you must think like a stone. I have listened to the singing of Muskoka sweetgrass in the amplitude of a hot summer day, and settled in the cicadas' shadow, indifferent to the vicissitudes of mortality. I have listened to snow deep in the Gatineau Hills, multifoliate sounds as familiar as time; my body's motion, frozen breath searing nostrils, defiant of stillness and the deprecations of death. I have spoken to anglers on the rivers of Ireland, listened to grass, and listened to snow. To be at home on the earth you must think like a stone.

As a Canadian in Ireland and a refugee from books I yearn to be absolved of language. I yearn to live not only in the future and past but in the present as well, where awareness and perception are one; to dwell invisible among ruins; to return at last to a place where my spirit is indivisible from the land. In recent decades, I have travelled the Arctic for vainglorious reasons; to go where others of my kind hesitate to go, reclusive on the awesome tundra, and for reasons more ennobling, to explore in splendid solitude the precarious limits of my own being and of my country's soul. In the Arctic and on the edges of language, where words most approximate the reality of things, I found myself always in a state of arriving, as if, sharing the curse of the Christian world, I could never quite get where I was going, say what I wanted to say. A contemplative adventurer, adventurous contemplative, I yearned to discover, in the vast open space of the Arctic and the echoing silence that holds a visitor transfixed between being and absence, murmurings of an unutterable connection between time and the timeless moment, to be, without words, free of history and truly at home. And in recent years I have found this, but as through a mirror, not a doorway to breach or a new place to live. Being an outsider in motion through the farthest reaches of my own country has opened perception on ways of connection with the whole of Canada.

I have not been in the Arctic an alien resident, as I am now in Ireland, but fixed as a hovering spirit at rest in the wind. Perhaps here, where language makes everything real, invisibility will fall away like a chrysalis and, reborn among words as a soul with the shape of the Canadian landscape, I will go back as a butterfly on rock, beautiful and brief in my passing.

You veer off a roundabout on the N25 just east of Cork, centripetal velocity as you swing north towards Fermoy flinging you onto a dual carriageway, the surface so new your tires hum, the patina of fresh macadam not yet settled, and after a few miles, or kilometres — in Ireland, you can never be sure. It's like temperature in Canada: those of us of a certain age get cold in Celsius but hot in Fahrenheit — after fifteen minutes or so, the divided highways merge, although traffic going north retains its breakaway speed, and after a while without warning the paved lanes narrow, the shoulder disappears under gorse and bracken, and at night in particular you feel you are hurtling beyond the decorum of gravity, and then as you rise on a great hill you encounter a sign beside the road and if you read fast enough you'll see that it says "Experimental Traffic Calming Ahead." Before you've had time to digest the text and assess the mortal implications of language so whimsically at play, you are confronted by the town of Watergrasshill in the middle of the road. And perforce you must slow down, willing or not. If church is going in or letting out or a service or mass is in progress, a Garda officer will be standing in the middle of the single lane, sorting out traffic as it funnels through Watergrasshill on its way to Fermoy.

We use certain words as if they meant the same for all of us; but as a Canadian living in Ireland, I wish to declare their categorical difference. The particulars of our experiences are often familiar, yet nowhere do we diverge more than when we think we are using a vocabulary in common to describe our similarities. When the Anglo-Normans first came to Ireland, they found the savage Irish could not speak their language. They were obliged to converse with the untamed islanders in Latin. It is curious how useful a dead language can be, and to whom. There is no such thing as a vocabulary in common, not between separate peoples, not even between the separate sides of an individual sensibility. Language is that precisely elusive.

Think of money, of paper currency. So long as two or more people accept that a particular scrap of paper has meaning, it has value. The meaning it has is not absolute; what it will do for you and what it will do for me bear no relationship. I might buy a pint of Guinness and get change; you might put a deposit on your eternal soul and pay for a mass. Let me read to you from the Irish ten-pound note the obverse inscription — supposing the likeness of James Joyce to be *verso*, if that is the word, for he is there, etched in green with a familiar scowl — words that if you hold the note to the sunlight appear at his side, ghostly in reverse, like reflections in an opaque mirror: "riverrun," they begin, "past Eve and Adam's, from swerve of shore to bend of bay," but you know the rest. It is enough that these words are happening there, on an everyday scrap of paper worth as much to the tinker as to gentry, to the traveller as to the prospering elite, although what they mean differs greatly; and who else in the world would quote *Finnegans Wake* just so? Some countries rely on the gold standard.

October 1997. Wind-hurled rain transforms appearance as I trudge the rutted muck of trails on Carrick Mountain, face thrust jaggedly against tumultuous air, masked with sweat and slick as ice, eyes peering awkwardly through slits in saturated leather, as if from salt spray of an ocean crashing on cold rocks. Below me, the veiled landscape of Wicklow is grand; huge rolling contours veined with narrow lanes and stone walls, and patched with networks of trees and sprawling fields. In this indeterminate season we keep a peat fire burning constantly, smouldering sweet-dry, and somewhere below

I've left Bev to read by the fire, nursing an incipient cough, and left a book where I was sitting, open at the final page, refusal implicit to be finished, waiting for the reader's return.

When I was seven, we had a green canoe; swift it was, alive in contemplation of the water's yearning for an edge to give it shape. Placed in the bushland of Temagami as it was, it shaped Temagami, and the wilderness rose up to it, no longer wild. Imagine wilderness. What is it you are imagining? Temagami is lush with secrets; when I was seven, Canada reached out ahead of me like an open invitation. Until I grew up Temagami was summer. Winter was a place of waiting; wilderness was a tangled garden. Is the wilderness you imagine sanctuary, or the certitude of Eden gone awry? And can you imagine, Hell for some of us would be a more appealing place to spend eternity than Heaven? Is it the utter absence of familiarity, a profound emptiness, where your language cannot grasp anything but your own indeterminacy? A place of banishment, of solitude so absolute even God is absenct? Think, what is it? What is wilderness? Now think: there are those for whom the concept of wilderness is unthinkable. We occupy our humanity from one culture to another in fundamentally different ways.

Ireland thriving as a European state is of passing interest. Ireland to Italy as Nebraska is to Delaware may bring benefits undreamed of in the economies of Irish heritage, without consequence to world order. But there is sweetness, here, now, in how casually the young prepare to assume in the future the ancient role of Ireland as the spiritual centre of Europe, geography not-withstanding, their confidence bolstered by a pride in origins which they see not as marginal or quaint, but real as earth itself. In Canada we cannot imagine such pride, not without flinching at our own reflection as we look away, to the south.

That Ireland is solid in the mind and Canada transparent; this means a Canadian in Ireland might see and not be seen. That Ireland is a place to come from, a place of mythic origins, and Canada is a place for arrivals, the apparently undiscovered country; this means in Ireland a Canadian may perhaps be more Canadian than at home.

That Ireland is held to the planet by a network of hedgerows and walls like Gulliver bound in Lilliput, while in Canada walls are conventions easily slipped off by a shrug to the north; this means that language and landscape and culture for a Canadian in Ireland are as different as ice from air.

Such precepts as these I learned in second-year university as faulty syllogisms. In my first year I learned other things; how far away I was from Waterloo County, an hour up the road. By third year at the University of Western Ontario I was more familiar with the banks of the Liffey than with the teller's wicket at the Bank of Commerce, more at home in Sligo, gazing in my mind past the thin stone marker on the poet's grave, up at the voluptuous rise of Ben Bulben, than with memories of my own childhood in the village of Blair across the Grand River flats from Preston, the settlement that Mennonites founded at the close of the eighteenth century, fleeing from Pennsylvania's democratic embrace, dealing for land with Mohawks who had moved in after the Revolution from the mountains of New York, the settlement that my Scotch and German ancestors shaped into a community of shops and small industries which English ancestors took under management until my Canadian ancestors, dying in Flanders, one death for every hundred Canadians, man, woman, and child, took as their own the language, the landscape, the culture. By historical fiat, they took it, Waterloo County, and removed it from the British Empire. After Dunkirk and Monte Cassino, where only one in every thousand Canadians died (and in the gas chambers of Europe, we lost our inherited innocence), we assumed sovereignty over our lives, too polite, too Canadian, to tell the Queen of England to go away, patient as India, willing to wait until the residual foreign tangle bent to the warp of history and original sin bound in the weft of our emerging postmodern design. I lived in those times in London, Ontario, and dwelled in the Bloomsday Tower and at Thoor Ballylee.

Afterwards, gradually, I emerged from the pages of books, to enter into the conversation of my times, but almost immediately upon engaging the world I began to write books of my own, to withdraw from time into text, where I could shape the narrative. Through decades, I carried on between memory and dream, forging the present as distinct and familiar, exploring the undiscovered consciousness of place, fighting always against the darkness of invisibility, writing to be seen, be heard, be illuminated among my own people. As I grew older, my own world in Canada often seemed darkly opaque, except when I occupied its extremities. I went to the Arctic, then came to Ireland.

We have just come from lunch with Paddy Hillery. It is December 4, 1997. However tenuously, we are now part of Irish history. For the record, we were hosted by the silvered elegance of John Kelly and joined by his colleague Noel Walsh, who has spent a decade of his natural life in Montreal. Back in my office, and not before, suddenly I have become aware how different it is in Ireland. Everyone connects. Lunching with the man who eventually succeeded his colleague Eamon De Valera as president of the Republic and who chatted casually about Oisín, and the difficulties the Empress of Japan had in pronouncing ancient Gaelic, as if Dev and the early Celtic myths and the wife of an Asian god were equally significant in his experience as an ageing Irish gentleman, for a brief moment Bev and I intersected with a nation's historical personality in ways impossible in Canada.

However socially obscure you may be, no one here is on the historical margin; the concept is inadmissible. Everyone shares in the experience of Ireland and that is your glory and that is your burden and occasionally, perhaps, that is your tragedy or shame. Everyone in the course of a life knows one version or another of Paddy Hillery, who for fourteen years was the embodiment of the body politic, and knows of Oisín, for fifteen hundred years a myth as personal and strange as virgin's milk; and conversations with a descended god in Ireland are quite commonplace. In Canada, a political encounter is an embarrassment. There is no politician most of us would admit to knowing without apology or explanation; there is neither history nor mythology from which we do not find ourselves on the edge, looking in, outsiders in our own collective narrative. And gods for many of us are a merciful absence.

Canada extends through seven time zones. Ireland closes for lunch. From anywhere in Ireland, you can go home for the weekend; Mammy and Da are never that far away. Canada's emblem is the stiff red leaf of a tree unknown through most of the land; Ireland's shamrock is useful to identify national monuments, to explain religious mysteries, a trefoil stained with blood. Green is the liturgical colour of hope. The red maple leaf is a flame, the brief colour of autumn; the white of our flag is the winter. Canadians are polite, arrogantly modest, the Irish are congenial and politically volatile. Canadians try to find and lose themselves in generalizations.

Imagine a deep kiss, now imagine making love. Imagine a kiss that makes your scalp tight and your toes ache, that sends spasms shooting through your entire nervous system in resounding arcs, so that you feel every corner of yourself, and everything is familiar. Now imagine making languorous love as every muscle in your body caresses from the inside out your melting flesh and slowly you resolve to ecstasy, and everything you feel is strange. The difference between the two is the proportional difference between Ireland and Canada; more allusive than saying their relative sizes are in the inverse ratio of a hockey puck to a football, or their population difference is in the same equation as that of Canada to the United States, one to ten. Canada is the second largest country on the planet, with several islands in its territory dwarfing Ireland, which could, in fact, fit within the Canadian land mass a hundredfold. There is sufficient freshwater surface in Canada for Ireland to float, buoyed up by its ancient history, along with all Great Britain and Japan, and be surrounded by margins wide enough to challenge Saint Brendan. Difference is not indicative of virtue. Both promise paradise for lovers; neither is a place to be alone.

The people of Ireland live among walls; the landscape and culture are inscribed with lines of stone, labyrinths of rearranged earth, proscriptions of denial and possession, sedge rows and hedgerows and relentless historical memories; and the often-rain of Ireland is a condition of life to be endured — of your lives, for I am speaking to the world as if it were Irish, to Ireland as if it were the world. Coming from a perspective of invisibility, where to declare my difference from Ireland I must co-opt Inuit reality for my own, to make my own reality apprehensible even to myself, I furl my way through the maze of Irish walls while, deep within, a yearning for the absence of human design thrills in my veins. I come from a country a continent wide and so wholly indeterminate at its northern edges that tracing tens of thousands of shoreline miles on a global map would not articulate our upper limits: imagine standing on the earth, trying to take in the illimitable depths of a clear blue sky; then, just when you think you have its measure, it is winter, the sun sets, and your soul opens to the blue-black night. You can impose constellations, but these signify only the limits of imagination. You are reduced to transparency and at the same time vision connects you with the infinite. This is what it is to be consciously Canadian, in a place where rain is often snow and where walls are only fences, merely conventions, and there is no perceptible limit to the circumscribing universe.

Our neighbour across the field below Ballymaghroe is the absent poet Seamus Heaney. His high stone cottage with Victorian brick casements and dark haunted windows is set close by the road, smack against walls and a hedgerow. It is empty the way absence of someone in particular can make a place seem deserted rather than only unoccupied, wanting to be filled with poetry, the smell of soda bread, the sounds of morning laughter. I have searched in his sonnets and cannot find myself there, nor in their music the cadence of landscape surrounding us here. I would like to write a learned paper on the future of aesthetics in the survival of Ireland; but Ireland seems in no danger of imminent demise. I would like to place Seamus Heaney at home in the neighbouring house, to soften the edges of Ireland. I would like to tell a story in which there is no plot, where time is spatial and dramatic decorum is governed by principles of rhetoric, where progress is in the meeting of thought and emotion, and the reader's memory is the text. The only way to break from the clutches of narrative is to refuse to begin. Or to begin again and again, to refuse the possibility of ending. Death is a given, but we cannot ask to be born.

Last night Liam sang. We were at Anne and Bertram's, our third Christmas party of the week in Donnybrook, Dublin 4. We had been talking until then and someone said, it's time for the singing, and we expected carols but Liam sang a Mayo song he heard from his grandmother about unconsummated love and a Galway shawl; and the sound was so sweet the others kept silent to give his voice room, until the third chorus, when softly they joined him, and together they sang his grandmother's song, though none of them knew it, and later some said they'd heard other versions in Wexford and Derry, but none that made them so homesick as being caught in the cadence of Liam's wavering voice.

The Irish Times, Saturday, October 11, 1997. Excerpt:

> We had to walk up and we had to walk back. We knocked at the door and Sr. Xaviera opened the door and she looked at us and I said: "What did you do to my baby? What happened to my baby?"
>
> So she turned around and said: "It was only a baby."
>
> I said: "That was my daughter, that was my child."
>
> But she had no sympathy, no compassion or nothing. She never even let us step inside the door, never even gave us a glass of water. She just closed the door and we walked off, didn't we?

Listen: your listening is a form of reading. Or if you are reading this, that too is a listening. Our voices merge. Given the immediacy of the process as I write in real time, and as you provide my words a text in real time, the present tense seems not so much an inviting rhetorical or narrative option as the inevitable condition of our coming together. Listen, I am about to commit metaphor. This will relate to my own life as much as to the ways language works, but personal revelations will be more obscure than the explication of creative endeavours and lateral thought.

These are not merely words drawn forward from mind, out of the cranial ragbag of our common vocabulary, from the infinite resource of semantics and syntax, those splendid evasions of meaning by which language conveys more than it ever can say. Rather my words are a tumble of water, into which by total immersion I struggle on the edge of the vortex, this then the whirlpool, and this the swimmer's moment, not to find what has already occurred as flotsam to cling to and spring free from the whirling descent and articulate my adventure, still dripping in exultation for having escaped with ideas intact, but to give myself over when the moment comes, utterly to language, and to plummet headlong into its spiralling depths, to drown among words, break free upon the reaches of the silvered estuary; and in such ecstasy as this, in being transformed among words to words, to rise and leave, now imminence, only, as you approach and enter the whirlpool yourself, in your own real time. In reading present tense you engage with a past that has not yet happened, you occupy a future that has already occurred, whether you read by the eye, or it is a listening.

My departure from Wittgenstein, from Heidegger, especially from Derrida who in the past has sanctioned so much of my autographic folly as to be almost accountable as co-author of my recorded lives, my departure from their company may already be apparent to you who care about language and consciousness, landscape and perception, culture and being. These cohorts of much thought have in common the Saussurean notion of language as the context and limit of knowing, the field in which we find ourselves real, the edifice in which we endure, and with all this I am in accord. But with Ireland and Canada held as mirrors, one to the other, each surface reflecting depths of the other, with me like Dracula between — that wily invention of Irish equivocation — present without presence, embodiment of undecidability in both places and neither, what seem evident are the ways in which language differs in Ireland and Canada as salt from water, light from air. It is not that we speak different languages, which is obvious, but that we live words in different ways. Language for the Irish as a place in which to know the world and dwell is not the same as language for Canadians. Language not only defines reality in different ways but allows different dimensions to reality itself, as surely as if there were an unbreachable gap between our common sojourns on the earth.

James Joyce wrote of being condemned, saying that his mother tongue was a foreign language, that he must write in English to be heard, so that he could listen to himself in the recesses of his own head and turn his words upon the page, harrowing as the furrow yields, alien and alive, his selfless yawping at posterity. How I admired Joyce when I was young. How splendidly Irish I would have been, had all the thousand thousand couplings that spewed me from primeval mud led, but once, through Ireland.

It was not until years later, when I had reached almost my present age, that vision, shifting from where I was going or where I had been, found me looking at myself isolated in immediate experience, that I recognized in Ireland my own language as a fitting place to dwell; language seized by Irish writers, throttled into revision by the sheer gall of their genius, in this I could hear myself think, feel my blood. It was not Irish English that did the trick, taking me in, foundling on a bed of phonemes, teaching me the ways of Egypt. It was not what they did, but that they did it at all and so well. In Ireland's air, as Irish throats twist English to their own cadence, I learn Canadian. And that is what I knew, without understanding, would happen, when I was still a young man and against my father's wishes longed to be Irish.

In Canada we are wary of language, considering it an impediment to communication. Our best writers do not love words. There are a few exceptions. But Alice Munro, who is generally regarded as our finest prose writer, writes pellucid prose so fine you hardly notice it. A sentence by Munro draws syntax and semantics into silent harmony, a perfect transparent plane through which the reader apprehends realities of the text as if they were memories recollected. Two of our best-known writers of fiction are also poets. Yet whether in poetry or prose, Margaret Atwood uses language as if she is in a rush to get it over with, to put the words behind her. It is attitude in Atwood that matters, that with unnerving precision takes her reader's measure. Reading Atwood we ourselves are judged. Michael Ondaatje renders fiction poetic, but that has to do with intricately detailed correlatives of discontinuity, not language; and poetry he writes with prosaic familiarity, writing of borderlines between the ordinary and the astonishing, intentionally deflating the promise of words. We are left with inchoate feelings that the poet's life has unacknowledged depths, not with the discovery of depths in our own. And fine; it is not his obligation to be our therapist any more than it is Atwood's to be our friend. Or Munro's to remind us of our separate lives. But I am perhaps less sanguine about their fear of language and rejection of the cultural imperative to sing in their own voices, so that others in their community may join in the chorus, be shaped by their sounds, sing lacunae, addenda, songs of ourselves.

Names: the Irish recite patriots' names as liturgy. The distance between signified and signifier falls askew. There is no such equivalent in Canadian experience. It would not be for us, as for Yeats, to write it out in verse: MacDonagh and MacBride and Connolly and Pearse. Nor could we devise sepulchral songs like the Clancy Brothers' lament for Bobby Sands and Ray MacLeish and eight more murdered at Long Kesh by the forces of history. Listen: Wolfe Tone, the name itself chills with a sense of loss — this is about language as context, a fitting setting for words that signify whole lives which together signify the struggle that signifies Ireland. But naming can also of course be a mausoleum, naming the dead more important than being alive. Perhaps we only, in Canada, recite in a similar vein the names of hockey players, a few of whom are still among us. Howie Morenz, Teeder Kennedy, Gordie Howe, Tim Horton, Rocket Richard, Jean Beliveau, Bobby Orr, Bobby Hull, Wayne Gretzky, Mark Messier.

And sometimes the mere mention of a name defines a national moment: Paul Henderson. Or an attitude: Terry Fox. When last October, on the way to Glendalough, I asked a man who had a poster in his shop advertising a Terry Fox Run for Cancer Research if he knew about Terry, he told me he thought he might be from up the road, about ten-twelve miles, there's three-four families of Foxes and he might be one of those; and I was proud of Terry but wanted to say, he is for us what Parnell is to you, and if you think a boy dying of cancer in the midst of his self-styled Marathon of Hope, loping his way across a continent, is any less, then you know nothing about the ferocity of Canadians, or about our modesty either. And Paul Henderson scored the winning goal in the final seconds of the first tournament between Canada and the Soviets in 1972, making us for ever hockey champions of the world.

In Dublin, I found in Waterstone's bookshop on Dawson Street — I would call it a book *store* at home; shop means little and quaint; but here I accede to the Irish vernacular; it is difficult to do otherwise, for the sidewalks of Dublin are emblazoned with pedestrian quotations from Joyce's Ulysses in sans-serif bronze, and when we arrived in September the walls of Trinity College and stonework along the Liffey, above the waterline, were festooned with iridescent snippets of Ulyssean wit caught up in blue twists of tubular neon lighting, and statues of Joyce are more common than waste disposal containers — I discovered Atwood, Ondaatje, Munro, and a few other of my compatriots on modest display. Ondaatje, of course, with the success of *The English Patient* as a film, was inevitable. Munro is so very good I would have been surprised not to find her, among the literary and the literati. And Atwood is ubiquitous, more so even than the nicotine-drenched voice of Leonard Cohen singing to the world from his tower of song.

I asked three different clerks in the Waterstone's shop if they had any Canadian writers and they said they did not, so far as they knew, but I could look around all the same and might find what I'm looking after. Setting off into the crenellated shadows cast by books of many sizes, in search of something as exotic and bland as a Canadian artifact in Ireland — books equivalent to a carpet of tribal design, perhaps a Qashqa'i done by machine in Donegal, or a Merlot blend in the proportions of Château Petrus from grapes picked in the Niagara Peninsula — I made my way to the best-sellers table. Beside Atwood and Ondaatje were novels by Jane Urquhart and Anne Michaels. There was nothing in any of the books to indicate they were

Canadian. But taking *Fugitive Pieces* in hand and thumbing its newly familiar pages I realized in Michaels there is no fear of language; even, at times, a lack of respect. The newest Urquhart I had not yet read but I have followed her discursions away from the splendidly centred language of *The Whirlpool*, her first novel, into borderless language, an international vernacular, in her second and third. Munro, I found in her place on the shelves, between Somerset Maugham and Vladimir Nabokov.

There is a direct correlation in Ireland between tobacco and language. Conversation here is a sport, it's been said; a spectator sport at that, for it is not uncommon to see in the smoke-drenched corridors of the Arts and Commerce Building at University College Dublin, where I hold a sinecure of a year's duration, a cluster of students gathered around two or three others in ribald debate or earnest discourse, listening proactively, evidence of their engagement apparent in the cumulus clouds of tobacco detritus swirling like stray plaster limbs of dismembered cherubs, evanescent in the louring gloom. Given the aura of death tobacco denotes, it occurred to me recently, walking past a parlous throng, conversation among the Irish has much in common with such apocalyptic sports elsewhere as bullfighting, cockfighting, bear-baiting, and American football. But goodness, I thought, overwhelmed with guilt for my runaway mind, even a fool could see the sophistry here, binding with hinges of rhetoric the effluvium of my distaste for an empirically despicable habit with superficial generalizations about a realm I know little about, the sport of words. Nowhere in the world is it so easy as in Ireland to lose track of the difference between literal and figurative realities.

I have written before of how difficult it was for early Canadian poets writing English to make language fit alien landscape, where it was not suited by literary or historical convention to the extremes of size and weather and grandeur we take for granted, in a place so far from its origins. As well as a history, language is a sociology: a vital record of people living in particular ways in a particular part of the world. When English was brought to Canada, it became on its arrival a foreign language. This presented difficulties of sensibility for those for whom it was the only language available. As a medium of functional discourse, it served us well. English is generous and accommodating, and we prospered under its aegis in economic and political terms, but at the same time we were culturally attenuated almost to transparency; stunted, at times, to the limits of opacity.

It was our poets, finally, and our painters, who gave us our difference, gave us snow, our nordicity. The Inuit have dozens of words for snow. The English have one. We had none. We had to define the term with modifiers. We would say, "The January snow is deep," when what we meant was that the snow was as it usually is in January. But we had no word for that. Not until the poets said to us, "Snow is snow is snow." Once we understood that Canadian January snow is, de facto, "deep," we started dressing for it, enjoying it, celebrating winter.

For Ireland it is not the same. English may be a foreign language, but it is appropriate to the landscape, suitable to the climate, and virtually subsumes the geography. Dublin is closer to London than Toronto is to Montreal or Calgary to Vancouver; Connemara, while related to the rugged terrain of Newfoundland and Labrador, from which it was wrenched loose by the continental shift that allowed the Atlantic to obtrude between them, preventing the Irish from being Canadians by geophysical fiat, is more akin to the Highlands of Scotland, the west country downs or the eastern fenlands of England, the hill country of Wales, different as they are, than is the rolling sprawl of Waterloo County, where I grew up, to the bushland and granite of Temagami, six hours north, where I spent glorious summers canoe-tripping through my adolescence. And English remains foreign in Ireland: how different are the words home, Christ, ale, master, on English lips than from an Irish mouth, different enough to make the soul fret and drive some to revolution, others to forge in the fires of imagination the Irish soul in language so vital, the English can barely gasp that their tongue has been abducted, then returned the better for its literary misadventures.

Irish writers have repeatedly reinvented English; more recently, Ireland has taken up the renewal of its ancient mother tongue, as

Israelis have of Hebrew. English is a native language only in England; Irish and Hebrew are native to their own places, the sources and reservoirs of their own cultures. In India English is useful, for there is no more better means to transcend the fissures between nearly two thousand linguistic groups than a language imported for the purpose, albeit to serve imperial ideologies now out of favour. In most of Canada, as in Australia and New Zealand and the United States, where the native peoples have been grotesquely displaced or disaffected, English has been imagined an indigenous tongue, but really there is silence behind an imported façade. We have no ancestral language to fall back upon, to assert our difference. The Québécois try valiantly yet deny the authenticity of patois and joual in deference to the alien origin of French, on another continent, in another world.

October 31, Hallowe'en, 1997. In a cottage northeast of Cork, after a splendid walk along roads narrowing to a single lane between overgrown walls embossed on the land in a meandering pattern for reasons lost in time, with a grass median running the road's centre and the selvedges of distant horizon rising to the sky beneath veils of rain, proving the world is not round, and after a simple dinner of potatoes, spinach, and pork chops poached in shallots reduced to a thick sauce, Bev and I settle in to watch the results of yesterday's presidential election. At the same time Bev is reading a novel by Kevin Major about the demise of the Beothuk, exterminated by English policy and Irish fishermen in Newfoundland two hundred years ago, about Shawnandithit, the last Beothuk for all time, her name plummeting through history, its lyrical sound a terrible and meaningless reminder of evil. I am caught up in the vagaries of a polling system I do not understand. Coming from a continent where results are conceded nationwide before voting comes to a halt in the west, it is strangely reassuring to see a vote-count hindered by fog off the Aran Islands and subject to multiple tallies a full day after the polls have closed. Procedures are explained and results are read from a stage at Dublin Castle, first in Irish and then in English. Think about this. Many Irish speak both languages. This is not a matter of appeasing parallel communities, as it might be with Flemish and Walloon or Canadian English and Québécois French. It is a refusal you have to admire to become extinct.

On the five-pound note there is an etching in brown of Catherine McAuley, apparently a nun by dress and habit, with dates on her collar, 1778 to 1841, eyes piercing as stigmata, inscribed without parallax to imply illimitable vision, hard as ball bearings. On the obverse: three children in a classroom, a map with Ireland on the edge of Europe, and on the blackboard a verse, lines in Irish which translated mean "I am the poet," and the walls are inscribed with designs drawn from stoneworks preceding the Celts. One child reads a book with great concentration. She is the present. One seems lost among dreams. She dwells in the past. And one, eyes fixed dead ahead, looks to what he will claim from the future, God willing.

I switch channels, find an English transvestite gabbling inanely, a dreary reminder of how dreadfully English men fear grownup women, so often do they dress in their clothes in public display, like shamans mimicking the awesome beast to diminish its threat. I switch channels again and find a cheery Irish talk-show host by the name of Gaye Byrne, known to viewers for being just like themselves, and he follows up an interview with Twiggy, promoting a book that seems intent on proving her as ordinary as one might have expected, by chatting with three panellists about their attendance upon death, it being the Night of the Dead, after all. An avuncular priest is amusing, dying in his presence an awkward pleasantry, an encounter with an amiable stranger. Another man, caught up in the profundity of his own experience, is painfully inarticulate. The third, an educated young woman, pronounces herself privileged to have been present at several dyings, and then launches into a charming metaphysical discourse: Jesus Mary and Joseph are always with us of course and that goes without saying but tonight of all nights we should give a thought to the fairies who are not, as people think, so small but only a little smaller than us and of greener complexion and will no doubt as we speak be on their way from summer to their winter homes without hindrance. Her vocabulary, her intonations, the beatific certitude with which she speaks, are constant. There is no need in her mind for verbal bridges or the armour of irony in her televised medley of deathbed revelation and Christian iconography and pagan fantasy, as if they are not all parts of the same world, as indeed they are.

The Irish Times, Saturday, October 11, 1997. Excerpt:

> The fate of baby Marion Howe in Goldenbridge Orphanage 42 years ago will have disturbed many people in the past two days. Some of these people are members of the Sisters of Mercy order. They will wonder what happened to transform a healthy, 11-month-old baby, within a few days of her arrival at Goldenbridge, to a child dying of dysentery and with an unexplained burn on her leg … The order issued a qualified apology in which it said it was sorry "if there was any lack of courtesy and compassion …" It is breathtaking that the acts of cruelty and bullying recounted by many former inmates of Sisters of Mercy orphanages, here and abroad, could be explained away in a phrase … The majority of nuns, brothers and priests who behaved decently over the decades will be overshadowed in the public mind by the minority who let them down.

Language imposes limits on experience. You cannot know what is not already known. What is not named has never been and, once named, what is named will live so long as the language endures, although perhaps only in the echoing din of words in conversation with each other. We live within language, that goes without saying; we dwell among words. In the music, the cadence, of syntactical equations we dream. Time is the invention of language. What cannot be named will never occur. Without the grammar of words we are isolated in the present, time merely the place of our being. Without words, death would be something we witness, not something we fear;

birth would be change, not beginning. Without language, experience would be in the present conditional, place would be where we are. You can see what I'm getting at here. Beyond anything else, it is language that makes us alive to ourselves and each other and our place in the world. If we know language as something different from one place to another, one culture to another, if we dwell differently among words, then we know different worlds. We are alive in different ways. Language imposes limits on experience, making it difficult even for linguists and semioticians to comprehend the difference. The difference is there nonetheless, waiting to be named into presence, given words to be apprehended.

Walking the Barrenlands in the summer of '96. A solitary traveller. Everything I needed for a month on my back: food, fuel, clothing, a 12-gauge shotgun for bears (polar, then grizzly, as I moved southward), and three books, Terry Eagleton's *Literary Theory: An Introduction*, Joyce's *Ulysses*, and *Anna Karenina*, in homage to a friend, Aritha van Herk, who rewrote Tolstoy's heroine on an Arctic island, as well as excerpts copied from books by explorers who had been over the same terrain, their texts showing through as ironically prophetic palimpsests on the blank reverse sides, which I planned to use for the field notes of my own experience. To cut down weight I left *Ulysses* behind in a cache on the third day out, to be picked up on my return. I built a small cairn to mark my place, a pile of boulders worn smooth by the weather, like an Inuit inukshuk in the shape of a stumpy man, and the wilderness rose up to it, no longer wild.

Some things we know only by their absence. Walking a logging trail high in the tangle of new-growth trees on Carrick, south of Ballymaghroe, among spruce planted so close even the rare sunlight enlivening the hills on a day such as this cannot penetrate to the dank levels where mosses grow in murky profusion, I feel strangely displaced, an emptiness inside as if unarticulated conviction called me somewhere else, and gradually it dawns in the gloom, what I feel is a lack of wariness, the unfamiliarity of an absence of fear. There are no bears. I do not smell the air as I walk for their rank scent, nor listen for the slow rush of their great bodies against the undergrowth. I do not look at my feet for scat on the path nor at low-slung branches for tufts of matted fur, nor do my eyes scour mouldering trees for the slash marks of claws, innerwood bug-bereft visible, crushed pulp scattered among shards of discarded bark. I have seldom encountered bears in Canadian bush, but they are there; you never doubt they are there.

Think of the continuity in Ireland between experience and memory, memory and history, history and legend, legend and myth, myth and primeval mystery, all in this place, superimposed layer upon layer, each layer poking through the ones laid over it, so there is a sense of it all as your personal past. Beneath the passage tombs of Knowth and Dowth and Newgrange at the Bend in the Boyne, are remnants of clusters of circular homes which crumbled over the bones of your earliest forebears, whose blood through lust or affection beats in your hearts, bled through with the blood of builders of pit-circles surrounding the tombs in the early Bronze Age, absorbed in the blood of migrating Celts, and then Vikings, and Normans, Anglo-Normans, and what else besides, who pillaged and raped, built and farmed, and are still building and farming, all alive still in the twist of an Irish tongue around vowels as old as language itself. For us, it is different. Discontinuity and dislocation, the emigrant/immigrant experience, throw us in a quest for origins directly upon imagination. We make up Ireland, but it is not a real place. When finally, we come here to visit, we look for ourselves among ruins, sort through the layers upon layers of your lives, and find ourselves absent. We were never here; this is your place. My ancestral bones lie buried not in the cemeteries of Munster or Leinster or Ulster or Connaught, or of Britain or Europe, Asia, or Africa, but in the landscape of home, the visceral, palpable, throbbing, unending Canadian earth.

Imagine paleolithic people, knowledge of themselves inseparable from their consciousness of the world. For them, language is an instrument of awareness, offering connection. To dissemble is an impossibility. Words reveal meaning; truth and understanding are the same. Language precedes presence; you experience yourself as an emanation of the world that has named you into being. This is a condition of purity to which poets aspire, who wish to make language sing with their absence. Paleolithic, the poet is primal.

Imagine Mesolithic people; recognition that knowledge of the world is power. Language separates you from the world, turns difference to advantage. You name yourself into being, articulate the world as a projection of fear and desire. The figurative becomes real; the lie is a way to the truth. This is the journey the storyteller follows, the shaman's dream-kingdom, the wild stare of the visionary close by the fire. Mesolithic: those catacombs in the brain where we wait, death's other kingdom.

Imagine neolithic people, naming the world into being. Language provides alternate realities, visions of compensation and transcendence, visions of consolation and control. You see yourself fated to endure, absolute and abstract as words. This is a land of walls and gates, the realm of the farmer, the metaphysician, the lawyer, the priest. This is a place where language is a boundary, containment, and an exit, escape; where truth gives way to the true. Neolithic: poetry is perpetually dying; story, a poetic device.

Imagin Technolithic people. Can you imagine yourself, or is it only someone in your body, inhabiting your life, you imagine? Language separates you from what you have become, words dissociate you from the earth. You exist on a parallel plane, you on your brief arc through an infinite cosmos and the world which barely flickers from the light of your passing. Words are technology. It is all very simple. Language is an illusion, and reality a mimetic contrivance. The poets have perished; no one remembers the nature of story.

And you have the poets. Ireland, you have the poets, the storytellers, and you have the lawyers and priests. We do as well, but we don't have the set of mind to listen. We turn to Ireland, I turn to Ireland, we should. In Ireland, there is poetry on the five-pound note, in newspaper columns, on television talk-shows; there is story in the language, built into the words and the grammar of everyday talk; there are 150,000 national monuments, more ruins than elsewhere are cemeteries, more burial sites than elsewhere are gardens, more walled garden sanctuaries than elsewhere are dreams. In Ireland, you dwell among words and history is the landscape of time; within ruins you find yourselves real. It is not so, in Canada, where reality is in flight. We are indentured to language; it occupies us. Only the land offers relief from history and culture that render us transparent in the larger world, invisible even to ourselves. The ragtag cultural tumble of time in this place, here, in Ireland, the capacity to live with your dead without embarrassment while we pave over graveyards, turn them into high-rise apartments, the way you sing to each other, and listen, could be the inspiration that redeems, absolves, translates, redeeming us from a past that is not our own, absolving us from a place we seized as if empty, translating what we have become into real apprehension.

Ireland, said the Maritimer and poet Alden Nowlan, is not my people's place of origin, it is their creation myth. You must understand this. We do not come from somewhere else. We originate in Canada; after a generation away from wherever, we are at home. We bury our dead in Canadian furrows, are born into landscape that others, even looking, can hardly imagine, it is so implacably beautiful. The stories of how we arrived have become separated from our places of leaving.

Do you understand? I do not mean to be patronizing but I do not want to be obscure. For you, ancestral memory is rooted in the land of your birth, the land that surrounds you. You look at the landscape about you, time is a human presence. For us, stories of origin are of another place. There is an element of post-lapsarian nostalgia in this, but we were not driven west from Eden by a trickster God, nor are we inclined to allow the old country as a garden paradise, though we may turn it into romantic myth. We are not on a diaspora; our place is where we arrived, by birth or by choice. It is not us but our stories that are dissociated, separated as they are from the earth. If we are not careful, this can make them seem sacred, the other place more real than our own. It is up to our poets to sing place into being, to be named by the world, until then, a dream; it is up to our storytellers to name us, telling tales of how we arrived and how we endure, to name the world ours.

The bookstore in Dublin Airport opens onto the traveller's concourse with the same anonymous familiarity you might find anywhere in the world. Across its back are rows on rows of magazines, their covers broadcasting the faces of impossible women, inviting either intimacy or emulation. On stage-right there are the usual fat novels in which depth of character would be an aberration, a compound sentence bad taste. On stage-left the whole wall is devoted to Irish books, the genius of a nation waiting in the wings. Having passed through the austere architecture of anticipation, you now find yourself on the other side of the proscenium, having crossed a boundary from the absurd reality of people preparing for flight into an illusory emporium of sentences for sale, courtesy of Hughes & Hughes, Booksellers. *Finnegans Wake* leans away as you reach, flinching from the verbal confectionery behind you, uncomfortably aligned with the novels of Maeve Binchy and Brian Moore, the former a famous best-seller, the latter an Irish expatriate born in Belfast, a Canadian by citizenship, and resident of southern California, a brilliant writer at home only in the country of words. You pick up Seamus Heaney's translation of Philoctetes, turn it in your hands, looking for Ireland, and of course it is there in the fineness of ironies. *Tristram Shandy* is there, a sudden reminder that Laurence Sterne was Irish by birth, if English by inclination and lifelong habit, an eighteenth-century postmodernist enthralled by textual affectation. You have been among books at Heathrow, La Guardia, LAX, Frankfurt, Keflavik, Bombay, Singapore, Pearson (you feel the need to explain, that Pearson is named after a Canadian prime minister who won the Nobel Peace Prize), and you have never found anything to compare. You run down a list in spontaneous order of international airports you have passed through, arriving, departing, in transit, Madrid, Abu Dhabi, Hong Kong, Melbourne, Tenerife, Tokyo, Nuuk, so many others, and you become distracted trying to perceive the pattern of their presence in your mind. Consciousness of your distraction brings you back to Dublin, to the wall of Irish books, to yourself scanning their covers, to the awkwardness of finding yourself on a stage so dominated by Ireland, where you as an inveterate writer had intended at most to shuffle forward and deliver a few modest lines, avoiding international vernacular, and you shrink back, escape into the concourse, and then notice you have walked off with *Finnegans Wake* tucked under your arm. Too embarrassed to return the book, you drop it on a plastic seat in Departures, to be retrieved by a traveller or a cleaner, and as you head out from the airport towards Ballymaghroe you promise yourself you will send Hughes & Hughes an anonymous cheque for the book, or make a donation to a Dublin charity or a funeral fund in Joyce's name.

While at Trinity College Dublin, Oliver Goldsmith, who came from Athlone, would sneak out into the night to hear street singers give voice to the vagabond songs he had sold them earlier in the day to earn his keep and tuition. Irony was not wasted on wit in the eventual works of the young writer, for *The Vicar of Wakefield* is unaccountably solemn, *The Deserted Village* is desultory, and even *She Stoops to Conquer* is as distressing as it is ribald or droll. Irish writers work with an advantage in English, for the language has never meant what it says, their roles as writers being always subversive. The great conflagration of war in this century has infused in all parlance an edge of suspicion, language the instrument of policy rendered unstable, so that irony is our only protection and weapon and mode of expression in discourse between self and the soul, whether in contemplation or public debate. But years before this, perhaps when Grace O'Malley pledged fealty to the first British queen, or all the peoples of Ireland to Saint Patrick's alien messiah, or when the righteous Cromwell swept inland on roadways of blood, or an Irish tinker sold an English soldier a sieve for a codpiece, the Irish have understood irony and language inseparable as a mode of survival, in the quagmire of words their means to endure.

August 19, 1993, Baffin Island: crouched under a blue tarpaulin, brewing tea on the camp stove. The rain is fuming; there is no word in English to describe the freezing pellets that swipe sideways against your face no matter how you turn. Bannock crumbles beneath stiff slabs of cheese as you lift it to your mouth; your face is a mystery, your mouth hard to find in the searing cold. Hot tea steams icily against the skin, burns the lips, drains heat into the pit of the gut. Squinting into the wind, you survey the Kuujjuaq Valley. Rain-light drenches the landscape in a spectral evanescence. You finish lunch and move forward through frigid turbulence, wholly connected to the world and strangely content. The Arctic willows clutch at your legs, the sopping lichens suck against your boots. To your right, the swollen river surges, crystal green, dropping perceptibly towards the horizon. To the left, the tundra rises in rolling fits and sudden bursts and disappears against the sky. You talk earnestly to yourself, out loud, about the precise moment when rain becomes snow and whether or not snow would be preferable to frozen webs of August rain whipping against your face, snatching at your unheard words. A motor-canoe appears, heading upriver. It is Graeme Dargo, Jawlie Akavak, and Elizabeth McIsaac: Graeme came over from Scotland fourteen years ago as a Hudson's Bay man, Jawlie is an Inuk outfitter, and Elizabeth is a researcher from Toronto. A second boat appears, carrying Matthew Akavak and Pingoatuk Kolola, who are learning the river, being asked to understand their ancient homeland from the perspective of strangers, to mediate as guides between their birthright and outsiders who will come to pay homage to what others call "wilderness." Both canoes pull over; Jawlie breaks out the Coleman stove. You drink hot hot tea and chew on frozen slices of raw caribou. Everyone is laughing. You make small talk, but the important thing is, everyone is laughing. When they leave, you feel good about sharing the river. That night you listen to the rain drive against the opaque tentwalls, and sleep beautifully until the blue light of morning.

You have the history, but where is the landscape? You have the poets; but I have delved inwards and downwards through anthologies of Irish verse and discovered a bogland of ancestral displacement, each layer as you drift deeper camped on before, the wet centre bottomless, what Seamus Heaney articulates as an absence of prairie, an absence of place, your unfenced country a land of descent. Where is the land but a landscape of words, your history the landscape of time? There is no horizon for the eye to see, the soul to contemplate; the natural world is always metaphor, only metaphor. Reading your poets, I find contiguity, each poem walled from the others, sharing occasional walls in common; enclosures like a churchyard with scenery surround as a backdrop, but no horizontal reach of the land and the wind and winter and the inaudible summoning for poems to be poems, in the lovely drift of open illimitable sky.

And where have all the women gone? Each to her grave, her life unsung. In Irish anthologies, some published as recently as the nineties, women are mothers and lovers and sometimes fiends, but none, not one, is a writer of worth enough to be included for her own verse. Women are, rather, a poetic conceit among men most concerned with how they themselves will die. What year will they write, utters John Millington Synge, for my poor passage to the stall of night? I have turned my face, says Patrick Pearse, to the death I shall die. Death was at hand, says Seán Ó Ríordáin, I said I would go. When under Ben Bulben I lie, mutters Yeats, Horseman, pass by! And Patrick Kavanagh intones: O commemorate me where there is water, where, by a lock Niagarously roars the falls for those who sit in tremendous silence, with no hero-courageous tomb, just a canal-bank seat for the passer-by. Declan Fitzwilliam avers the androgyny of death's embrace, declaring, I shall be nor man nor woman in my grave, while Thomas Moore invokes Avoca's vale as a burial place, should its merging waters serve adequately as a conceit for love. With grandiloquent modesty, Jonathan Swift anticipates the news of his death at England's court: the Queen, so gracious, mild, and good, Cries "Is he gone? Tis time he should." Only, of all I could find, does Samuel Beckett bear in mind that a writer dead no longer writes. He finds it better to grieve than be missed: I would like my love to die, he says, and the rain to be falling on the graveyard and on me walking the streets, mourning.

Inside the symmetrical elegance of Newgrange, deep within the mounded contours that stand away from the adjoining rough hills and proclaim its human design, surrounded by absolute darkness so close it encloses your flesh like an amorphous carapace, your body disguised as inchoate sensation, inside this most famous of Ireland's many passage tombs, the illusion of having descended into the depths of the earth, although actually you have risen as you negotiated the narrow corridor into the burial chamber, jars you from your lodgement in time. Before the tour guide turned off the lights you examined the cut patterns in a range of lithologies, swirls confounding the solidity of the medium, deep lines denying the inefficacy of stone tools on stone, but only in the absolute dark and the depths of the guide's voice does the mystery of their intricacy enfold you and, quelling panic, you listen not to her words but to the ancient lineage of her voice itself, its shades and inflections filling the darkness with people alive for hundreds of generations, living for that brief moment in the caverns of your mind. Leaving the tomb, stepping carefully out into the green and golden day, you are reminded in the chatter behind you that not only is the shamrock a symbol of Ireland, but also the harp, a musical instrument in which songs of souls of those long-gone hover among the strings, waiting to float, as they are called upon by music, into the light.

The millennium closes less than two years away. Our Christmas tree, a hybrid spruce, is bedraggled now, heroic in its refusal to expire. It is the end of February, and the tree has not yet released its browning needles so that we in good conscience can strip it of plastic Kinder Egg shells that dance without movement from its branches among oddments of ornaments, beading from China, hand-painted pine cones from North Carolina sent by my daughter Julia, painted by my granddaughter, Clare, a papier-mâché effigy of Grace O'Malley, in full pirate gear and ready for sea, bound to its uppermost tip, and a lone French hen in handcrafted Waterford crystal hanging close to the light of the fire , can strip it clean and toss it aside. It has been through the gale-forced blackout of Christmas with us, dark times when much of Ireland came to a standstill, and now as I write I look over its shoulder at the first real snow we have seen, not counting the occasional flurry, thick wet flakes splatting on the windows, shrouding the Wicklow landscape in white swirling equivocation, and we are a little homesick, and anxious to go out for a walk before the snow resolves into rain and the green emerges more so than ever. It is a tree of great magic and will perhaps stay with us until Easter, when the Kinder Egg ornaments will truly come into their own.

A month after the Terry Eagleton lecture on Yeats that was lost in the hush of the National Library, we went back to the little restaurant off Grafton Street where we had eaten a light dinner beforehand. The restaurant, despite the name, Tosca ... (a word followed by three dots), is a clean well-lighted place, less smoky than most, and the early-bird specials, where you pay for your entrée the time on the clock when you ordered, were wondrous. When we returned, this time to order at 5:45, the waitress who poured our water enquired how we had enjoyed the Eagleton lecture last month and, when we said we had not, because we were unable to hear, she sympathized, saying how much she generally liked his writing on critical theory in spite of the neo-Marxist cant and it would have been a pleasure to hear him on Yeats. I said she must be a student and it was amazing she remembered us; and she said, No, I just heard you talk, I'm a waitress. Such is Dublin; and we, being close to Trinity College, didn't know whether dissembling was postmodern strategy and she was constructing a fiction of her life for a class project, with us as part of the subtext, or if in fact she was what she said and we were marginalized, for being surprised. Such is Ireland, just so.

TEMAGAMI

This piece was originally delivered at a conference organized by Nipissing University called "Visions of the North, Voices of the North," held in Temagami, Ontario, in 1999, with contributions published by Nipissing University the following year as Visions and Voices in Temagami. *The editor of the book, A.W. Plumstead, wrote in his Introduction with telling insight about the intended chaos of my contribution. "Is it fiction, autobiography, literary criticism, philosophy, history? ... What are all these doing so interfused in this essay/tone poem/lecture/reminiscence, murder-mystery-in-progress?" It is postmodern metafiction, whatever else it may be. Some of it is true. I am amused at how advancing age and the imminence of death are woven throughout, given that I am now twenty-five years older and, as I write, not dead yet.*

Whenever I am in Temagami I think of murder. Not abstractly, and not with pathological intent. It just seems to me that if I were going to murder someone, this would be the place to do it. When I round the corner on the highway driving north and first catch a glimpse of the town-site opening ahead of me — -rising from the shore with roadways and buildings set in angular response to the primordial lay of the rocks and the water — -my mind immediately turns to the disposal of bodies, the choosing of lethal devices, the selection of an unsympathetic victim. At my present age, I am not likely to kill anyone; it is enough to cope with my own precarious mortality. But I am a writer of fictions. If I were going to write about murder, this is where I would set my story.

Nothing in my life prepared me for getting old. It was inconceivable to me at twenty that I would ever be sixty, just as it is inconceivable now that the world will not be appalled at my death. Facts we know with certainty often remain unreal. That is the difference between true and the truth. It is true I will die; but the truth is I cannot imagine my absence. I can envision a world without me in it, but it is only imaginary, a projection of my own mind. If I were not here, it would collapse into nothing. And therefore I write. To make the world real.

Perhaps only now, while there is still time in my life, has the desire to shape the world into being achieved such urgency. Perhaps only in Temagami do I associate place so strongly with murder, where intimations of mortality first entered my mind when I would struggle against sleep as a child on our rocky one-acre island, in a tent pitched over a soft patch known as 'the Englishman's grave.' If my brother left to go into the cabin or into the darkness for a nocturnal pee, I could feel the corpse beneath me drawing me downwards into the dark mossy earth. This was the only spot on the entire island where the soil had depth and it took on a sinister character when my father refused to dig the hole for the new outhouse there. That was his way of honouring the story that passed like a rumour from his own father to him before I was born that this was a place of interment. Instead, the outhouse was straddled across a small crevasse on the far side of the island with a spectacular view through the open door down the northeast arm.

Even when Richard and I were very young we would drive the kicker from island 108 into Temagami for groceries. We would land at Ernie Smith's and take our list to Doughtie's Store, then walk to The Store of Little Things for popsicles, circle back to pick up our groceries and ice, then drink glasses of well-water which Mrs. Smith would have waiting for us, along with a smile she would hold effortlessly and without words the whole time we were there. Then we would climb back into the five-horse outboard for the long trip home. Richard would drive; he was older. I would sit up against the half-deck at the front and watch for shoals.

One summer, when we arrived from the south and scrambled out of the car which we parked beside the canoe-works shed at the Smith's, Richard and I listened while Ernie told Mom and Dad that we would have to buy our groceries somewhere else this year. Mr. Doughtie had killed Mrs.Doughtie and Mrs. Doughtie's mother. He had set fire to the house and then shot himself through the head; and the fire had smouldered for days before they were found, the three of them smoked dry like pemmican. Mrs. Smith served us cool drinks of well-water on the front porch overlooking the dock where the kicker was gassed and ready to carry us with our new baby brother down to island 108. We never had a name for the island other than its registry number, although Ernie and my grandfather, Austin, and his friend, Archie Belaney, and a man from the States had built our cabin two generations before and it was teeming with stories through our childhood, until Mom and Dad sold it in the mid-fifties and bought a sailboat on Lake Ontario which could be moved from place to place on a whim and by the wind.

Old as I am, as the narrative voice I can be as young as I wish. When the Doughties died I was six or seven. Since Steve was a baby, I must have been six. The melodrama of their deaths seemed awesome and exciting at the time, overheard on the Smiths' porch. I could see through the trees the roof of the house next door where it happened. I could not imagine anyone else living there again, with the smell of smoked flesh embedded in the walls, but another family moved in. From that summer on, no matter who was living in the Doughties' old house, it always looked empty to me, as if the gravity of past events had more weight in my mind than the present. The summer I returned with my own children, after an absence of years, to see if the Smiths were still there, the Doughties' house was gone. It had burned to the ground the previous winter with no-one inside. Mrs. Smith, I was told, had died, and Ernie had retired from making canoes to live in a small house down the highway. When we found him, I introduced my children but Ernie spoke only Ojibway by then so we left after a few minutes and proceeded on the canoe trip that had brought us there.

Every story must have a setting. Today I am in Temagami. I write that down and the fact becomes fiction, a truth to which you accede by narrative convention — you, by convention, lending your life to the text to affirm its veracity. The story at this point is simple; it is about me in Temagami contemplating murder. But nothing has happened. I have established a location in your rational mind, but probably not yet in your imagination. I have indicated a temporal context-today — although it will always be today in my text, so time is elusive. I have seeded your curiosity, perhaps, with a passing reference to Archie Belaney, a name which gained much prominence years later when it was associated with the man who became famous as Grey Owl. I have suggested emotional conflict, my concern about age; I have shared my implicit intention to ground consciousness in the world through language, simply by acknowledging your presence in my discourse. Of greater significance to us both, I have proclaimed my desire to make the world authentic through fiction.

If you are offended by solipsism, consider: it is the poets and painters who shape where you live. If you look out the window in northern Ontario, you see tall pines, the cedars and birch, articulated as Tom Thompson saw them, as surely as crystal on linen is ordered in your mind by Vermeer, sunflowers by Van Gogh. The equations proliferate. Do you remember that evening you spent drinking red wine by lamplight on Piazza San Marco, or is it the geometric precision of Canaletto you recall? The first time you visited England, sitting on a train sliding through English countryside, the windows framed Constable landscapes. When you went to the Arctic and each time you return, you see echoed the paintings of Lawren Harris and Doris McCarthy, Tony Onley and David Blackwood, and you wonder what Americans see.

Before you dissent, proclaiming yours to be an untutored sensibility, pristine or unpracticed, consider: painting, like grammar, brings a random vocabulary to order. The fact that you do not know parts of speech, cannot parse a sentence, does not mean you do not speak words that Shakespeare spoke, contemplate thoughts that Milton wrote. Print and paint have etched in your mind deep structures of aesthetic response; you only see what has already been seen.

From the perspective of Temagami, I realize my life has increasingly become a struggle to keep on the surface of time, without flying off into dream. At an age when memory so often distracts from experience, no place seems more than a projection of my own personality. The world has become a protean concept, its myriad forms in my mind more substantial than my present location. That is how I know I am old: places from the past seem more real than the present. That is what Temagami has made me realize, because Temagami is the one place in my life where time is ephemeral, flowing by me like mist on a wind, while I remain constant, as inseparable from the land as an inlet or a promontory. Place here is the constant, and time is unreal. In such a setting, murder seems possible, although my choice of a victim, even in fiction, from this point seems arbitrary. It is like going to sleep and no matter what you intend to dream, the dream will determine what's dreamed on its own.

Let me sum up, for summations should never be left to the end. Those versed in such things may find echoes here of Husserl and Heidegger, Saussure perhaps, and Wittgenstein, and even Derrida. For the rest of us, more comfortable in the libraries of our minds among volumes less weighty than those that the vestiges of these men inhabit, all of them but Derrida being presently deceased, I will attempt clarification.

Temagami, the lands of the Teme-Augama Anishnabai, is so much a part of my sense of self; when I am among the lakes and rocks and trees I am most truly at home with my mortal condition, a creature of consciousness inseparable from the immediate world around me; and when I am away from the bush, the vital waters, the outcroppings of stone in the sunlight, I return to their configurations as landscape in my mind to locate myself where time and space merge, the one place in the world I am real.

Temagami is without boundaries or limits, although maps may put edges on it, which land-claims dispute. It is seen by outsiders as empty, although there is not a trail through bush, a route over water, a cliff-side vista, that has not been experienced by humans for thousands of years. Temagami is vast and intimate; I can travel its terrain for months on foot or by canoe and always, the tree I lean against to ease my burden, the lake I cross to make my way, the rocks I shift to set my tent, are so familiar, I seem to be their holy emanation, not they projections of my personality as humanists would have it.

Descartes founded all knowledge on the immodest premise that consciousness is proof of existence, a proposition not unlike my own declaration to write the world into being. I designate Temagami as the place where objective reality and I, as its human witness, converge. Temagami transcends my own life or my death. Some places precede us in the world, and others only exist as we become aware of their presence. Think of an English manor house and Agatha Christie. Think of Tombstone, and the Erps and the Clantons. Think of a tall ship caught fast in Arctic ice. Death as diversion, as American melodrama, as the force of indomitable nature, imposes on the imagining mind a powerful sense of place. Certain settings anticipate our discovery of the deaths that occur in their midst. Then by the efficacious logic of a well-turned corollary, a place that is most splendidly real invites the contemplation of death, as the human activity that most engages individual consciousness with the implications of being alive.

Nothing affirms our authentic being in the world like a reminder of mortality, and nothing reassures us so much as confrontations with death contained within narrative design such as we find in a well-wrought story of murder, mythic violence, or the indifference of nature to the vainglorious aspirations of human endeavour. If I write about murder in Temagami, I had better do more than describe the eruption of the Doughties' domestic dispute — even when offered from the oblique perspective of a child, it seems a violation of privacy to give the terrible fate of those people a context of fiction that might place their suffering within a spectrum of understandable behaviour.

Domestic violence does not make good fiction. That is true, but of course the truth is that *King Lear* is a domestic tragedy. Much fiction originates in or reveals family life. What makes it good, however, is not domestic revelation; it is the design of the story, the moral and aesthetic structure by which the violence achieves meaning. In my account of the Doughties, there is only artlessness. I remember in Temagami the time a woman drowned her two children in the boat-house slip, then tied an anchor to her feet and drowned herself. I knew the family. There was no meaning to this event, either, no story to redeem the lives lost, no narrative absolution. Only the stunning finality and the infinite pain.

To make murder tolerable, to make it cathartic or exciting or amusing, it must be placed in an unthreatening context of moral coherence, described in a context of narrative closure. Story, in other words, must be sufficiently removed from real life to make sense, yet anchored in experience enough to engage. If I am to situate a murder in Temagami, the one place in the world more real than the past, then I must provide you with character and plot as incentives to remain with the text.

Plot: I am suddenly old. Character: think of me as a spectre from another dimension. I can lie dormant indefinitely in a configuration of words. But I am able to cross over successfully from potential to being only so long as I can hold your attention. If you have ever watched *Star Trek* or *The X-Files*, you will know how it works. I have no qualms about my fictional status. Whatever I am while I arrange these words, in their arrangement I am something else. Like Descartes, my presence in language has more substance than my life. I have already suggested that you are fiction, insofar as you permit yourself to participate in my rhetoric. You have the advantage, of course, the power to annihilate me as a textual entity by closing the text, refusing to listen or read. But I would remind you, the butterfly and the carpenter see different trees. Why not give my being as fiction its due.

What we need to sustain a relationship is common ground where you and I are equally authentic. I propose Temagami. But suppose you had never been here before my words urged the necessity of your presence. You need story, you need facts. You need atmosphere and perspective. You need time. It will always be today in this text. The present, where the past and future divide, depends on when the text is revealed. You need a temporal axis to locate yourself, for when you enter a text it is like stepping away from the north pole into a time zone determined by the direction you choose. Once committed to time, you will need parallels of latitude to determine location. These come from story and place.

As an astute reader you will be wondering impatiently, haunted perhaps, by my early reference to the Englishman's grave on our island; wondering why the word Englishman was seeded with meaning and then seemingly dropped. The problem is, I do not have a plot in mind which I intend to reveal as the fiction progresses. The opposite is true. Fiction will create plot, not reveal it, from memories evoked by the Temagami landscape in conjunction with the urgency by which I measure each passing moment as the murder of time.

There were two Englishmen in my childhood. My grandfather was one. He died before I was born. He was my father's father. My mother's family, and my father's mother's family, were Canadian hybrids: Mennonite, Presbyterian, Lutheran, United Empire Loyalist, Church of England, Viking. My father's father and his friend, the other Englishman, met in Toronto in the early years of the twentieth century. Austin had been a ranger in the Boer War. Archie Belaney was younger, an idealist. From our perspective they were practically pioneers. In their own era, they found Toronto an inhospitable fusion of the new and established, and within a short while after their arrival in Canada, they fled paradox, north to Temagami, where they both found refuge from the New World amidst the vestiges of a civilization as ancient and elusive as their own, the one they had left behind because it seemed more the subject of books than experience, and here they embraced native culture in which people and place, the sensibilities of the people and the authenticity of land beyond any consciousness of its presence or worth, were indivisible.

My grandfather and Archie teamed up with Ernie Smith, who liked them because, for their different reasons, they were both eager to be just like him. They built canoes together. Ernie tried to teach them Anishinaabemowin, or Ojibway, as he called it. When a handsome hawk-faced man from the American southwest appeared, he was hired to help with the work, chopping wood for the rib-steamer. After a season of apprenticeship, he became an equal partner as it did not seem right to have three bosses and one labourer. The stranger learned Anishinaabemowin, which he spoke softly, quite unlike the two Englishmen, and soon spoke it better than them. Ernie said he was an Indian. The man said nothing to confirm or deny his origins, except to speak earnestly sometimes by the dying light of the boiler fire, late at night when the men would share a mickey of rye, about being born out of death, that he had been cut from his mother's womb as they prepared her for burial. I know this because Ernie would stay over sometimes in the cabin on island 108 and tell us stories in the flickering lamplight, and that is one of the ones he would tell.

In those days, a trickling of tourists moved into the area in the summers and even after the Great War, as the trickle turned to a seasonal torrent, it seemed that the vast open arms of Lake Temagami could embrace everyone. When Archie and Austin returned from the War, the four partners resumed their business and prospered, and were soon building cabins for outsiders as well as canoes. Things changed when kickers arrived. Suddenly the drone of outboard motors severed the silence. That, of course, is speaking poetically, for the land is never silent, the lake breathes with a resounding and subtle dissonance of wind and water, and you can hear the sky. It is only poets who hear nothing in nature but the sounds of their ear-drums beating and the echoing haunting melodious yodel of the loon.

When I was a young man, I worked as a bush guide and we used Temagami cedar-strip canoes, some of them old enough they might have been crafted by the original team which broke up long before I was born. We sometimes paddled past cabins they had built; you could always tell their cabins by the way they were set among the trees and the rock like natural events, not propped up on cliffs or crowding the shoreline. Of the four partners, I knew only Ernie. Austin died the year after my Mom and Dad were married. Archie Belaney died in various ways, depending on which story Ernie chose to relate. The most chilling was the one he sometimes refused to tell, sometimes sending us out to our tent on the Englishman's grave so terrorized by his reticence that we would try to stay awake all night. The stranger from America married a local woman, Anahareo, and took an Anishinaabemowin name and did some writing and it was he who became known as Grey Owl.

Now if you were attending carefully, even before my sentence came to a full stop you were thinking of murder. All my life, I have been wondering the same thing. I have never said anything about this, not even to my brothers. I have heard nothing about it from anyone. What actually happened, the years closed over. Time itself is a conspiracy. If people in Temagami registered interest or alarm, nothing of their concern is recorded. Four partners went out to build a cabin on island 108. They hauled their equipment over the ice, including a boat, the prototype of their new line of outboards based on the classic Peterborough design. After the break-up, only three came back.

Years later, following his own death, Grey Owl, who had become a famous "Indian," was revealed with considerable fanfare to have been the manufactured persona, some would say fraudulent persona, of the Englishman, Archie Belaney. When I first heard that, my impulse was to write fiction, to correct the record. But I thought about Ernie and realized he would be amused, or more likely would think the confusion not worthy of comment. I remember once asking him, when I was still working as a canoe-trip guide, who Grey Owl was, since even then there was some confusion about his authenticity. I used that word, authenticity. Ernie ignored my query. Not exactly ignored. He weighed it and left it unanswered. But Mrs. Smith spoke. It was the only time in all the years I knew her that she ever said more than a greeting; I had no idea how much English she knew. She said, "His name was Wa-Sha-Quon-Asin. He is authentic, he is Indian. I knew two wives. Anahareo, she is my cousin. Her husband, he tells good stories."

Since hearing that Grey Owl and Archie had apparently become one and the same, whenever I am in Temagami I now think of murder. Place here is more knowable than time. If there is a world that does not need to be written to be real, it is here. When I return, even in imagination, it is always waiting, just as it was, although the particulars change. If I went to island 108, I know what I would find in the Englishman's grave. Archie Belaney would be saturated with bogwater in a mossy cleft deep under the soft dry layers of pine needles and fragments of lichen that are matted from years upon years of tents being pitched over his earthly remains.

His skull would be split and the bandage that was used to hold it together would fall away if his grave were opened and the two halves of his skull would come apart in the air. He was not killed by Ernie or my grandfather. If he had been, we would never have grown up knowing our island campsite as the Englishman's grave. The secret would have been absolute, with no room for irony. It was the stranger who killed him, the man who took the name Grey Owl. The man who after his own death was given Archie's identity. It was a quarrel. It was about Archie trying to be Indian, and the stranger, refusing. Ernie and Austin would have returned from the mainland with a load of stripped saplings for chinking the logs and found the murderer sitting against the giant white pine in the middle of the island, cradling Archie across his lap, staring into his empty eyes, trying with both hands to hold Archie's head together.

This revelation is not an epiphany. It is, after all, part of a fiction. I am older now, and no longer text. I have gone on to other things. You may linger a bit in the today of your reading, to contemplate the implications of being present in a fiction that offers itself as a witness to murder. But it is Temagami this is about, not you, not the pathos of a man who killed his mother-in-law, his wife, and himself, ineptly, not about a hawk-looking stranger who became, perhaps, what he had always been, and not about an Englishman who perhaps said the wrong words at the wrong time, and has become more a part of Temagami than Grey Owl could have imagined. It is a story about arriving finally at a certain age and discovering I would rather be in Temagami than old. It is about shifting identities through time, and about the efficacy of place as a plot device; and it is about the presence of death as an absence in your life, like a grave on an island in the back of your mind.

THE IVORY FLUTE

Inevitably, it seems, I turned to fiction. My last novel, To Set the Stone Trembling, *(2023), is a dystopian intellectual thriller, where the author is simultaneously present but absent. Nowhere is this more evident than in Book Two, called "The Invisible Labyrinth." There, there are discontinuous bits of narrative set fifty-thousand years in the past, when grammar forced language into meaningful abstraction and the notion of metaphor became real, all conveyed as a metafictional vision. I have arranged these pieces into chronological coherence and done one radical thing with them. It may seem little enough, but I eliminated all commas. The language flows, at once disjointed and as fluid as time. While not as extreme in my devotion (subservience?) to punctuation as* The New Yorker, *I generally find commas, especially, to be useful. I'm a firm adherent to the Oxford comma, which many regard as superfluous — yet here the breath-pause implied by the comma seems inappropriate.* To Set the Stone Trembling *has been read by few, appreciated by a few of those, and awaits appropriate recognition in years to come, should the world endure.*

This is a time before everything means something else. It is when words are things and there is no difference in the mind between 'stone' and a stone. There are no tenses no parts or figures of speech. Lies and metaphors are inconceivable. The graphic design on the wall of a cave is an auroch in flight. The rock breathes and snorts and clatters with hooves over rubble as the animal perpetually runs. Words and images struggle to break through time carving cracks in the darkness. The human brain is preparing to explode with radiant and murderous light.

***

A woman stoops and enters her shelter. She remains bent over after her head clears the pole holding an auroch skin in place to keep out the cold. She has been gone several days. She is looking at something in the mottled darkness. Her eyes cannot focus and she rubs them with the backs of her hands. She kneels tentatively beside a rumple of shadows which is the body of a younger woman on a bed of sphagnum and she touches the cold lips with her fingers then slips her hand under the covering and feels the hard chilled flesh. She stares for a moment at the dead face of her daughter revealed in strands of light that penetrate the sides of the shelter animated by wind scattering sunlight through wavering spruce.

The woman rises to her feet and stands for a moment then leaves and the door falls closed behind her. She stands full-throated in front of the shelter letting the sunlight warm her breast. Her eyes are moist and her lips tremble until she closes her mouth and draws them tight over her teeth. When her eyes become dry, she turns and walks along a narrow path past several homes in dead-fall spaces among storm-battered spruce. When she arrives at a skin door that is larger than the others she stops and draws herself tall and then stoops and enters.

A man her own age strongly built with good teeth glances up. He continues to stroke the girl lying against his outstretched legs soothing her as if keeping her still. The girl is the same age as the woman's daughter. She looks frightened but the woman showing her own fine teeth touches her face and the girl shrinks submissively and lies quiet.

The woman utters a sound to the man that reveals a story they both understand although the details for each are different. The man shrugs. His lips form a snarl accentuated by his beard. The woman lowers herself pushing the girl to the side across the sphagnum. The three of them touch skin to skin. There is no further movement until the man reaches out and stirs the small fire in the centre of the shelter. The man spits into the flames and wipes the drizzle from his beard.

The woman forces herself more firmly between him and the girl. As soon as the man's hand falls away from the girl she gets up and quietly leaves. The man rises to his knees and positions himself over the woman and briefly invades her body surges and rolls away. He falls asleep. She leans forward and picks up a blackened boulder from the hearth weighs it and brings it down sharply cracking open his skull. His eyes flare wide in the moment of his death.

She pulls a charred stick from the embers and holding it close to her mouth she blows it into flame and then reaching out she touches the flame to a brittle tendril of the uprooted spruce that forms the skeletal structure of the dwelling. She rises and walks into the dappled sunlight.

Behind her the wood and dried mosses and desiccated skins blaze into an inferno that roars for some time and then collapses over the smouldering body. She picks up chunks of dried log that have been smashed into manageable pieces and throws them onto the fire. Bystanders move close and a few heave wood into the flames until the charred remains in the collapsed shelter are no longer identifiable as a corpse then they drift away. A few others hold chunks of meat skewered on green sticks over the embers and cook them to succulence.

The woman walks back to her own shelter carrying a glowing coal on a small flat rock. She sets that shelter alight as well and sits close so the flames scorch her face and eventually she gets up and stirs the embers until her daughter's body collapses into fiery pieces and mixes with burnt detritus and scarred clumps of earth.

It is evening when a man approaches and takes her roughly by the hand forcing her to her feet. This woman whose daughter was murdered and this unlikely man who acceded to the leadership of their community are now a couple. Neither has a name. They have known each other since infancy.

The man she killed had been powerful and perhaps handsome. This man more supple is well adapted to hunting for aurochs on the plains above their valley. He had once impaled a lunging sabre-toothed tiger on a thick length of dry spruce he had sharpened in a fire offering his own body as bait. He wears the tiger's skin draped across his shoulders. She is slender as a reed silent and quick able to snare rabbits with her hands and to strip the skin from frog's legs with a single tearing motion as she breaks them away from their quivering bodies.

Inside his shelter he touches her gently. She opens herself to him. Afterwards they sleep. Frozen rains begin to whirl outside in a high-pitched wail and their fire crackles in defiance beside them. Dusk turns to darkness. The flames of his fire shoot wavering bolts of light through chinks in his shelter out into the night. Toward dawn the air is thick with sound and they do not distinguish the earth breaking along the ravine's upper edge nor the groan of stiff clay slurry as it slides down the hillside like a rumbling wall and smashes into their shelter and buries them, clasped in each other's arms and they disappear for fifty thousand years.

***

Imagine the primeval woman who suffocated under the unstable earth. She is creating words with her infant daughter. It is fifteen years before they die. They amuse each other tossing sounds in the air. It is a game with no rules. As the girl gets older the two of them sit in the sunlight or in front of the fire and click consonants ululate hiss sibilants resonate vowels and whistle delighting in distinctive patterns. Sometimes the patterns are strung together. The woman and her child play with sound-clusters until sonorous shapes slip into memory where they are invoked at will. Music comes before words. Words come before meaning. The permutations seem endless. Sometimes the sounds attach to objects through imitative affinities aural evocation emotive stimulants.

After a few years the woman and her daughter share a vocabulary that allows preternatural communication between them. They live at the edge of their commune but others are enthralled overhearing their music and words. Being gifted with curiosity and imagination they imitate the sounds in the privacy of their auroch-skin homes sometimes roaring with laughter or screaming in fear at the unintended capacity of their efforts to invoke things even when the things are not there.

Soon words become the currency of play among the children and creep into the primal activities of adults as they hunt and gather and struggle against inclement weather. Within a few years their group has achieved a consensus on sound equivalents for many of the items around them and that changes forever their relationship to everything. The girl and her mother meanwhile formulate verbs that enable divisions of time as well as procedures of logic and abstraction. This changes their relationship to themselves.

By the time the girl is half her mother's age and her closest friend they have taught by example and imitation their entire settlement to communicate in ways that neighbouring groups of humans will find useful to emulate as the new tool of language spreads exponentially eventually to the farthest reaches of the world although at least one robust branch of their kin with sloping foreheads and recessive chins cannot comprehend the new phenomenon that enables the weaker more cautious *homo sapiens sapiens* to prevail at hunting large and ferocious animals whose fat stores are essential for survival as ice encloses their environment.

The younger woman becomes anxious by the ways their words give them command over the world but separate them from it. She ceases talking except when no one but her mother can hear. It is too intimate and estranging an experience to share. On a particular day, she disappears.

Predators in the woods surrounding the valley are rare. Most have been driven to extinction or wariness by the wiry interlopers who chatter with furtive urgency then fall into menacing silence only to leap from the shadows screaming and flailing with weapons that extend their strength and their reach. Always the humans are outsiders. Their talk and their tools make them perennial invaders. It is not exceptional for them to vanish although few venture far from the cluster of homes on their own. They hunt or gather fruits of the earth in the company of others. Occasionally a couple will run off to live by themselves or to join a gathering of humans more amenable to their own peculiarities. When one person disappears it is often because the lone hunter the solitary gather has been assaulted by his or her own kind and left to die.

The young woman's mother searches for two days and on the third discovers a crack in the earth where odours of burning pitch drift upwards into the open air. She walks to the edge of the nearby ravine and descends, clutching exposed roots for support and settles by a cleft in the rock face. After a period of consideration she ventures into the mottled gloom. She had lived in this chamber herself after her own mother died. It is here that her daughter had been conceived and was born.

She moves back from the main chamber and darkness closes around her pressing from every direction. A crevasse near her feet echoes from pebbles she kicks as she shuffles across accumulated guano scat rushes and brittle dried hides. She stops and calls and receiving no answer returns to the harsh sunlight outside. She finds a gnarled branch with a knot on the end where it had broken away from a struggling pine. It is caked in dried resin. She removes a small case made of perforated shells that is hanging around her neck and blows across the tinder inside until it bursts into fire which she touches to the resin, transferring the flame before smudging the living coal and retying the pendant restoring it to its place as an ornament.

Passing through the initial chamber with her torch flaring wildly carefully avoiding the gaping crevasse she proceeds into the darkness and discovers amidst the leaping shadows an unfamiliar corridor that leads deeper and deeper away from the entry. There are layers of loose dirt under foot and evidence of bears who have dragged killed prey into the earth. Her torch casts erratic shadows over a patina of pawprints and bones and dried faeces as she edges forward. She is surprised that animals would eliminate waste where they eat. She detects the occasional fresh human footprint superimposed over the detritus. They are leading in only one direction deeper into the bowels of the earth.

The woman scans for flakes of ash on the cavern floor. If her daughter has a torch she will be safe from bears. The woman is relieved to find ash. There is only one set of prints. She shuffles on gazing in wonder at the rock formations. She creeps through low passageways and sidles along narrow openings always keeping the footprints in sight until she hears a soft wordless song emerge from the flickering darkness. Thrusting her torch ahead of her she crawls under a low-slung boulder wedged between two sheer walls and comes out in a chamber with flaring light limning the body of the girl who is facing the wall singing softly and shuffling in a slow and erotic dance.

When the lights of their torches merge the girl turns. She acknowledges her mother with a shy smile then steps to the side and gestures to an auroch racing on the stone with her palm curiously held in the direction of the wall as if she were making a gesture for the animal to stop. The auroch is a living thing caught in mid-stride with its massive head flung back against an outer flank in wild exuberance as the slender forelegs paw the air and its hind legs kick out at the emptiness in pursuit. The woman gasps to see a sentient creature transformed from rock into flesh. Her daughter reaches and touches the auroch and the woman shudders as their torchlight sets the stone trembling. The girl caresses the animal's shoulder with stained fingers reaches down between her own legs and scrapes congealing blood from her inner thighs mixes it in the palm of her other hand with spit and charcoal from a burnt-out torch and dabs the mixture onto the flesh of the beast making it flex and ripple with movement.

This is the girl's first blood. This is the word made flesh. The woman's daughter has given birth to something authentic that stands for something else and the woman suddenly understands how the sounds they have filled with meaning since her daughter's infancy have given them power. She understands how language works how symbols are as real as their referents. Stone painted with blood and ash is still stone but the auroch exists. In her mind it is a living beast caught in a moment of time. She understands that she is a human aware of herself in the world and with this new power, *homo sapiens sapiens* is forever estranged even from itself.

***

The girl who creates aurochs avoids people. She refines compounds made with animal fat blood clay ochre and charcoal. Her mother brings visitors into the depths of the cave to witness her creations but only when the girl isn't there. This desire to work undisturbed translates into magic. The girl is thought to make flesh from her dreams. She is believed to conjure an auroch from nothing grazing in flight at bay. The paint flows with finesse from the tips of her fingers as she turns it to flesh and sinew and bone. To the girl it is the auroch itself that is magic.

The more people who arrive from distant communes to witness her work the more desperate she is to retreat. For months and then years she hides deep in the cave where sunlight can't touch her and her skin turns the colour of ivory with a luminescent sheen from the smoke of the fires her mother keeps stoked for warmth while she contemplates aurochs. Periodically, she ventures to a place near the cavern entrance where a sliver of sun penetrates through a narrow crevasse and she watches as it slowly sweeps across her legs and torso.

Sometimes she sits on the fur mats on the floor of her cave and arranges pebbles in the dust in rigid designs, sometimes she rocks herself asleep and awake and asleep until she collapses onto her side and her mother covers her naked body with an auroch robe. Sometimes she eats the berries and meat that her mother provides and she gazes into the middle-distance teeming with aurochs. Sometimes she and her mother chatter while they eat together trying out phonemes contriving modifiers verb tenses metaphors.

***

One day in an indeterminate season with no warning the mother brings three young men into the heart of the cave while the girl now a young woman is dreaming of aurochs. When she sees them approach she turns her back and addresses the stone searching for creases in the rock face that promise the curve of a twisted neck the surge of a shoulder or haunch any part of an auroch waiting to be freed. She mixes pigments and begins to paint and the arm muscles of one of the three young men twitches in unison with her movements and he looks past her nakedness to the metamorphosis of rock into paint into pulsating flesh as she manipulates the shadows and spectrum of light and he cannot separate what she makes from who she is as she works in the firelight. The other two watch her pale body flicker and they shrink in annoyance and fear and contempt.

The woman who brought them into the cave pushes the boy most stricken with repugnance towards the pale apparition. The girl drops and he moves forward and takes her with little more than a clumsy thrust rises and stands apart in the shadows. The next shrinking boy is pushed forward and falls on the girl while she is still down on the fur mat resigned to the breeding ritual orchestrated by her mother. He takes her in an instant and rises triumphantly then recedes into the shadows to join his compatriot. The third young man without urging steps forward and first touches his fingers to feel the auroch alive on the wall then bends to the young woman and gently touches her skin until she moans softly against his shoulder and spreads to invite him into her, where he lingers and then comes with a quiet surge. He rises and joins the others. The girl's mother leads them away through the tunnelled convolutions of rock out past the crevasse where the bodies of two of the girl's fathers had been cast into bottomless darkness only moments after conception. The third the woman had allowed to survive. These three she now discharges with a perfunctory shrug and prepares dinner for her daughter and herself of tubers cooked inside a roasting goose. The girl rises and goes back to the auroch and fashions a calf stumbling in its tumultuous wake.

∗∗∗

In another season in the chamber near the opening outward into the light her newborn shivers gasps howls in a single cry and dies. Her mother takes the dead infant from her arms and wraps the small body in a lamb's skin and sets it away from the fire. The girl rises and walks with her mother to the opening of the cave and is blinded by the sun. As her eyes adjust she sees colours she has long forgotten and shapes that move with the breeze. Her pale skin quivers in the open air. She picks wildflowers in bloom from close to the entrance. The two women turn back into the cave.

The girl picks up her baby cocooned in its wool and cradles her burden against the flowers pressed to her naked breast and walks alone deeper into the earth carrying a small torch in her free hand. She makes her way through the cavern teeming with aurochs. When she finds a secret grotto in the darkest depths of the earth she sets her bundle down wipes away tears from her cheeks and unwraps the shroud. She plucks petals from the flowers and spreads them in delicate patterns over her baby gently wraps her again and places rocks around her to protect her from the idea of predators then crawls back and walks out into the firelight where her mother wraps her in an auroch hide.

And the stone comes alive as cave lions emerge in endless succession around the cavern circumference while the girl paints frantically in the concealed chamber where she has laid her baby to rest. The stripes on their fur are visible in rippling shadows. Their massive size is shown by undevoured carcasses of aurochs and elk beneath their leaping contours. Their speed and agility are caught in a whirl of torchlight swaying in the darkness while the grieving young woman exorcises their furious beauty into colour and movement that sets the stone trembling. Her mother tends to her with supplies of ochre and charcoal and blood mixed with animal fat or with food and water to be shared amidst the feline threnody for the dead infant child.

One day and she cannot know when since days inside the cave are indivisible her mother arrives pushing her torch and a bundle of food ahead through the narrow crawl-space into the chamber and finds the girl seated in the dwindling glow of her fire which she has not stoked or replenished. Their eyes flicker as the girl soundlessly directs her mother to survey the completed chapel a distillation of genius so vast and intimate the viewer becomes pure consciousness transcendent and inseparable from the power of the vision conveyed. Mother and daughter filled with fear and awe from the lions around them turning and turning in a widening gyre stop when the girl breaks away and leads to the exit. She urges her mother to go ahead through the narrow passage. Her mother complies with trepidation fearing the girl will block the way between them and perish surrounded by her whirling memorial but the girl follows and together they close off the chapel with boulders and gravel and wads of clay worked into mud with drinking water carried in a beehive sealed by layers of its own wax. Even to them it seems the chamber might never have existed.

They clamber over rockfalls and through hollows and fissures into the cavity that was the girl's first studio and then further towards the surface of the earth to the chamber that had been her mother's refuge after her own mother died in a fire before the girl was born. The girl has crafted a few aurochs here to engage with her mother and be shown to visitors who don't warrant a deeper tour into the depths of creation. The older woman has spent a lot of time on her own making clothing from hides in this chamber while the girl was working on her lion project which they both recognize is meant to displace the loss of her baby not the infant herself but the harrowing gap left by her absence not to honour cave lions which are the human's chief predator but to honour death which is more powerful than lions or love.

The girl does not pause by the glowing coals of the hearth but continues to the gap in the rock that opens onto a vista of the valley below. She kicks a piece of woolly mammoth ivory off to the side as she goes. Her mother picks up an awl made of elk antler and a scraper of cracked human bone a few pieces of ivory along with a rolled bundle of membrane to make sinews and together they venture into the sunlight and traipse down and over the worn forest path by the side of the river until at the edge of the commune they come to the ageing shelter of auroch skins draped across logs propped against a cliff that the woman years ago built on top of the charred remains of the funeral pyre of her mother who herself was feared and thought mad because her mind was estranged from reality around her.

For the next few months until winter falls upon them the girl joins her mother in sewing clothes for the hunters whose partners are better disposed to gathering autumn berries and to drying fish flesh and skinned fowl in the wind and the sun. With the first snow the girl takes three lovers and conceives. In the seasons that follow mother and daughter share companionable chatter creating word patterns that signify parallels to details of their lives. Occasionally their sounds conjure the carousel of lions still whirling in perpetual darkness their eyes gleaming their silent roar deafening. They sing by the fire and chew hides into leather and their song keeps the circle from ceasing to turn.

Late the following summer the girl gives birth to two boys and a girl. One of the boys is stillborn. The families of the fathers attend the birth and the girl falls into abject sorrow as two of the families each take an infant to suckle with aunts because the girl is depleted and does not immediately lactate and the lives of the babies are precarious. The girl does not recover and is distracted by visions of lions as they swoop through the depths of the earth which she never again enters or smears with contours of charcoal and blood. Her mother who had killed two of her own lovers discourages her from further progenerative encounters.

She is surprised when several years later a powerful man comes in while her mother is absent. He reveals his intent in the streaks of light that penetrate the sides of the shelter animated by the wind scattering sun through a stand of wavering spruce between her home and the river. Sex and death seem to her much the same and she is murdered for her apparent indifference. When her mother finds her daughter's body she goes to the man's home and kills him. By the next morning she too is dead smothered by the restless earth in another man's arms.

Twenty thousand years later after glaciation reaches a maximum and begins its rapid retreat melt-water run-off floods the valley and scours the landscape of soil and vegetation. Another twenty thousand years and more sees the waters dwindle as the ice recedes northwards and the river flows much as it had eons before. Lichens and algae mosses and grasses bird droppings and natural detritus build up the soil until trees take root first alders and trembling aspens then towering conifers and finally beech maples and great oaks in abundant forests. *Homo sapiens sapiens* had fled the cold while the hardier Neanderthals stayed and adapted until it was too late — they did not have the skills or technology to hunt the diminishing fauna and they perished. When the others return carrying remnant Neanderthal genes within them they flourish occasionally discovering echoes of their distant heritage. No one finds the cave where the woman had made clothes from animal skins while her daughter made art until palaeoanthropologists from the evolved new world dislodge a few boulders causing a small landslide and discover the entry revealed by the adjusted surface of the planet.

***

Through a narrow subterranean fissure deep in a nondescript passage a woman pulls away rocks to clear an opening. Prying with her spade she hits an oddly displaced chunk of river clay and feels a momentary breeze on the back of her neck as it crumbles. As she clears a space large enough to squeeze through the smell of charred wood and oestrogen emerges from the darkness ahead. Her colleagues and assistants have retreated for lunch near the river. She herself skips eating. She relishes the time on her own in the bowels of the earth where every discovery is mysterious and generates wondrous emotional stirrings. The discoveries of colleagues are facts to be catalogued deciphered and stuffed into boxes for future withdrawal in support of a theory. Her own are episodes in the continuity of human experience. She knows from odours wafting out of the narrow passage that she will find ashes ahead and walls scanned by her flashlight beam will reveal heart-rending flourishes of movement and colour. This is not something she wants to share. She knows she is being subversive.

She crawls forward hesitates as she enters a small chamber and moves carefully illuminating her way step by step on the fine-powdered floor until she reaches the centre then stands tall and shines her flashlight beam on the wall and turns slowly turning and turning in the direction of the animals' movement until she is dizzy and switches off her light. In the palpable darkness she can hear the rush of the lions' fur whirring in the breeze the hush of their breath throbbing in rhythm with her beating heart. She has never felt more human.

She switches on her flashlight again and slowly circumnavigates the room mesmerized examining each lion in turn pausing to identify the carcasses of elk and aurochs that they leap over in a steeplechase with no beginning or end. There are so many lions some superimposed over others that they seem like innumerable facets of one large whirling animate creature with her perceiving surrounded by rock and energy inseparable from their terrible beauty.

Her feet strike an object and she flashes her light down to see boulders in a tight circle and knows this must have been the hearth where the artist warmed pigments and drew light. The dusty clay is discoloured with streaks of carbon near the rocks but lies undisturbed as it has been for tens of thousands of years. Nothing no person or animal or elemental disturbance has penetrated this chamber since the artist had conjured a whirl of lions to fill the void that engulfed her.

On the far side of the fire's dark residue the woman's light catches a strange configuration in the dirt. When she moves closer she recognizes the hint of a human footprint. Giddy with excitement appalled at her unprofessional carelessness she sweeps her light across the entire floor and recognizes her own bootmarks standing out from dwindled contours that turn out to be a chaos of footprints indicating two people from their size likely women with the smaller ones fully arched suggesting youth. In the shadows away from the hearth another mound of rocks reveals by its shape the grave of an infant. The woman starts toward it and then stops. The sound of her own weeping fills the chamber and stirs the lions to leap faster and higher until they seem to overwhelm and she sinks to the floor fists clutching at clay as it sifts through her fingers.

A voice calls through the rock. Suddenly she is at the opening of the passage she came through stepping carefully not to crush footprints and crawls the long passage to the entrance of the tunnel and gazes out shining her light into the eyes of her colleagues. Nothing she declares. Dead end. She urges them to return to the principal dig deep in the crevasse by the side of the main cavern where they have found human fossils and curious bits of antler with rings etched into their sides.

Once she is alone she piles rocks across the narrow low entry behind her and pushes dirt and rocks and a paste made from clay dust mixed with cold coffee from her thermos into the remaining fissures until a seal has been made that will resist even the seepage of air. Then she walks away as if the cave of swirling lions never existed except as a trick of perception.

Back in the outer cavern with the voices of a work party wafting up through the crevasse dulled to meaningless phonemes by the churning sounds of a propane generator the woman sinks onto the soft floor of sand guano and vegetative detritus. She gazes at aurochs that leap on the walls as if in rehearsal for the riotous profusion in the secret chamber created by the same artisan who brought the brute power of lions to life with such feverish intensity — she knows this in the same way she would have recognized a recovered painting by Michelangelo from the ways flesh pulsed beneath painted skin. The artisan was an artist long before art migrated into an end in itself and the artist was a woman. She knows this by the way the smaller footprints covered the floor from every perspective with deliberate randomness the larger prints being of a mature woman more flat-footed possibly a caregiver. She knows the artist was a woman by the subversion of anatomy to motion as form becomes function that speaks of a visceral truth she is convinced few men could grasp however moved they might be by the facts.

Swarming in concentric circles like the scratchings on a reflective surface that arrange themselves neatly behind a candle in patterns owing more to perception than the source of the light what she had seen in the funerary chamber merged with the maelstrom she had endured long ago a memory so appalling she had refused it admission to consciousness in the interim and yet fused with the riot of lions it came forward as an ordeal she no longer had to endure.

Feeling secretive and free she struggles to suppress her explosive heartbeat to subdue her turbulent breathing. She envisions the young woman as a visceral memory ecstatic in the throes of creation a young woman at the base of an opening gyre that includes all the women who lived in the period between them a young woman who was perhaps among the first humans to be aware that she was aware — and this woman fears she herself could be among the last. She walks out into the broad valley and along the well-trodden path by the river determined to shield her progenitor's soul from the implacable light of science in the brave new world that foretells an end to their species.

***

Before the girl's mother the woman who was buried under the earth-slide reaches puberty long before her daughter is born the home she shares with her own mother turns into a funeral pyre. She has been foraging for berries left to dry on the vine by migrating birds and when she returns their lean-to hovel has buckled. Tendrils of flame flick along protruding lengths of shattered poles smoke seeps from beneath auroch hides that gather the body of her mother under their acrid folds. The simmering haunch of a giant elk lies heavily on top. The girl gazes at the smouldering ruin enthralled by the carnage confused.

The infirm or inept receive a share of the communal bounty before hunters are replenished or their own families fed. Her mother deemed eccentric perhaps even mad has received a generous portion of the most recent kill but the weight of a gift tossed carelessly and the force of the snow and the weakness of rotting supports have collapsed their shelter. Glowing embers on the hearth have turned their home into a seething furnace.

The girl pulls hides from the wreckage keeps the least damaged and throws the remainder aside. When she reaches her mother's remains seared and roasted like the slaughtered elk the corpse smells succulent. The girl touches her fingers to her mother's seared breast and to her own mouth but instead of salivating she gags. She wraps two skins around the crumbling body as winding sheets and ties them securely.

Then she hauls the grisly bundle along the base of the cliff to a narrow opening in the rock and manoeuvres it into a cavern littered with layers of dried animal scat. In the gloomy depths of the cave she peels the shroud back and looks at what's left of her mother's face before rolling the wrapped body into what seems a bottomless crevasse.

She returns to the site of their devastated home and tears chunks of flesh from the roasting elk and eats without satisfaction until she is satiated. Only then does she realize how cold she is despite warmth rising from the ruins. Her grease-covered fingers are frost-bitten to the bone. She pulls a smoking remnant of auroch from the wreckage and wraps it around her hands. The pain as her fingers thaw makes her scream but no one can hear. Their home is away from the deepest part of the valley where others live and no one has noticed that her mother has died swathed in billows of smoke and the aroma of cooking meat.

The girl moves into the outer chamber of the mortuary cave. She does not venture deeper into its recesses until years later when she is searching for her own lost daughter. No one she knows lives inside the earth recognizing that caves are the homes of bears and cave lions and ghosts of the dead. She lays out salvaged skins over the scat on the floor. They are late winter auroch hides filled with holes from warble flies that have gnawed through the animal's flesh from the inside to drop and pupate in the warming spring earth. The hides have been cast off by the families of hunters as worthless. Arranged in layers they serve adequately as shelter and robes for mendicants who cannot supply their own. The leathers and furs of smaller animals which the girl has captured as long as she can remember do not cover sufficiently to be useful except for the swaddling of infants but they are soft to lie upon stretched over sphagnum moss.

The girl forages for food close to her cave setting sinew snares for rabbits and wrapping their skins around her feet. She binds several auroch hides that are scarred by smoke and perforated with holes around her thin body and begins to follow the hunters at a distance and watches them work together to make their kills and flense the skins from the carcasses and strip the flesh from the bones.

Sometimes when she approaches close enough they throw scraps of meat her way and she devours small uncooked bits but saves larger pieces to take back to her cave and roast on a stick and the savoury smoke finds its way through fissures in the rock overhead and eventually out to the open flavouring the crisp winter air.

Winter rounds into spring spring warms into summer summer dwindles as autumn descends. With urgency brought on by the shortened days and the growing chill she gathers discarded skins of wild sheep bringing them back to her cave from the hunting fields. Their hair is still dark but beginning to thicken and the warble flies remain subcutaneous. The skins become supple by scraping away residual flesh with the sharp edge of a cracked human shin bone retrieved from a stranger's cadaver. She places them on top of the smaller hides to make luxuriant bedding. She would not be allowed to carry off the auroch skins or elk at this time of year nor the rare woolly mammoth skin which the hunters use to clothe their own families so they can survive the searing cold wrapped in bulky folds that are loosely bound with sinew made from shredding the dried membrane stripped from their kills.

When the girl walks through the village in the depths of the valley many cringe in their hovels until she passes. She cannot know how they fear her courage. She lives in a cave like a beast. She cannot understand how oppressive they had found her mother's behavior dwelling at the edge of the community like a half-domesticated grey wolf with her cub. She cannot know how threatened they were by her mother's disappearance or unsettled by her own unnatural capacity to live by herself.

In a world where imitative behaviour generally offers the best assurance of survival for all living things the most minor infraction could easily mean death. Yet the girl resists conformity. Being raised by a mad woman, she has never learned the essential behaviours that allow her species to thrive. Driven by the same appetites as the others but free from absolute constraints to conform she is eccentric defiant resilient liberated through ignorance empowered by curiosity innovative aware of herself fearless and she endures.

***

Mostly the girl keeps to herself. Sometimes she imitates the world around her. She stands in the wind on clifftops swaying like a tree. She emulates deer prancing and rabbits leaping. She gurgles and giggles like spring run-off coursing down the cliff-face to enter the stream in the valley below. Sometimes she follows a trail of leafcutter ants carrying bits of foliage under dense thickets she has to claw her way through. She watches spiders for hours and days as they create their webs twitching with fascination as they bond one strand to another. Sometimes she observes female spiders devour their mates during or after copulation. She knows which is which because she understands the females deposit eggs the males die. She monitors her own menstruation she feels awkward at first but empowered. She identifies with the female spider. She knows her blood will make children. Perhaps from observing her mother perhaps it's just something she knows. Her mother was still bleeding with the cycles of the moon when she died. Menopause is an incidental factor of age in her species and seldom achieved but when it occasionally happens the gift allows mothers to mother beyond their gestational limits.

The girl is intuitive observant inordinately free to think as she wants. Although she and her mother wears cast-offs she has observed women in their village scrape and dampen and knead the auroch skins over and over each time letting them dry in the sun before working them further until they are supple enough to drape over human bodies the first layer with the hair turned in and the second overlapping with the hair turned out. It is as if human flesh has grown fur providing they move carefully so the coverings don't slide free. She sprawls between bringing in loads of dried wood on fly-riddled auroch skins and gazes at the holes left behind when the flies drop to earth. She examines their patchwork of moulting fur and despairs of a winter confined close to her cave for want of adequate clothing.

She picks up a length of sinew that has dried crisp from being left too close to her fire and pokes it through holes near the edges of two dilapidated skins and draws it forward until a kink in its lower end catches and the skins come together by magic and undulate as she tugs on the thread. She plays with sinews using more supple strands and binds pieces of hide together until they seem like the skin of a single large animal which she draws over herself as if hiding and marvels at the sight of firelight shining through perforations like stars among low scudding brown clouds on a moonless night.

The next morning she selects quality skins of smaller animals from her bedding and sets about forcing holes along their outer edges with a stone-sharpened shard of elk antler. Then she retrieves sheets of dried backstrap membrane she has scraped from chunks of retrieved meat and shreds them into sinews which she works with animal fat until they are pliable. Finally she threads softened sinew through the holes to make smaller skins bigger and roughly in the shape of two humans as if they have been skinned from the corpses of hirsute giants with their hands and feet and heads cut off and she begins to sew these together leaving openings in the envelope of leather for arms and legs to slip through from the inside and a slit wide enough at the bottom to admit a person's entry.

Her fingers are nimble and her broken nails are thick and sharp and no one has shown her that what she is doing following intuition is aberrant behaviour. Living the meanest of lives gives the girl time to create. Living alone gives her freedom. By dusk of the third day she has added tubes of hide for arms and contrived a warm coat that extends from her neck to her feet. With a bandana of fur tied over her ears and rabbit hides bound around her feet she ventures out into the chill autumn air and breathes in the cold and excited by her own body warmth she strides down the narrow path into the village.

Seeing an unfamiliar beast approach with movements that belie its gigantic size, most villagers flee to their shelters although the braver among them take up sharpened poles and burning brands and stand their ground. They are not a timid species. They do what is necessary for survival hiding or fighting as their nature demands.

A boy throws his spear while the monster is still out of range. The spear clatters on the frozen ground at its feet. The great beast laughs and they are amazed when they realize who is inside the strange animal. And frightened. But curious. They approach cautiously. A few tug at her coat. She smiles. She has never smiled before in public. She is invited into the best hunter's house. She has never before been in anyone's home but her own. She sheds her coat like a moth slipping out of its chrysalis and stands naked in the firelight as the villagers crowd into the dwelling to gasp and grunt their amazement at the transformation. The men feed her choice morsels of meat softened in the flames the women anoint her newly formed woman's body with grease from a bowl made of a mastodon skull with the holes stopped up by wads of grass and clay. They wait politely until their ministrations are complete then all examine her coat. Some press the edges of their own robes together but when they release the pieces fall open again leaving gaps exposed as expected. They laugh and slip out into the cold autumn air. There is much to consider.

Before the winter solstice the girl has shown the village how to sew. She still lives alone in her cave but now she receives choice pieces of meat and the most succulent tubers in appreciation and is growing round and plump. She is sad her mother is no longer alive except in her dreams to share her contentment and revel in her absence of fear.

One spring evening as she sits by her fire, binding two small prongs of elk antler to short lengths of sinew before slipping each prong through a hole on different sides of a robe to make a fastener she hears a commotion near the cave entrance. The sounds are strange but familiar.

She thinks of the female spiders she has watched. She waits and a man enters. He is the first person to venture into her cave since she made it her home. He is young her own age. He is nervous. He lies down beside her. She helps take him in. It is over quickly after a surge of discomfort neither had expected. He rolls away. She reaches closer to the fire and wraps her hand around a shaft of sharpened antler and brings it forward and plunges it through the side of his neck. There are noises still gurgling from his mouth and his wound when she drops him into the crevasse at the back of her cave. She returns to her bedding. There will be two more. It is believed that three are necessary. The second enters. He is twice her age. He takes so long he begins to weep. She plunges the antler into his gut as he lolls to the side. She disposes of him in the same fashion as the first waiting by the crevasse this time until his body smashes into the bones and debris at the bottom.

She calls softly and the third man enters. Firelight shimmers off the walls of her cave making the stone seem fluid luminescent. He looks around for his predecessors peers into the shadows then shrugs and proceeds kneeling by the girl and stroking her hair away from her forehead. He bares his teeth. It is an ambiguous gesture. Although he is older than her and a powerful hunter he is wary. She smiles. He strokes her breasts experimentally squeezing them gently to test their consistency. He touches her between the legs he touches himself gently. He lies down beside her and invites her onto him. She draws him inside and he stays utterly still until moving slowly she explodes in unexpected elation. Then he grinds under her weight until they both come together. He grasps her wrists and spreads his arms holding her pinioned from below. When their heartbeats fall into synchronicity he shifts her to the side and rises. He stands looking down. She is not a woman to live with but she will be the mother of his child. She and her infant daughter will move out of the cave into an auroch-clad shelter that she builds for herself on the spot where she and her own mother had lived the place where her daughter will eventually die. The man will never lie with her again. It is too dangerous and he already has a woman in the village but he will hunt for her and keep others from intruding on her solitude. He will accept that his two missing friends have disappeared. He has begun to forget them already.

After he leaves she squats close to the fire. Tears roll down her cheeks. She does not understand grief. She misses her mother. She slides the small prongs of antler from the skins they are holding together. Their bindings of sinew slip off and they fall to her mat. She picks one up and with a sharp edge of obsidian carves a groove around it. She does the same with the other then binds them again a little apart with fresh sinew. She inserts each toggle through holes in two separate skins. Satisfied with her work. Confused. She begins to doze off then awakens abruptly and detaches her new contrivance and tosses it across the chamber where it slides over the edge of the narrow abyss into the gravesite below and a paleoanthropologist digging through the detritus of time will find fossilized antler pieces scored around their circumference the sinew long gone buried under bones turned to stone and thick layers of rubble and dust perhaps fifty thousand years closer to the end of the world.

***

After the girl who was an artist is murdered and her avenging mother suffocates with her new lover beneath the shifting earth, her infant children, a boy and a girl, are carried away by their adoptive families in a great trek across warmer plains that stretch to a vast river flowing between the rising and setting sun. As the seasons progress their party migrates to a great saline sea where they settle on the estuary. By the end of their arduous journey the children are approaching maturity. The boy has learned to be an excellent hunter and is welcome company in any shelter but the girl while strong and exceptionally capable is not at all social. She keeps to herself as much as possible sharing in food shelter and work but spending a lot of time on her own on solitary expeditions foraging for sustenance and sleeping under the stars or in shallow caves carved by the elements into the soft stone of the area.

On a midsummer day when she is far from home exploring the steep hills sloping away from the sea she sights a cave lion slinking through the underbrush. At first she thinks it is a furtive shadow but when she sees an eye flashing through the leaves her fears are confirmed. The lion is tracking her on a parallel course unfamiliar with the scent and behaviour of this strange nimble animal with flapping skin. Even with its massive size and jaws that can seize a deer in mid-leap and break its neck on the run the lion instinctively anticipating the unexpected is wary. In the interval provided by this defensive anomaly the girl has time to think which is the primary defence of her species.

She can't see the ruff around his neck but she knows he's a male. Female lions pursue their quarry in groups usually in the open while males are solitary hunters and use the layout of natural terrain to their advantage. She turns his strategy against him by clambering higher up the slope into tangled scrub forcing him to drop back and follow the course she sets for them both. When she is confronted by a sheer bluff she searches out a small plateau at its base between two large outcroppings of rock. The lion can only approach from one direction and at the same elevation.

She moves with deliberate composure and gathers an armful of twigs and sticks. When she reaches the back of her plateau she removes a case made of perforated clam shells that is hanging from her neck and blows across the tinder inside until it bursts into fire. She touches the flame to a cluster of dry twigs and smudges the living coal inside the shells before restoring her ancestral pendant to its place as an ornament.

Once her fire is blazing she takes advantage of the temporary respite from danger to haul a pole from the edge of her safe zone back to the fire. The pole is dead pine the wood is dry but firm most of the branches are broken away. It is large enough she can only lift one end but light enough she can wield it quite easily when the lower end is braced against the earth. She repeatedly sears the tip burning and scraping until she smooths the charred wood to a point.

She roasts and devours the hind quarters of a rabbit she had snared the previous day and carried in a sling over her shoulder. She has no water. She needs to force the issue with her predator before thirst makes her foolish. She extinguishes the protective fire and drags the pole forward in front of the smouldering coals planting the blunt end with a few roots still showing against a boulder piling stones to secure it in place. She pivots the charred end upwards and slides herself under it until the point is poised well above shoulder height. She temporarily fixes the pole in place with a brace of sticks lashed with sinew. The landscape will force the lion to attack within a projected wedge of open terrain but when it happens she will have to bear the weight of the pole in order to aim the point with lethal precision.

The surface of her fire grows cold the vermillion embers crumble gall themselves black. There is not even a wisp of smoke to indicate where the few remaining coals cling to their warmth. She waits through sunset. The dark of a moonless night closes around her then opens to a skyful of stars. She listens. She can hear the air breathing or is it her own breath or the restless breathing of the lion? She can hear his heartbeat. It seems to be inside her chest. She is desperately thirsty she wants to sleep. She can hear the lion sleeping its rough breath purring in dream. She smiles. There is a bond between them. She dozes sitting upright. She awakens abruptly she senses movement. The stars are washed out of the sky by the first hint of dawn. She moves under the pole next to the brace.

When he comes he comes swiftly. The only sound is the muffled thud of the brace falling away as she raises the weight of the pole on her shoulder. She peers into the blur of darkness as the lion leaps high through pale air at the furious centre of a blood-curdling roar. She shifts her weapon as the arc of his flight expands and his massive form turns to a whirl of destructive energy. She lurches back and a few degrees to the side. There is a piercing scream — the lion the girl agony terror. The lion caught in mid-air impaled through the gut hovers above her in a maelstrom of rage and despair and then lion and pole both irreversibly broken crash down pinning the girl under a mound of throbbing flesh whimpering blood charred wood.

He twitches and shudders in violent death throes. The girl cannot tell where the heaving carcass ends and her own body begins. She is drenched with warm blood. The lion's head is twisted his face is close to hers she can see herself in his eyes she can feel his hot ragged breath. She pushes to free herself the lion cries out. She lies still and waits. His breath washes over her. He moans she weeps. His breath smooths out. Then he is dead. She flexes and fidgets and worms her way from under his body. She drinks blood from his wound lifting it to her trembling mouth in cupped hands.

She lights another fire. It is not necessary the sun has risen but it gives her comfort. Other mammalian carnivores with the exception of the unscrupulous wolverine will recognize the feline scent of the mighty leviathan and scatter perhaps catching a scent of death as they turn away. But wolverines are opportunistic and tend to binge storing fats to cope with inevitable privation. They are scavengers and the smell of the lion's spilled guts will attract although the scent of the lion itself may keep them wary especially when reinforced by the smell of his human companion who herself reeks of death.

The girl sleeps on the open ground but is awakened by the screeching of carrion birds and the buzzing of flies. She stands and gazes at the animal she has killed. Even sprawled on the ground he rises halfway up the height of her body. She takes an obsidian blade from her sling-bag and after the difficult initial cut, she flenses the lion with meticulous flourishes slicing deftly under the skin and peeling it back proceeding solemnly showing deference to the great beast even in death. She cuts carefully around the head and pulls the skin back removing residual flesh with a scraper made from a cracked human tibia.

No one in her community has killed a cave lion before although a decade ago a woman had been carried off and devoured in front of her adopted daughter. The incident was never acknowledged. That was the best way to honour such passing. The wilderness consumed as an expression of power allowing a form of transcendence.

Her daughter was nearly five at the time nearly old enough to fend for herself. The entire community watched out for her making sure she did not starve and had sufficient clothes to survive the bitter cold that descends further upon them each winter but no one knew how to salve her wounded psyche assuage her bitterest fears. The lion became the girl's secret talisman for the incomprehensible fury with which it merged with her foster mother.

When she was ten she carved the crude shape of a lion from a stone small enough to nestle in the palm of her hand. The carving showed the fearful lineaments of a voracious animal while the edges were softened by what seemed like a flurry of flames transformed in the girl's memory from the screams and blood spewing out of her mother's body. She worked a hole through the stone and wore it as an amulet. Abandoned by the woman she knew as her mother she walked alone under the grace of the lion.

When the girl who is now fifteen and has killed the beast awakens in late afternoon she chases away the carrion birds and rolls the skinned carcass into a depression in the earth. She digs a loose canine tooth from the skull surmising the lion must have been quite old perhaps losing a little of the cunning that might have given it the advantage. She looks to its claws that are fully extended in death. Lions walk on sixteen toes. With no concept of numbers she recognizes symmetry and admires his feet even with the fur stripped back to the pasterns. He must have been magnificent in his prime. His claws are smoothly curved and razor sharp but his toes are calloused and worn. She decides there is more honour to her prey if she leaves his claws than to take one. She rolls a sheet of congealing blood onto a smooth piece of stone before piling rocks on his remains in a huge mound.

She sits by her fire and pokes a hole through the root of the canine tooth and taking a cord of leather from around her neck she adds the tooth to her clam shell casing and the pendant that could be a lion amid flames that she had fashioned from stone when she was ten years old.

She picks up the shaggy head which she has removed from the skull. It has been baking in the sun but it reeks when she holds it high in the air. A zephyr sweeps in from the distant sea and displaces the smell with memories of the lion's warm breath washing over her while he died. She smiles. The skin of a lion contains its invisible essence and she is determined to keep it to make robes and to keep the skin of his head to stuff with dry grasses.

She spends the night close to the fire working on the skin singeing the remaining tendrils of flesh and scraping its inner side smooth and pliable. When the sun appears she bundles her skins and moves away from the direction of its rising. She walks for days chewing the lion's congealed blood drinking water from puddles and rivulets. She knows there is a lone wolverine following her desperate to attack but a wolverine is the most cunning of animals and will keep its distance until certain of its own safety. It will follow her until she shows a moment of weakness and then it will strike. She wears the lion skin over her shoulders. It drags on the ground behind her. The head-fur is rolled up and strapped with her sling to her side. She is confident the wolverine will not attack so long as she keeps moving. It has been a good summer. Meat has been plentiful. He will not be desperate. When she finally approaches the river she knows he has slunk away to find a quarry not protected by the scent of a lion.

Swarms of flies have been attracted by the animal skin that has not been fully worked into soft leather and by her own sweat-streaked skin beneath it. After she fords a branch of the river onto the estuary the flies become worse. She stops by a slough to smear mud on her body but still the insects attack so she drapes the skin over her shoulders again and draws the lion's head over her own with twigs inserted sideways to give it shape and allow her to breathe. She continues walking exhausted like a beast slouching towards home hardly able to see through the eyes of the lion guided by the feel of landscape passing beneath her feet more familiar the closer she gets to the end of her journey.

A cry rings out that a lion approaches. She is too depleted to wriggle out from under the skins. A band of boys and young hunters who have been grooming themselves in the shade recognize that the lion is strangely injured and offers no threat. They rush at her with spears poised but she seems so feeble they leap over her and on top of her working themselves into a frenzy and they kick at her with bared feet and they scream with excitement when she groans which confirms the beast is alive giving proof of their courage.

The entire community is watching uncertain what the death of this strange slouching creature will mean. After a powerful blow from one of the boys a hand emerges from under the lion and flails at the air followed by a mud- and blood-soaked human head with blazing eyes. There is a collective gasp. The lion has swallowed a human whole and is releasing her. The oldest man and woman rush to the girl and draw her free and she is born again into the world. A young man her same age comes forward and lifts her in his arms and carries her to a shelter he shares with his adoptive parents.

No one seems to recognize the girl. It is as if she has been transformed born into adult being from the womb of a male lion. The girl she had been seems forgotten. The young man cleans her and cares for her and after a few days he carries her to a new shelter he has built from driftwood and auroch hides and lays her on a bed made of her lion fur which he has worked to chamois softness. After a few more days she awakens fresh and powerful and gazes at the lion's head which he has filled with grasses and shaped like a living lion except for the gaping eyes and hung on a supporting pole. She reaches for the necklace and grasps the small case of perforated clam shells. It is cold. The tiny fire inside has burned through the tinder. She touches the canine tooth of the lion then holds the flaming lion amulet in her palm and squeezes feeling its power and with her other hand she takes the young man's hand and squeezes. She smiles. There is a bond between them.

***

The young man and his lion-bride pack up their skins and tools after their first child is born and turn away from the primal community where they are feared and revered and walk to the left of the rising sun until they have climbed rolling hills past where the lion is buried to a height where on a clear day the horizon shimmers from the distant sea. They settle into a shallow cave with a cleft near the back that draws smoke up through the rocks overhead and with a small stream tumbling through the rocks close by. Together they pile boulders into a wall across most of the front and drop auroch skins from the upper edge making a barrier against inclement weather but allowing the balmy zephyrs sweeping in from the far-off sea to embrace them when the weather is good. They have seen a few humans on their journey a single Neanderthal hunter and a great deal of game as well as gardens of berries and grains fruits and nuts all within easy reach.

    In the evenings they sit by their fire inside the cave or outside in midsummer and share sounds with their baby their child their children. She uses words but he is awkward with language so he makes music sometimes from his mouth sometimes with sticks and bones and then with fledgling flutes. Imagine this primordial family in front of their home resting on skins the older children having dragged the cave lion's head out from its niche playing ferocious giggling games. The woman is sewing hides into warm clothes in anticipation of winter which is still a long way off. The man has had a good hunt bringing back the haunch of a deer — he left the rest for wolverines or the humans who he knew watched from the shadows. He sits partially in the smoke to ward off insects. He takes up a shaft of ivory the length of a child's forearm and begins working it with a shard of obsidian. The ivory is from a wounded woolly mammoth his birthmother and her mother long ago had put out of its misery. He does not know this only that it has been the one possession that he has always had. The lion-woman carries in her folded sling a small piece of ivory from the same tusk as her own ancestral inheritance. On a shelf in the rock near at hand are earlier versions of the man's work a polished tube he had carved from the femur of a young cave bear and a length of bone from a mute swan wing both with holes along one side. He has been experimenting with sound that will speak in ways the limits of his words cannot reach.

After he has finished hollowing and polishing the ivory he takes up the other tubes one at a time and plays them as flutes testing the noise made when he moves his fingers over and away from the holes. Then he grinds two punctures into the ivory and tests the sound. He takes up the other flutes again and plays. He is searching for a true correlation of the distance between holes and the quality of sound. He grinds out a third hole then a fourth and a fifth all within finger reach but at variant spaces to each other. Working on into the night with only the fire tended by the woman to fend off the darkness he achieves a diatonic scale with the eighth hole. As dawn obscures the night sky with first light with the children asleep and the lion-woman at his side he polishes the ivory reaming out the detritus inside and smoothing the holes. Then he puts the flute to his lips and the notes drift down the long valley picking up resonance as they curl like smoke through the trees and the underbrush. Animals stop and listen. A few humans gather close to their fires and smile. The lone Neanderthal who will never see his own family again moves closer stalking the sounds to their source. When he breaches a cleft in the forest he sees children playing in the grass. He stoops low into the shadows and waits.

***

In the evening the woman stands languorously in the diminishing sunlight. She caresses her man's shoulders while he plays his trilling mellifluous tune then she goes into the cave to retrieve a robe for each of them. The children follow her without being summoned and climb into their bedding of auroch hides and a lion skin that is getting old but exudes an odour of primal warmth. She sits with the children for a while humming along with the strange ethereal music of the ivory flute. When it goes silent she thinks nothing of it. She caresses the baby's forehead hoping she wasn't coming down with a fever.

The woman with robes in her arms pushes the skin door back and goes out. There is still enough light to see the Neanderthal hunter stooped over her man passing the flute back and forth from hand to hand apparently trying to determine where the music had come from. Her man lies sprawled with his head smashed open in a dark stain that glistens in the sunset like a pool of flames. She roars with incomprehensible pain she staggers backward into the cave and gathers her children behind her. She and her oldest girl and boy each grab a stone-tipped hunting shaft and hold them poised with lethal unwavering intent at the door.

The Neanderthal does not try to come in. The woman moves slowly to a slit in the door. She shivers with rage. The killer has pushed her man's body to the side and taken his place on the stone bench. He still holds the ivory flute in his fingers. He turns when the woman comes out. She moves slowly towards him. A large club lies across his knees. It is made from a branch sheared from a tree with the knot still attached that had been shaped into a murderous protrusion by repeatedly burning the surface and rubbing the charred wood against rock. The bulbous end glistens with the blood of its victim lying sprawled at his feet.

He beckons her to come to his side. He seems oblivious to the hunting spear in her hand. He runs his own hand across his throat in a gesture of vulnerability. He holds out the flute in her direction and rattles it as if trying to shake the music free. She moves backward into the cave drawing her children with her. She has never encountered a Neanderthal at close quarters before. She knows he is the lone hunter who lives in the valley below. She and her man had sometimes left a cache of meat for him although he seemed to fare well enough on his own. They had shared the knowledge of him with other humans imitating his slow powerful gait and no one seemed to hold him in fear. Nothing in his behaviour indicated aggression. Perhaps he had been driven to murder by loneliness and the haunting strains of the flute.

During the night he remains on the bench gazing out over the valley. At dawn the woman and the older children walk out ignoring the interloper and gather her man's body which they drag to the grass sward on the closest slope and bury with a mound of rocks piled over to keep him safe from scavengers. When they return to the cave the Neanderthal has gone. He shortly returns lumbering up the hill with a broken branch laden with ripe figs which he sets down on the stone bench and offers with an open-hand gesture. Warily the woman eats and her children follow suit.

After a few days when their stores of dried meat are diminished the Neanderthal leaves and returns with the haunch of an auroch freshly killed and crudely slaughtered and they roast the entire piece on the fire and feast tearing chunks free and smearing grease that oozes from the meat across their faces and rubbing their hands through their hair.

That night the Neanderthal and the woman sleep under the same robes at the back of the cave. Near dawn she slides out and walks to the front of the cave where she takes up the lion's head and quietly removes the branches and grass stuffing and draws it over her own head. She picks out a spear feels the sharp stone tip with her fingers and slips stealthily through the flickering darkness back to the stranger. He rolls over looks up offers a fleeting grin then sinks back under the lion-skin covering as she drives the spear through his chest deep into his heart.

The lion-woman with her gift for language had listened closely watched her man closely and teaches herself to play the flute. Before long music fills the valley again and east of Eden their family endures for two thousand generations possibly to the end of the world. And when a paleoanthropologist one day holds the flute in her hand the ivory still feels warm to the touch.

IMAGINE TAHITI

The following is a stand-alone chapter from Lindstrom Unbound *(2019), the third in a mystery trilogy published by Iguana Books. I've included it as an exemplar of my ventures into unmediated fiction, with the author being wholly absent (or wholly there?). It purports to tell itself. While context within the larger fiction is not relevant and the whereabouts of the author is of little importance, recollection of the actual crimes this story evokes will perhaps find Canadian readers on common ground. If not, it is only a story; and that, perhaps, is enough.*

During the evening of her last night on Huahine, Teresa MacPherson cut her hair short. She bleached it and coloured it honey blonde and lightened her eyebrows. In the morning, she switched her lipstick from scarlet to pink and put on a pareu printed with a profusion of blood-red hibiscus blossoms, worn long, with a shot-silk blouse on top.

Arriving on the short flight to Tahiti, she walked through the open-air lobby at Fa'aa Terminal to a taxi stand and hired a taxi to Papeete where she settled into a room at the shabby genteel Hotel le Mandarin on Rue Colette. For the next few days, she kept to the bustling core of the city, lingering over breakfasts of *café au lait* in the sidewalk patios on the Boulevard Pomare overlooking the harbour, having pick-up lunches in the art nouveau market surrounded by tables of fresh produce and tourist curios, and in the evenings eating at one of the innumerable food trucks parked between Boulevard Pomare and the water.

On Thursday, Teresa MacPherson made a local call on a public phone. After lunch, she booked a flight to Paris on Air France for the following Wednesday, paying with a credit card that identified her as Celestine du Maurier, then she caught a ferry over to Moorea where she had reserved a room at Motel Albert, across from the Moorea Bali Hai. She took most of her meals at the Bali Hai in an open pavilion overlooking the incomparably majestic Cook's Bay, eating alone. She was not bothered by other guests. Like many attractive people, she projected an aura of inviolable solitude.

On the Sunday evening a boy delivered a package to her door. She tipped him and unwrapped the package, removing a pair of surgical gloves and a pistol-shaped object shrouded in folds of blue cotton. The next morning, she returned to the Hotel le Mandarin in Papeete and the following morning, wearing her silk blouse with the red pareu, she rented a small Renault to be dropped off at Faa'a airport later the same day.

She drove along the Tahiti shore road counterclockwise past the airport and through three coastal villages before stopping for a small lunch, including a Pernod over ice, in the rambling village of Mataiea on the opposite side of the island. After lunch she doubled back a short distance and turned inland onto a ragged dirt road that rose steeply through a ravine extending down from the folds of Mount Orohena. She passed a few cottages along the way. Most of them were ramshackle but several were in good repair.

She slowed in front of one of the more substantial cottages. A signpost bearing the hand-lettered name, "Rochecoeur," identified the occupants. She edged the Renault higher up the slope until she found a widening where she could turn it around. She coasted back to a level spot on the shoulder just above the cottage and parked in the shade behind sparse shrubbery, allowing her to observe the cottage and the small clearing in front of it where three hens and a rooster picked lazily at the ground. A red wheelbarrow lolled on its side next to a worktable littered with carving tools. A couple of half-finished stone tiki sculptures sat to one side. The tools appeared to have been set down in a moment of distraction but not abandoned, as if the artisan had run out of energy or inspiration and was biding time, waiting for renewal. A lame cat hobbled out from under the house, reconsidered, and slipped back into the shadows.

After an hour, the cottage door swung open and a petite woman with long mouse-coloured hair emerged from the depths inside. She was wearing a faded cotton sundress but had nothing on her feet. Her hair was tied back with a colourless bit of frayed ribbon or string. She was a nondescript age; her face had been pretty but was lined and cross-hatched from smoking and sunlight. Her eyes appeared sleepless; the lids drooped at the sides. The pupils were unusually dark. She held an infant against her breast as she pushed two small children out into the yard. She said something to them. Their bland faces showed no emotion but as soon as the woman backed into the shadows and closed the door, they squatted down in the pebble-strewn dirt and started to play. The woman who called herself Celestine du Maurier watched them. Little girls, two and maybe three-and-a-half, small for their age and untidy but not malnourished; they were soon lost in some incomprehensible fantasy and began to exchange pinched smiles, as if smiling were a secret language they shared only between themselves.

In mid-afternoon, as the sun crept through the glade of shadows, threatening to engulf the Renault, a man came trudging up the road and passed through the gate. The little girls ignored him. He paused to watch them play for a moment, said nothing, and entered the cottage.

Celestine waited another half hour, then withdrew surgical gloves from her purse and put them on and got out of her car which by now was unbearably hot. She removed her damp silk blouse, hiked up her hibiscus pareu and re-tied it as a dress. She tossed the blouse into the back of the Renault on top of the carry-on bag she had picked up in the market and walked down to the Rochecoeur gate and through it into the yard. The girls stopped what they were doing and looked up but sat perfectly still, as if she might not see them if they did nothing to attract her attention.

Celestine walked to the door and placed her hand on the latch. There was no lock. In her other hand she held a compact Glock semi-automatic that she had withdrawn from the folds of blue cotton which she stuffed back into her purse. She cocked the gun and slid the safety off. She depressed the latch and pushed open the door. She stepped inside and closed the door behind her.

The woman with mousey brown hair tied back with a string looked up. She was sitting at a grey arborite table, bottle-feeding her baby. She glanced at her baby, she remained expressionless. The man standing by the sink moved his right hand towards a large knife on the counter. Celestine watched him. His fingers touched the knife but didn't close around the handle. Acknowledging the gun, he turned and gazed out the window at the sun-dappled hillside sloping down to the cottage.

"What do you want?" said the woman in a tired voice. She spoke French out of habit, then repeated her question in English.

The man hissed something unintelligible.

Celestine glanced down at her gun.

"My children are here," said the woman.

"He will look after them," said Celestine. "I waited for him to come home."

The man turned slowly and faced Celestine. His English was awkward. "Cannot you leave us alone."

Celestine du Maurier looked around her. There was no squalor. The cottage was orderly, but not immaculate. Lived in. Poor, not impoverished. A few clippings from French magazines were pinned to the walls. Several uninspired tiki sculptures sat heavily on the floor near the woven partition separating two cramped bedrooms from the living room-kitchen. There did not appear to be a bathroom. A single faucet hovered over the cast-cement sink.

"You should take the baby." Celestine addressed the man and pointed her gun towards the door.

The man looked at the woman. His pale features seemed permanently exhausted, apprehensive. The woman appeared resigned, a little annoyed.

"It is okay, Hugo. You take the boy and go with the girls. It will be fine."

She stood up and pushed her baby towards the man. For a moment, it seemed like the baby would be released in mid-air, then the man reached for him, leaned forward and kissed the woman on one cheek. He drew a snow-white gardenia from a wine-bottle vase and tucked it behind the woman's left ear. With the muzzle of the Glock following him, he stepped out through the door into the sunlight. Chickens scurried. The little girls were seized by the tension and moved close to their father and baby brother.

When the door closed, the Glock swung back to the woman.

"This will not give you satisfaction," she said.

"No," said Celestine.

"You did not know them."

"Not personally," said Celestine.

"I did," said the woman.

"Your sister," said Celestine. "Not the others."

"Will you be paid?" the woman asked.

"No," said Celestine.

"Then why do this? My children," she stopped.

Celestine sidled close to the kitchen counter and picked up the knife. It had flecks of melon stuck to the blade. She set down the Glock within reach and washed the blade clean, then picked up her gun and moved directly in front of the other woman.

"*Your children.*" Celestine repeated the woman's words, cutting them so precisely they fell through the air like a judgement.

"You do not know what I feel," said the woman. "You do not know me."

"No," Celestine agreed.

"It was my husband."

A shadow passed across Celestine's features. She breathed deeply, inhaling the rancid odour of cigarettes.

"My husband," repeated the woman.

"Yes?" said Celestine.

"It was not me."

"You watched."

"Sometimes."

"More than that."

"Sometimes."

"You took pictures. He took pictures of you."

The woman's mouth tightened.

"Yes," she said.

Celestine said: "Their bodies." She stopped. Her words filled the room.

The woman with mouse-coloured hair turned away briefly, her features were in shadow, her eyes pale discs in the sliver of light seeping around the edge of the door.

Celestine said: "He will die in solitary confinement."

"Segregation," the woman clarified.

"Your lawyers withheld evidence. You served twelve years. Four years for each."

"Six. There was no charge for my sister, it was an act of God."

Celestine stared into the woman's eyes.

"I took no parole," said the woman. "I paid my debt."

"No," said Celestine.

"I am a mother now," the woman said.

"What about him?" Celestine gestured with the Glock towards the man outside. "Does he know?"

"That is why we are living here."

"Your children, when were you going to tell them?"

"Perhaps never."

"They will find out."

"Possibly."

"They will hate you."

"I am their mother."

Celestine's eyes momentarily narrowed.

"You are not any better," said the woman. "You with your gun. You like to kill."

"No," said Celestine. "I don't."

"It is not difficult," said the woman.

Celestine moved closer to her, exchanging the knife and the gun, one hand for the other. She pressed the knife tip against the worn cotton stretched across the woman's breasts, then let it slide down a few inches before thrusting the blade through the cloth into her torso below the rib cage, tilting and twisting the blade, lacerating the lungs in search of her heart. She watched light fade from the woman's eyes, then wrenched the knife upwards as the woman's dead weight collapsed on the blade.

She lowered the woman's body to the floor and extricated the knife which she washed carefully in the kitchen sink. Wrapping the body in a sheet from the bed she carried it to a child's cot, where she laid it out taking care to cover the open wound and conceal the blood. She rinsed her bangles and bracelet by holding her arm under the faucet and used two tea towels to clean her hands and blood-red dress, and to scrub the blood pooled on the floor, and threw them into a garbage canister under the cement sink. She picked up the white gardenia which had fallen to the floor and tucked it backwards behind the woman's ear so that the smears of blood on the petals were obscured.

When she opened the door, the man was clutching his children in the shade by the gate. Celestine brushed by them and walked up the road to her Renault.

She dropped the car off at Faa'a Terminal, deposited her silk blouse and surgical gloves and the unfired Glock wrapped in folds of blue cotton in a refuse bin. She had already removed the bullets which she dropped into a different bin. She changed in a washroom and discarded her soiled red pareu, slipped on a black wig made from Polynesian hair, and had time for a Pernod over ice before boarding her flight to Los Angeles with only her carry-on bag. It was Tuesday evening. She was flying business class under the name of Teresa MacPherson. The Air France flight from Tahiti to Paris the following morning would have an empty seat in the Voyageur section, booked and paid for by Celestine du Maurier who would apparently have disappeared from the face of the earth. At about the same time, Teresa MacPherson would vanish from LAX and late Wednesday afternoon

Jennifer Izett, travelling Tango Plus, would disembark from an Air Canada Airbus at Pearson International in Toronto.

Her sabbatical was almost over and it was time to prepare lectures for the coming term.

RESISTING AUTOBIOGRAPHY

Here the writer is fiction but also a fact, drawing as honestly as possible from his own, my own, lived-in life to explore facets of Carol Shield's novel, The Stone Diaries, *from what I hope is an enlightening perspective. Sometimes the facts are distorted to convey feelings; sometimes emotions are suppressed or distended to let facts speak for themselves. I hope the reader will find more in this critical fiction than I intended, as I expose the tensions between nostalgia and grief. It was originally published in the collection,* Being Fiction *(Tecumseh, 2001, reprinted 2005, 2007).*

An authentic autobiography must necessarily conclude with the death of the author, otherwise it is merely an interim report. That is perhaps why I have resisted writing my own story, although I have lived a full life among words and over the years have envisioned my demise from a rich variety of perspectives. Much as I would like to shape my past into a narrative that would illuminate my entire existence with an aura of significance, it would be a violation of form and a repudiation of my responsibility as a protagonist if in the end I were to avoid a simultaneous departure from both text and the world. Suicide as a literary device, however, holds no particular appeal — my dedication to the requirements of genre is not absolute and the chance of natural expiration at the moment of closure is beyond imagining.

After my great uncle hanged himself from an oak tree in the back garden of the family home, we all went to the funeral. Following the service, there was a reception at the house. It was winter and the interment would not be until after the spring thaw. I was eleven and flattered to be engaged in a conversation with the bishop, who was very taken with the grandeur of the estate in such an obscure part of the country and with the sumptuous table laid out for the guests. Taking me into his confidence the bishop told me it was he who had cut my great uncle down from the tree. He had been summoned by my great aunt and being new in the diocese he presumed it was a matter of a major bequest.

In fact, she had no idea of who else to call. The police seemed a sordid option, a doctor was beside the point, and our regular minister was not quite important enough. My great aunt had heard people sometimes called the fire department in an emergency, but since she herself had tugged at his feet and knew her husband to be perfectly dead, emergency action seemed wasted. When she telephoned my mother, my mother confirmed that she had been right to summon the new bishop. By the time the authorities arrived, my great uncle was laid out on the sofa near the front door, the last rites had been given, and my mother had begun to supervise kitchen arrangements for the visitation, which would take place in the front parlour, off the library, after my great uncle was returned from the mortuary.

It is difficult to die in a vacuum. Daisy Goodwill comes close; Carol Shields eliminates Daisy in *The Stone Diaries* with so little fanfare the reader hardly notices her passing. The autobiographical format of the novel, which has been distended and distorted from the very beginning when Daisy relates the grotesque circumstances of her own birth, dissipates into trivial particularities following her death that seem to obscure the event, as if Daisy has simply run out of story to tell. The effect is paradoxically powerful, for the true story is metafictional: a sustained challenge to the limits of the autobiographical novel. Out of an ordinary life comes an extraordinary work of imagination, devised by an author who revels in the breaching of genre conventions and with sly dexterity consigns her protagonist to a minor role in her own account. Daisy does not lose narrative authority at her death — it was only a playful illusion that she ever had it. Left to her own devices, she would have been at most a figure of inconsequential pathos. She does not die so much as she falls from view as the camera pans to a higher level and the credits roll, which prove not to be credits at all but a casual obituary consisting of fragments from a life lived largely unexamined.

In writing my autobiography rather than having an author like Shields write it for me, I would have to slip away from the final scene like a victim of drowning. It would be my responsibility to dispose of the body, so to speak. The trick would be to relinquish control, embrace death, write silence, with appropriate subtlety, appropriate flare. I am uncertain about the annihilation of self as an act of creation.

When I was an undergraduate, I thought suicide a seductive alternative to reality. An arbitrary exit from the world would 1) draw my ill-formed personality into focus around the particular moment of my passing; 2) inform the random particulars of my life with the design of retroactive inevitability; 3) give me absolute control in a life where absolutes and control had steadfastly remained out of reach; 4) expunge in a singular action my innumerable fears about dying; 5) fulfill my romantic notions drawn from Scott of the Antarctic that death is intrinsically heroic if the cause is sufficiently banal, and from John Keats that death confirms genius; 6) make me the object of mourning, haunting all the young women who resisted my advances with suspicions they might have done more. I contrived termination scenarios from the mysterious to the spectacular, but I did not have sufficient discipline or resolve to follow them through.

Suicide, then, struck me as a literary device, the lives of writers and their works seemed inseparable. I thought a lot about stones in the pockets of a drowning Virginia Woolf, more than about *Mrs. Dalloway* or *To the Lighthouse*, although "A Room of One's Own" crossed gender to fill me with anger and empathy. When Sylvia Plath died in 1963, I had finished a bachelor's degree, knocked around Europe for a couple of years, and was considering graduate school.

That words could etch such horrors as she endured on the nerve ends of her reader's mind, horrors that only death could finally bring to submission, impelled my application to a program of advanced literary study, a field for which I am by temperament ill suited.

I now teach, I now teach at a university and have raised two children who perpetuate a few of my idiosyncrasies but I was born to be an autobiographer, not just an academic or a genetic link. Like John Glassco in his notorious *Memoirs of Montparnasse*, which he began at seventeen, I have lived my life in order to have something to write about. It follows, then, that my lifelong fascination with suicide is not a predilection for death but a morbid obsession with the complexity of being alive. It astonishes me that the universe unfolded as it has to admit me. Had an ancient forbear sneezed during orgasm, I would not be here. At the same time, it is tenuous, this business of living. Right now cancer cells may be gathering momentum in my viscera, or a driver dreaming who will one day roll his truck head-on towards a place to which even now I might also be *en route*.

As you may have divined, mine was an indulgent childhood. My parents indulged me and I indulged myself. Not surprisingly, I learned very early to express dissatisfaction by declaring I had not asked to be born. My parents gave me brothers and sisters to soften the sting. Two of each, whom I loved in my fashion, although they diffused the focus of affection. I ran away from home twice before I was ten. The first time I sneaked out in the middle of the night but returned for my skates by midmorning. The second time I fled across the field behind our house to a forest grove beside a millstream, and when my father came home from work, he found me, waiting. He had brought a tin of pork and beans, an opener and some matches, and we warmed the beans over a fire of dry cedar twigs and poured them out onto pieces of birchbark cupped in our hands and ate with our fingers. Only years later did I realize how much I loved my siblings or what a good man my father was, for all that we conspired against him.

I am still haunted by the bedtime prayer my mother occasionally had me recite:

> Gentle Jesus, meek and mild,
> listen to this little child.
> Guard and keep me
> through the night,
> let me see the morning light.
> And if I die before I wake
> I pray the Lord my soul to take.

This upsets me now more than it did then, that I should have been so bound by death. I became an atheist before I was old enough to ride a bike.

You do not grow up in a family like mine without a preternatural sensitivity to guilt and responsibility. My parents were lapsed Anglicans, which is perhaps a redundancy, but we were genetically Presbyterian. Any discussion of suicide is less a betrayal of religious decorum than of my mother's affection. The greater betrayal, however, would be not to give her appropriate status in my autobiography — the deepest sin in my mother's cosmology was to violate the appearance of fairness. If one of her children inspired pride, then so did we all. If one fell from grace, the others did too. I know the importance of fairness; I cannot introduce my father in a text without giving my mother equal representation. If she were here now, her eyes would water and her beautiful face, even more beautiful when she was old, would resolve into a mask of forbearance, letting me know without words that being consigned to a minor role in the narrative of my life is a small price to pay for having brought me into the world.

By my time we had settled into the middle class, somehow as if it were a fallen state. The new-world fortunes of my family attenuated as they were subdivided over the most recent generations until by now I have little to leave my own children but memories, a modest academic reputation, and a few ancestral furnishings that survived the dissolution of successive estates by virtue of being painted or scarred or crafted in the country style, items that paradoxically are worth more now than the high style pieces that replaced them. I leave them with recollections of childhood shaped in part by the urgency of my ongoing struggle to assimilate the imminence of death, which seemed at times my only constant witness, so much so that I held it almost in affection. Gradually it took on my personality, a doppelganger who shadowed my life, my runcible twin. My children grew up with a man who could not step away from his own shadow.

II

Contemplation of suicide is the best antidote to morbidity. It combines an acute awareness of death, essential to living a full life, with a sense of sovereignty over a condition that is otherwise arbitrary. It is not mortality that gets you down. Dead is dead, whether flights of angels sing you to your rest or worms consume you in a jester's grave. It is the indifference of death to your personal requirements that appals. You do what you can. Those truly engaged with being alive, for instance, usually have a vivid idea of where they wish to be buried. You may daydream of burial in a sacred place or of ashes scattered in lyric eloquence. The rhetoric of time, however, prevents your presence to appreciate the actual event. Instead of enduring the possibility that someone might decide to flush you down a drain or discard your body outside the city wall, I suggest it is preferable to reverse the order of things, bring death forward to confront the moment, contemplate on a sustained basis your own wilful demise. Suicide has a purpose in the well-ordered life as much as cemeteries and premonitions of eternity.

This has been my line of reasoning for the last several years. As with most such eschatologies, I came to my beliefs through induction, not theoretic conjecture. It started when I was constructing a bookcase in my basement workshop and lost a finger to my table-saw. I did not actually lose the finger. It lay in a pile of sawdust on the floor at a beckoning angle for several moments before I realized through the shock what had happened. Jamming the stump against my diaphragm to staunch the bleeding, I retrieved the errant digit and hurried with it to the freezer where I deposited it among the blanched rhubarb. I had some idea they could sew it back on if it were adequately maintained on ice. However, by the time I drove myself to Emergency, where I passed out in the waiting room, and was revived and able to explain where my finger was, the wound had been cauterized and the stump sewn over, and I was informed that cellular damage from freezing would by now have rendered the flesh irretrievable. Two weeks later I reduced the finger to ashes in my backyard barbecue, and on a whim placed the ashes for future disposition in an urn my wife kept in the back of her closet after the dispersal of her first husband's mortal remains.

Commandeering this repository for my own ashes began as a tasteless jibe, born out of morbid jealousy and the vague uneasiness that I had thus conformed with her ultimate intention to recycle the funerary paraphernalia she had so painfully acquired before we met. I did not tell her what I had done until she asked one day with what I thought was contrived decorum if I had seen her missing urn. At first I bluffed, asking which urn that would be; this was to force the embarrassment of a clarification that would feed emotional masochism on my part as I would attempt to estimate from her tone how much she missed him more than she valued me; but she is good at disarming my immaturity with studied equanimity, and she said merely that she could not find her dead husband's funerary urn, thereby placing the sharp divide of mortality between my predecessor and myself which did not warrant further consideration. I confessed the urn was now in my possession, and solemnly requested it remain so.

My wife cuts my hair and for some time I had been gathering the clippings in plastic bags. I had an odd sense of affection for what I knew rationally were merely remnants. Perhaps as justification I nurtured a vague sense that the wisps and tufts and motley strands grown from my head might someday prove useful. Since encrypting my finger remains, however, I came to realize the value of my bags of hair was more than symbolic if less than practical. The hair although worthless had intrinsic meaning; it was me, material of my earthly being. It took some time to devise a way to transform the hair into ashes without a terrible stench, but I did so by building a backyard food-smoker and then reducing the hair, handful at a time, to a dry brittle consistency that crumbled to the touch. This residue I added to the urn.

I could not help but think of Daisy Goodwill. Reading her quasi-autobiography brought my own haphazard existence into focus at about the same time that my fortuitous accident occurred. As all the fictions of her life accumulate in Shields' account, each rendering of Daisy revealing more of a ubiquitous and elusive narrative persona than of Daisy, her life merely an accumulation of intersecting arcs shed from the circles of other peoples' lives, it becomes apparent that Daisy is less than the sum of her parts. She could not ever be the author of an autobiography. Perhaps no-one can. Autobiography is an anomaly, a literary genre that succeeds in direct proportion to its violation of the conventions that define it — it will seem most authentic, most truthful and complete, when it most engagingly gathers a thematic, dramatic, schematic collection of facts adhering to one personality into a narrative design answering all the requirements of fiction. Emboldened by this revelation which I attributed to my reading of *The Stone Diaries* I determined thenceforward to live a fictional life. Without Shields to write my story, I would have to gather myself together for future disposition with assiduous care. I would mark the line of demarcation between life and death, fiction and ephemerality, with small ceremonies. Who knew what parts of me would eventually sustain my story.

Hair, perhaps? Nail parings? I could not bear to part with palpable souvenirs of my mortal presence in the world. I took to doing all manicure and pedicure procedures over the bathroom sink, after which I would gather and sort the clippings from bits of accumulated grime and render them with my hair into ash in the backyard smoker that I had discovered also made excellent sausages, some of which we gave away as Christmas presents to friends and relatives. One day a thumbnail of considerable size slid down the drain and I had to remove the stopcock under the sink to retrieve it, which I did on my own as I had no desire to involve a plumber in my esoteric plight.

I thought of skin cells and excrement, but like sweat and urine they seemed to be less me than the by-product of my functioning. The urn in any case was filling at a rate that would soon allow sufficient room only for the addition of my final cremated remains. I stored my urn, for I now thought of it as mine, in a corner of the basement among some bottles of fine wine I had laid down over the years. Each time I looked at it alongside the unopened classic vintages of Chateau Mouton Rothschild and Chateau d'Yquem, I would experience a subtle delight in quelling my sense of self-congratulation.

You might ask what all this has to do with suicide as a palliative device. Just as the pleasures of a wine cellar derive from musty odours and smoky haze that arouse anticipation, after which the consummation merely affirms the wisdom of your patience, so too with the accumulation of bodily remnants. Knowing the time could be determined by an act of will when these residual bits would be combined with my cremated residue, making the sum of my parts an impossible whole, as it were, gave me great satisfaction.

The value of my collection, as with wine, was in the dark promise it implied and the power that accrued from my decision to abide, until the time was right.

One day when I was away and my wife was at work a thief broke in through a basement window, smashed the priceless bottles of wine and scattered my accumulated ashes across the cellar floor before finding himself unable to breach the door upstairs to gain access into the rest of the house. After further malicious damage he absconded with a cordless power drill and an old pair of ski poles. My wife had a cleaning service come in and with a powerful vacuum they sucked up old wine, fragments of glass, priceless labels, and my scattered ashes into their machine. When I came home, I was bereft and locked myself into the pristine basement where I contemplated sorrow.

Within two or three hours I came to the realization that this catastrophe had been a blessing in disguise. I felt free, liberated from the weight of my endeavour which had lately taken over my life. No longer would I be the source of a personal reliquary. Life would be an end in itself. Slowly, and in increments, I had been trying to commit suicide-but without the commitment. And without the finality. In the photograph my wife took for insurance purposes, the urn lay demolished on the floor like an admonition — at first I thought I deciphered meaning in the lay of the shards, directing me to seize the day, live each moment as if it were my last, but that seemed as depressing as the habit I had left behind. Then I realized, as I contemplated the shattered urn and in my mind gathered its pieces into a coherent pattern, their message was more specific — I would dedicate my remaining days to the repair of funeral devises. I ascended from the basement with images of toppled gravestones to be righted, neglected cemeteries to be weeded, records to be updated, paupers' graves to be identified, mausoleums to be restored. In the detritus of death I had at last found my calling, a purpose for being, the will to endure.

III

You may by now have perceived conflicting philosophies emanating from the same narrator that are so fundamentally in opposition their only resolution will be through suspension of your own personality. Be wary of such deprecation. This is not a modernist plot. Consider the possibility that opposing ontologies are equally tenable. The problem is mine, not yours. I think life has no meaning but is what it is. I think life has meaning. I would not reconstruct my life unless it were significant; but, paradoxically, my job as autobiographer would be to make the inchoate particulars of my life coherent, to give them significance. I am my own semiotic conundrum. Although you cultivate my presence through the generosity of your conscious attention, this is not about you.

It is only illusion that I am in control of my story. When the words end, by reverting to my place in the temporal continuum I yield to mortality. Even though what I write may endure for eons on library shelves and in the minds of sympathetic readers, I will eventually die. Beyond the text, I will become transparent or fade to opacity, they are ultimately the same, so that readers will casually observe, oh yes, I believe he is dead; or maybe not, but he is very old; or he died years ago, if I haven't confused him with someone else, a character perhaps in one of his esoteric fictions. Readers may remember the exact point at which my autobiography concludes, but concerning my life the point of departure will seem trivial at best. There is pathos in this, from my perspective. And fear. I would rather prolong the moment of my demise interminably than achieve narrative perfection.

Daisy Goodwill has an advantage. There is no real pretence in *The Stone Diaries* that she is constructing her own account. Yet her story is not fictional biography, not an authorial imposition of narrative form on a life that has been lived beyond text. Despite the inclusion of photographs that imply authenticity in the real world, Daisy's story is a novel. It is a novel in which the author refuses to yield textual authority to her protagonist, yet fosters the illusion that the protagonist is engaged in self-revelation. Shields invests Daisy with an articulating consciousness that is paradoxically not self-aware. We read her life as innocent voyeurs, our innocence the measure of Daisy's lack of moral engagement with the world, and we are charmed. But we are never moved by Daisy, only astonished by the anarchy of her author's achievement, as Shield's defies conventions of literary form, and especially of what is truth and what is true. Daisy has the advantage. She can recede from the text in the end and there is nothing left behind, no other Daisy who must deal with death beyond the final pages of her narrative.

If I were to write my autobiography, you would be my necessary witness. Some people find God an appropriate witness. Myself, I need you. Suppose I brought my story and life to simultaneous conclusion, you would now be more real than I. It is an odd notion, generally accepted in theories of reading, that you, my reader, enter my reality. But no, it is otherwise. In the infinite theatre of your mind, I come alive. Perhaps in you I find myself quite different from what I intended. If so, it is a revelation your mind permits. I exist because you think me so. And like the God of *Genesis*, you need me to affirm your power.

To end autobiography without the author's death is a wilful plunge into the absurdity of time. Paradoxically, to bring any piece of writing to an end is a form of suicide, annihilation of the self, caught up in the act of writing, sustained in the moment of creation where the past and future converge. If I continue in the conflicted moment of spontaneous engagement with language, I remain alive. But I do not know how long I can go on. I suspect there are many who hover all their lives between yesterday and tomorrow as if today were of no consequence. But some of us, you reading this, me writing, by our conspiracy to subvert time, we affirm the absolute poignancy of being here, now.

There's no time like the present.

Each passing moment is a theoretical point in a continuum, having no duration itself. But the past is past, whether two seconds ago or millennia. The future is equally beyond reach. The past and the future, as well as the present, are factors in a geometric theorem. They cannot be said to exist in a three-dimensional world. Nothing exists beyond time. Nothing exists within time. Time does not exist, except as a measurement of something else, an object or event, context or duration, point or perspective.

Unlike Daisy Goodwill who thinks she is real, I know I am fiction. Although I may never write my autobiography, like John Glassco I have turned my life into an *objet d'art*. I am fiction because I cannot bear to be real. The only evasion that allows me to live is writing, knowing you will read this. It is like dialysis. If I cannot cleanse my system of the poisons invading from without and within, I will perish. It is not enough to write; I need to know that you will read. You will not succumb to my malaise, for the filter is virtually by definition resistant to the deleterious effects of the effluvium. But the intersection of your life with mine will allow me remission until we both reach the end. Does this seem contrived, a narrative paradigm for the relationship between writer and reader? It is not. Trust me on this.

Consider my argument an ironic commentary on the lover-poet's ploy to confer immortality through art. The odd thing, of course, is that the beloved is invariably disguised by artifice, and the lover submerged in the art. We are left with a paradox, the poem itself as evidence that its argument is false. Only the reader is alive for sure. That is what I want, your lifeblood as a reader. My conviction that you are here keeps me alive. You cannot stop my death, but you can help me to endure the intervening hours before it occurs.

IV

When I was twenty-one, Hemingway died. The next summer I ran with the bulls in Pamplona. From Spain, Hemingway's suicide seemed both ignoble and inspired. A Spaniard was killed in the corrida; I had a fling with a flamenco dancer from New York who talked to me in Yiddish and thought I understood. After she left, I fell in love with Barbara Moxley from Palo Alto, California, but nothing came of it. Those of us who had already partied on Ibiza sat apart and drank quantities of vino tinto in honour of Hemingway, not for the writing but the man. That's what people have to understand who lament his becoming a figure from fiction, that's what we loved. It was not the writing, any more than it was Kerouac's writing, it was the way he constructed a life. As with Kerouac, his reputation was the projection of what he wished to see of himself in the mirror. We envied the authenticity of his artful deceit. This was before the sixties began in earnest, when we were in flight from the fifties, and the twenties were still the age we admired.

"Requiem" was one of my friend R.K.'s favourite words. We shared a room in West Kensington for a couple of months, hung out on Ibiza watching itinerant Americans smoke pot, and sat for hours in the main square in Pamplona talking about Hemingway's death. While we were there, Faulkner died. R.K. was the only close friend I had in those days who had not gone to university. He knew everything Hemingway and Faulkner had published, could quote terse riffs of Hemingway dialogue, whole paragraphs of Yoknapatawpha prose. He had never learned to be embarrassed by enthusiasm. This made him exotic. He would sometimes hold words up to the light. "Look," he would say; his thin face would break sideways into a grin. "Listen, you can see the letters dance," and the sounds from his lips of a single word would inscribe the clear sunlight over the plaza. "Sanctuary," he would say, "requiem," he would say, shaking his head as if saying such words brought him closer to Faulkner. "Dos cerveza," he would say to Manuel, the waiter — not because he wanted beer but because he did not understand Spanish and was gleeful each time "Dos cerveza por favor" brought beer to the table. At least twice a day we drank beer; and the rest of the time brackish red wine which came without asking. Thirty-five years later I was walking west on St. Clair near Bathurst when in a chance encounter with an acquaintance she mentioned R.K.'s death a decade ago, by his own hand, which implied a gun rather than poison or hanging. All that time, I had thought he was alive. People do not die for us until we know about their deaths.

When I think about R.K. now, he is in the ceremonial dress of a samurai, and with unwavering precision he cuts into his own entrails as he has done in his mind a thousand times. He is in a story by Yukio Mishima. It is called "Patriotism" and he is the protagonist. As the sword enters his body he cannot distinguish the pain from the ritual, it is not his pain, the ritual absorbs the shock and leaves his mind lucid, allowing him to cut in the right direction, over and then up, while he still has the strength to guide his meticulous blade. His wife observes, her modest death will follow, she is his witness. Before she plunges a small knife into her body, she unlocks the front door so they will be found. Ten years is a long time to be dead without notice.

One night in the Colonial Tavern on Yonge Street, R.K. and I compared suicide notes. He had been back from Europe for a year and I had returned home a few months later after two years of wandering, both of us world weary and yet strangely untouched by all that we had seen and done, denizens of Toronto now, the world remote. We both had ordinary jobs and often met to drink draft beer in the evenings, sometimes bringing dates but usually alone. The Colonial was murky and we were cheerfully morbid. Even when he showed me the wound between his fingers which in the dim light looked like a birthmark, and told me how his mother had smelled burning flesh from his cigarette after he had lost consciousness and sent him off to have his stomach pumped; we laughed. But that was too close, and we drank more than usual that night. Saying goodbye at the subway, I asked R.K to promise if he ever reached desperation again, he would call me. It's a contract, he said with a conspiratorial grin and descended into the subway. We met less frequently after that, and then not at all. Neither of us attended the other's wedding. I do not know if he had children or ever took the night courses he talked about when I told him I was going into graduate studies.

Recently I had lunch with another friend from my discontinuous past. He had been R.K.'s childhood neighbour. His name was H, a signal distinction in a world of whole names and double initials — T.S., G.K., W.H., A.S., V.S., R.K. Usually single letters without punctuation are names only in fiction: F in Beautiful Losers, K in Kafka, the Countess of M-. H had shared Pamplona with R.K. and me, and Ibiza, and I had travelled with H to Istanbul and shared great adventures, but we had not been in touch for a long time. And H told me R.K. used to ask about me sometimes in the hospital where he spent his last months before he died from emphysema. When I said I had been told he killed himself, H said yes, he might have done, but no, he died of emphysema. I did not think it possible to stop knowing someone, but I felt I had lost R.K. then, as if in my confusion he had slipped irretrievably away. The reality we had shared during the explosive intensity of those brief years when our lives ran parallel suddenly vanished. It was not death but the confounding of stories that did it; because each passing was as plausible to me as the other, the possibility remained that he was still alive, or that he had never been, and so his death was fiction and his life unreal.

I found it difficult to reconcile my grief with an unsettling sense of disappointment — whether in myself or R.K. I could not tell.

V

Today a man I know at the University where I work died because his estranged wife had the affection of his children and they turned against him. He killed himself in a rage of despair and self-pity, both emotions familiar to me. He was not a close friend, but I am in shock. I look to my own life, weigh his decision in the light of my own experience. His children are very young. I did not know his wife or the terms of their estrangement. But I do believe he died for his children; we would, any of us, die for our children.

Most of us do not have the opportunity for such appalling sacrifice. Could I restore to life my child who died, or could I give my living children back their innocence, I would. But even laying out my life as fiction, I cannot comprehend the ways to change what having happened has become inevitable. If Daisy Goodwill could have seized control of her story, sidelined Carol Shields, she would have told it differently, but it would have been the same in the end, she would have died in Florida. The plot might deviate depending on perspective as our lives unravel but the outcome is the same.

Since every conscious moment effects a reconstruction of the past, and inscribing life at the moment of our passing is impractical, it is only possible to tell our true stories by arbitrarily suspending the experience of duration, writing out of time, as if time were merely a literary device. Even then, we would need infinite autobiographies to achieve the truth. There is no library large enough to hold the books of consciousness emanating from my own unexceptional knowledge of the world. Imagine each of us an autobiographer, furiously inscribing our accounts of who we are for those few readers who will act as witness to our separate lives. We could not move for manuscripts as numerous as molecules, we would expire in a suffocation of words. If our minds were libraries, they would be labyrinths jammed with books of our own devising, the corridors stretched to vanishing in all directions. We could not move for fear of minotaurs, the monsters of imagination sprung to express finitude in the galaxies of our knowing. We cannot endure too much reality. To survive the onslaught of our myriad past in the passing moment we each select our autobiography best suited to the present, and revise as future needs reveal themselves, revising and revising until the end.

The problem is, as autobiographer you do not know what you think until you write it down, or what you feel, or who you are. I do not know the person writing until I read his story, even when it is me who invests the words with authenticity and makes them breathe. As creator I cannot tell the difference between the desire to end my account from an appetite for oblivion. I need to read the finished work.

The ambivalence of my present condition makes me suspect my own conceit. Could it be that in my recent life I am content and therefore mad, or perhaps mad and thus content. I do not want to end my life. I want my life to end. It is my autobiography I want over with, I do not want to finish writing. I want control of my story, I want to cede control; I want absolutes and absolution. I have not lived tragedy, for all the sadness I have known affects my personality but is not its emanation. I have not lived comedy, for all the joy I have known has been seized by acts of will. I have not lived romance for I am an ironic man, nor irony, for I have a romantic disposition. My life is satire, perhaps, but incomplete for it postulates neither an alternative nor remedy. Ambivalence as I write becomes ambiguity: I must consider not the story told but how to tell my present story. Rather than resolution, bear with me, let us deal with revelation, with what has been left out.

In truth, I have had two lives. Certain factors overlap and interpenetrate. I have memories and artifacts from my previous life still with me, some haunting and some affirming, some connecting me with yet another life, when I was a child and growing up among the remnants of several squandered small-town fortunes, amidst the sprawling affectations of a large eccentric family, and some reminding me of wasted opportunities and lives not lived. The mother of my surviving children is a professional woman. Out of the crucible of a volatile relationship both she and I achieved much; not least of our accomplishments was the successful negotiation of our children's growing up. But after they were safely grown and on their own, I felt perpetually in a state of exhaustion, as if my many lives were a crowding of strangers and only the context seemed familiar and there was nowhere I could rest. I left for solitude and discovered someone waiting for me; it seemed we had both been waiting. I miss the home I built like a work of art or other self. I miss the continuity. I have broken the past and for this my children never will forgive me.

While I have courted suicide all my conscious life, it seems in times of greatest pain a misguided indulgence to consider arbitrary closure. On the saddest day of my life, I resisted the solipsistic evasions of invoking either God or death. In a fit of rational discourse between my soul and self, I determined that to call upon a deity who will not take responsibility for unhappiness is foolish, a nasty metaphysical conceit. What possible respect could I have for a master of the universe who craves adoration, demands subservience, and dispenses grace or annihilation like a madman plucking angels' wings? Suicide stood up little better to scrutiny, for if life is not bearable, its negation can hardly be preferred. Such thinking left me comfortless.

I have not recovered from the death of my infant son. Not a day or an hour, not a moment of conscious awareness, do I endure that I do not grieve. I miss the easy familiarity I once had with my surviving children, but they occupy a place within me of visceral complexity that will remain until my mind goes empty. From my dear dead son, I have only the memory of holding him for a short time as his still body, warm from his mother's womb, grew gradually the temperature of air; and memories of our single winter as a family, the three of us, me touching his movement through his mother's flesh, him reaching to the sounds of our affection.

I wrote poems to him that winter. I sang to him with my crooked voice. Nothing can shatter the love that we wrapped around the three of us like a cocoon, not even his death. But there was no metamorphosis, only an absolute end. I miss him so much, I sometimes know I am broken.

Then his lovely mother, my beloved, takes me in her arms, and breathes into my broken heart, and not shamed but moved by her courage we come together and we share gratitude that we had him even so briefly. She carried him, and it must be unutterably sad to remember his birth, yet they were so much part of one another for the whole of his living that she can remember with joy the promise of his surging inside her. I did not know him as well, but in his mother's eyes I see all that I miss and all that I will love as long as we remain alive.

For them I abandon equations of autobiography and being. I resolve not ever to write myself out of the story, I will not submit to despair. That does not mean I won't sometimes stare at an oncoming truck and as it goes by wonder that it could have been over with a swerve of the wheel. I will probably never cross a bridge without looking down to imagine my trajectory and feel the thud like a premonition in my bones. But these are vain thoughts and I will let them vanish like voices in the air. Each new moment will declare my autobiography subject to revision. It is an impossible genre, but inevitable for those of us who cast our lives in letters and sometimes confuse the written word with being alive.

A PARTICULARLY LOVELY PROJECT: THE JOURNAL OF CANADIAN FICTION

The following is an historical footnote, drawing from memory more than imagination. A pleasantly sinister story called "Waves Break Stone," published in The Paradox of Meaning *(Turnstone Press, 1999), was a critical fiction devised around the same two characters featured here, versions of David Arnason and myself. This one originally appeared in Canadian Literature #202, 2009, UBC. It was written a decade later and was meant to be trusted; the former, of course, was not.*

In the late spring of 1971, New Brunswick was the centre of the world and anything was possible. Sitting at the inevitable kitchen table in Nashwaaksis, across the St. John River from Fredericton, drinking morning coffee that in other jurisdictions might have been declared illegal, David Arnason and I decided to create something which to give our banter appropriate gravitas we named the *Journal of Canadian Fiction*. Dave's coffee was made by pouring boiling water through a rancid bag full of grounds that then soaked in the pot. It was either an Icelandic contraption or Ukrainian. Dave was from Winnipeg.

We had finished our first year in the legendary University of New Brunswick PhD program in Canadian literature. We were both in our early thirties with families in tow; not exactly young and perhaps not quite geniuses together but astonished by the possibilities of a life in letters. I wonder if the TISH bunch had the same irrepressible confidence only a few years earlier? In the spring of 2009, I overtook George Bowering on a street in Vancouver and we talked for a while. Of course, they had the confidence, he still does, and they had an agenda which changed the way we talk to ourselves in this country. Dave and I didn't have an agenda, no manifesto to nail to the doors of CanLit. We abhorred the term CanLit. We just had an inspired restlessness and an encyclopaedic enthusiasm.

There once was a time when it seemed both important and possible to have read almost everything. We were still in the thrall of the Great Tradition, but under the influence of Desmond Pacey and Fred Cogswell, Bob Gibbs, Don Cameron, and others at UNB, we were immersed in Canadian literature as a legitimate if improbable academic pursuit. Students and faculty talked together in a comfortable scholarly context about our own country's literature from its earliest beginnings to its current achievement as if it all mattered, and talking made it so. It would be hard to convey just how unusual this was.

Taste and judgement had magically become matters of cultural awareness, not the measures of a prescriptive sensibility. Dave's prairie bias, and our shared immersion in what was then called Commonwealth literature that came from an inspired course we had taken with Tony Boxhill, struck a lovely dissonance with my own Upper Canadian background. Yes, we were informed as graduate students by Empson and Leavis, but reading Achebe and Ngugi and Rhys and Lamming and Rasipuram Krishnaswami Ayyar Narayanaswami, better known as R.K. Narayan, gave us different possible contexts within which to experience literary fiction.

We were not Frigians. That is one of the great myths perpetuated by god knows who (Frank Davey), that we who were wallowing, perhaps, in thematic criticism were acolytes of Northrop Frye. I read

Frye on Blake, but his commentaries on Canadian literature I skimmed — checking, I suppose, for distortions and omissions. I found him inimical to my own critical project and my personal experience of Canada. Our Canadian world was both infinitely larger, more cosmopolitan and complex, and much smaller, tighter, more provincial, close-up, and personal. We were more influenced by the eclectic commitment of Carl Klinck, the casual authority of Malcolm Ross, the critical generosity of Clara Thomas, the dissident worldliness of George Woodcock. Frye was brilliant, effete, given to alarming generalizations, and had not really read all that much Canadian writing — we had, or thought we had, which at the time amounted to the same thing.

We had read Frances Brooke and John Richardson, James De Mille and Laura Goodman Salverson, Ethel Wilson and Thomas Raddall. Writers like Grove and MacLennan, Moodie and Carr offered a significant context for the critical consideration of our own country's literature alongside Austen and Faulkner. Not because they were as good, but because they spoke in the voices that were already inside our own heads. Notions of mirrors and maps may seem quaint, now, putting literature in the service of psychosocial and cultural needs. Then, it was a revolutionary necessity.

Sitting at the kitchen table in Nashwaaksis, drinking David's toxic brew, we talked about bringing down the wall between writing and literature. In a town where the hugeness of Alden Nolan formed a raucous counterbalance to literary pretension, such walls seemed absurd. Each weekend, Alden, kept barely in check by the diminutive grace of his wife, Claudine, hosted the world at their little house on Windsor Street. Academics appeared as writers, writers from up and down the valley and across Canada appeared as themselves, and gifted readers, debaters, scholars, and clowns were welcomed in a scotch-laden air of flamboyant erudition and biting good humour. The classic divisions between students of literature and its practitioners perished.

While David and I each went on to have an academic career, we were both at heart creative writers. We wanted to publish a journal that would feature new fiction along with critical and scholarly writing, covering the whole gamut of Canadian literature. We wanted context. We wanted reviews of fiction and of academic criticism. And quite arbitrarily we wanted to pay $100 a short story, a vast sum at a time when little magazines rewarded contributors with free subscriptions.

George Woodcock's *Canadian Literature* was iconic, but it was not our model. It was genteel; despite the editor's anarchical predilections, it was thoughtfully indispensable and therefore conservative. *TISH* wasn't our model. Too strident. *The Fiddlehead* and the *Malahat Review*. Too writerly. *Alphabet*. Too Reaney. There were experimental reviews available, as there always are, all radically chic and ephemeral. There was *Mosaic*, trying to be all things to all readers, and there were the university journals which dabbled in Canadian content: *Dalhousie Review*, the *Queen's* and *UofT Quarterlies*.

Our timing was right on: there was room for, a need for, the *Journal of Canadian Fiction*. Hybridity based on genre; creative, critical, whiggish, confident enough to think Grove was important and informed enough to know why. By the end of that morning in 1971, as the coffee leached into our bones, we had formulated the basis of what was to become a radically successful quarterly with a circulation of around 2,500 by the end of its first year.

Before leaving Fredericton to its own resources for the summer, we invited Fred Cogswell and Desmond Pacey to serve on the editorial board. From my Ontario base, by the end of the summer I managed to inveigle a diverse crew to serve alongside. While talking to Clara Thomas on the phone, she handed me off to an unidentified woman who waxed enthusiastic about the possibilities of our project: it was Margaret Laurence, and she signed on to become one of our most active board members. Northrop Frye generously loaned us his name, as did Roch Carrier. Others, like Rudy Wiebe and Dave Godfrey, became actively engaged in the editorial process. Both Margaret Atwood and George Bowering made numerous suggestions, although both declined to be on the board. Literary journalists like Robert Fulford offered to contribute, then faded; others, like Pierre Berton, came through.

Sinclair Ross wrote to express interest, as did Hugh MacLennan and Hugh Garner and Dorothy Livesay. The irrepressible Robert Kroetsch, then still living in Binghamton, NY, got involved. So did John Metcalf, in the days before he became god. Matt Cohen sent us a carbon-smeared coffee-stained copy of a brilliant story. Bill New and Sherrill Grace and Laurie Ricou connected, as did the incredibly gracious George Woodcock. UNB undergraduate David Adams Richards phoned me at home periodically, hoping we'd publish a story, which we eventually did. A relative unknown from Vancouver Island sent us a manuscript that was impossibly long but David insisted we publish it, and we did: Jack Hodgins. And so it went. Canada, from a Fredericton perspective, came together.

During the autumn of '71 I wrote personal letters to every library in the country, to every high school and college and university, to writers and critics and scholars, as well as to anyone else suspected of being even remotely sympathetic to Canadian writing. Subscriptions poured in, stories and essays poured in. Without understanding what a Ponzi scheme was, I basically juggled the books to make us seem financially viable. After our second issue, Canada Council came through with, as I remember it, a staggering $17,500 grant — almost as much as we had asked for. We were alive.

The UNB English Department gave the journal office space. Sherry Dykeman abandoned her secretarial job in the president's office for a part-time position with JCF. I must be among the few graduate students in UNB history to have had a private secretary who could take dictation in shorthand. Sherry went on to become Cheryl Bogart, one of the best artists in the country.

That was a different era. I recall receiving a formal letter from someone at Canada Council asking us to fill in the gaps in our financial statement. I wrote a pompous note back, saying I was an editor, not an accountant. Over the next five years the Council gave us their fullest support. We in turn distributed hundreds of $100 cheques to writers ranging from Hugh Garner to Clarke Blaise, Hugh Hood to Miriam Waddington. Another government agency underwrote significant expenses — a situation about which nothing more need be said (except that my intentions were not in the least bit larcenous). Somehow, we fared well for five years.

I took the editorial offices of the journal with me to Montreal in 1973, when I joined the faculty of Sir George Williams University during its transition to Concordia. Dave continued his irrepressibly prescient role as fiction editor from his aery at St. John's College, University of Manitoba.

After three years teaching, I decided to move to the margins of academe, something that proved disastrously temporary. During the Learned Societies Congress at the University of Toronto in 1974, Jack McClelland and Anna Porter approached me to take over the New Canadian Library. Sadly, no one told the NCL founding editor, my former mentor, Malcolm Ross. Nonetheless, on the basis of a handshake and a promise, my family and I moved to the country where I could focus on revamping Ross's astonishing but stumbling achievement. Managing Editorship of JCF was turned over to John Robert Sorfleet, who had been reviews editor from the first issue, and who succeeded me at Concordia. David was now deeply involved with the fledgling Turnstone Press in Winnipeg. He and I retired to the wings. Over the next few years, the *Journal of Canadian Fiction* faltered and somewhat ignominiously expired.

From the beginning, it had been an amateur project in the best and worst senses of the word. Covers were generously provided by Tom Forrestall, Greg Curnoe, and several of the country's leading cartoonists, all for effusive gratitude and a $100 gratuity. The first few issues were laid out in my dirt-floor basement on Charlotte Street, with Letraset, Exacto knives, wax, a hand-iron, and awkward patience. Along with an energetic undergraduate volunteer, Judith Steen, I taught myself rudimentary principles of design. Glueing large font, letter at a time, onto the title page, Judy and I managed to represent one of our editorial board members as "Margret Lawrence." In the first issue off the press, autographed by most of the writers involved, one autograph stands out. In her firm hand, the great lady of Canadian writing signed herself, "Margret Lawrence."

The *Journal of Canadian Fiction* didn't change very much in the world, but we were very much part of the times. David Arnason and I, if we are remembered at all, will be remembered for other things. But for a while, our project that warmed into being over rancid coffee, connected with readers and writers, critics and scholars, in a particularly lovely way.

TWO FROM OTHER PERSPECTIVES

SHIFTING INDENTITIES:
A CONVERSATION WITH LAURA FERRI

My Conversation with Laura Ferri called "Talking with John Moss" was recorded in Peterborough, 2002 and published in Englishes: Letterature Inglish Contemporanee *(Rome), the same year. Laura was cultural coordinator of the Siena-Toronto Centre at the University of Siena. She makes my words more coherent I'm sure than they actually were. She and her husband were gracious hosts when Bev and I visited Siena. Some of that experience finds its way into fiction.*

Laura Ferri: In Invisible among the Ruins you write, "… we are a northern nation. The white of our flag is the winter; the Arctic, a condition of our imagination. As we become increasingly a part of the global community, as our history, written by geography, is rewritten by ethnic diversity, we cannot survive as a people without coming to terms with how we imagine ourselves. The white of our flag is the winter, but the Arctic has seasons. Those who live there know that. For the rest of us, who visit or who read, we must explore beyond winter, find what is there and what we think is there, find what we missed." The illuminating perception of a postmodern critic and the daring experience of the man who has travelled the Arctic conflate here into a whole vision of Canada's identity: its multi-ethnic growth, the possibility of its global future. Could you expand on this?

John Moss: This is a most difficult question. In effect, in your very astute reading of the passage I articulate my position and feelings in the clearest way I am able to. Canada is evolving as a multi-ethnic society in ways my grandparents, and even my parents, could not have foreseen, and perhaps would not have liked. They were comfortable with British privilege and welcoming to all, so long as outsiders conformed to the standards of the Empire. Curiously, this sure sense of their own presence in the world placed even First Nations people as outsiders, and therefore inevitably subject to assimilation, as the price of belonging. This is reminiscent of Rome, conferring citizenship to people in the provinces in exchange for fealty to the Imperial centre. All that has changed, as Yeats said, changed utterly. It is irrelevant whether the change is good or bad, or from which perspective it is measured. It is what happened. And Canada evolves into a multi-ethnic nation with unknowable prospects. In our time, it is important that we come to terms with the cost of transition, that we accommodate new ways of seeing and being ourselves. There is a tendency, however, to dismantle the past, our cultural and historical heritage, and to see ourselves in the present as simply a holding ground for future development. Ministers of the crown, leading thinkers, sometimes deny Canada's real presence in the world, perceiving us risen from a past that is irrelevant to most and incapable of a coherent vision into what lies ahead. Perhaps this is why we are governed by political pragmatists. There is no room for ideals, for memories or for dreams. As the world's nations converge under the cultural hegemony of global economics and as traditional family and communal relations inevitably collapse, individual human beings more than ever will need to sustain a sense of belonging through identity with the nation-state as a cultural home. Place of being will become more important, not less. If Canadians cannot relate to their landscape through history or culture or vision, then

Canada will fade away. We will not be destroyed by barbarians at the gates or among us. It will be our own lack of focus that does us in, our inability and lack of desire to see ourselves not through ethnicity or power but as a gathering place, a good place to be.

L.F.: Would you consider this passage appropriate for use in an anthology for Italian students, to give them a sound sense of what Canada is? Which others would you suggest?

J.M.: Yes I would. I think often students connect more through metaphor and allusion. Just look at the lyrics of popular songs!

L.F.: What do you consider peculiar to Canadian literature? Could you offer a statement which may best describe the Canadian literature of the last few decades?

J.M.: I think there are many things particular to Canadian literature but, as with all literature, few things peculiar, that is, unique. Culture is infectious. It settles in, where conditions are similar, and assimilates. It seldom expires on its own, or spontaneously springs into being. Canadian literature in the 19th century was largely a delayed response to British literature, in part emulation and in per hybridization. In the 20th century, it came much more under the influence of the Americans, but by the 1960s it was developing a voice of its own, what might be described as the cosmopolitan parochial, exemplified by pride in being the same and yet different from the rest of the world. This quickly gave way to the post-colonial expression of our individual experience in a borderless world; the Canadian reader as 'Everyman', the writer as only him or her self.

L.F.: Which Canadian authors would you recommend for the teaching of literature in high schools?

J.M.: David Adams Richards, Margaret Atwood, Jack Hodgins, Jane Urquhart, Robert Kroetsch.

L.F.: You have recently moved from post-modern criticism, through critical fiction, into Borgesian short stories. Could you say something about this turn in your writing?

J.M.: At this point it is difficult to comment. When I was writing those stories, that was the only way I could write.

LE: Is there a risk that critical fiction, as exemplified by your Borgesian stories, for all the power it has to extract responses subversively from those who are widely read, may be too demanding for young students and put them off literature at all? Or do you think that students should be exposed to this kind of maieutical challenge rather than remain subject to prescriptive critical commentary?

J.M. No; yes. I couldn't have said better. Of course, it is demanding. But liberating, too. Read a story like "Peggy Be Good." There is more critical thought in response to Atwood's writing carried in that piece of fiction than in everything else I've written, and it is far more accessible. Teaching is sharing, providing access. In this story, the reader is invited to form a relationship with Atwood's canon and the authorial personality that informs it and holds it together. Students will make the leap if given the opportunity; they will respond to her writing through direct experience in my text. I think prescriptive/proscriptive critical commentary can deaden the sensibility, whereas critical fiction can bring it to life.

L.F.: In *Being Fiction*, in the chapter on James Joyce, relating to the Irish question you sound disappointed by the fact that "The Irish who condemned specific acts of terrorist brutality would invariably wind up their exhortation against the most heinous crime with an explanation of why it was, just so." Isn't it ever possible that accounting for the historic origins of a terrible event, rather than a mode to offer violence sanction, may be a way to help the civilized world find the correct, I would say honest, response to it. I am obviously referring to the heinous attack on the Twin Towers and the Western World's reaction to it: Enduring War.

J.M.: Ah, you ask penetrating questions. First of all, it would seem accounting for the historical origins of events has done little in the past to reduce the horrors of which we are capable. Sometimes it seems, those who know history are condemned to repeat it. But what I was getting at had less to do with history than about the confusion of moral and theological context. If the activity of righteous fanatics is perceived on a religious spectrum of good and evil, then response will also be placed on that spectrum, at the opposite extreme. This kind of reductionism immediately degenerates into such dangerous absurdities as "the axis of evil, and Satanic epithets, all of which perpetuate the conflict. It becomes a simplistic Bushite notion of "my god is better than your God," and "my readings of Scripture are better than yours." But on the scales of secular justice, all crimes are unconscionable. Then, in a search for right and wrong, the pathology of an act of terrorism may both be evaluated in absolute terms as unacceptable, and seen, in relative terms, continuous with the conditions that brought it about, conditions that may be addressed. Human beings can far more easily agree on what is right and wrong than on what is sacred and what is profane. The Twin Towers tragedy is wrong; that is why it was deemed a holy achievement, precisely because it was a theologically justifiable wrong. Both sides agree, although those of us outside the sphere of religious zealotry regard it as a profanity. I would rather humanity struggles to right wrongs than to justify action through deference to an infinitely malleable God

THE END OF ALLUSION: AN ESSAY BY CRYSTAL CHOKSHI

Crystal was among my very best undergraduate students at the University of Ottawa. We have corresponded from time to time over the years and she is now a professor of Communication Studies at Mount Royal University in Calgary. This essay grew out of a conversation we had in Peterborough in 2023. In a prefatory note she says, "John Moss's latest novel argues that what generative AI really heralds is loneliness." Precisely; and her essay provides a good way to round out the themes of this book.

An underrated Canadian writer recently published what seems to be (by virtue of the pseudo-obituary appended to the text) his last book. *To Set the Stone Trembling* appeared quietly, as much of John Moss's work has in recent years, the tail end of a comet that once illuminated the skies of Canadian literary circles.

Speaking with me in the darkened living room of his 1850s farmhouse in Peterborough, Ontario, Moss laughs in an effort to be lighthearted about the fizzle-out at this stage of his career. "I remember speaking to [fellow Canadian writer] Bob Kroetsch about this, and he said, if you and I keep on the same trajectory, we're going to end up selling no copies because each book sells a few less than the last. And he may not have been serious about his books, but it was true for mine."

The fade-out is ill-timed because Moss's latest book is more relevant and urgent than anything he has written before. Whereas his earlier work was preoccupied with debates that, arguably, mattered most to English professors ("but what does postmodernity *mean*?"), *To Set the Stone Trembling* sets its sights on a topic that has dominated global headlines in recent months: generative AI. The book features two protagonists desperately working against a tech company not altogether unlike Elon Musk's Neuralink, and the blurb on the back cover describes the novel as "a dystopian [take on] the terrifying genius of language to define the limits of human experience." By my account, we could put it like this: *To Set the Stone Trembling* is a book about writing, AI, and why never the twain shall meet.

That is Rudyard Kipling, of course, which means my previous sentence makes use of allusion. Both allusion and reference are entirely the gambit of Moss's work. In the opening pages of the text, there is reference to Ferdinand de Saussure, James Joyce, Carl Jung, Franz Kafka, and Marshall McLuhan. And this practice — saturating his own work with the words of many others — continues throughout. There is hardly a paragraph that does not call attention to another writer. Some,

Moss returns to frequently: Lewis Carroll, William Shakespeare, Friedrich Nietzsche, Jorges Luis Borges. They hover closer to the centre of the novel than its margins, and their frequent cameos suggest that reading Moss's book means piecing together not only its thriller-based plot but also the story's relationship to the texts woven into it. The reader's task is not just to sort how characters in *To Set the Stone Trembling* relate to each other but also how they relate to ideas from other times and places and works, which, in turn, impact — and I would go so far, here, as to say dictate — what they can do for, and with, each other.

"I wanted to write in the vertical and the horizontal. The horizontal is developing characters, developing plot, developing story, and the vertical is all the things I wanted to bring into that... The vertical is what I think of as the semiotic side. While I let the horizontal story, the narrative, take me along, I just loved what I kept bumping into — everything from *Hamlet* to Geoffrey Chaucer to *Beowulf*. There's stuff in there that I don't even know is in there because it's just part of me, part of the education system I went through."

That education system counts the University of New Brunswick, where Moss's PhD thesis was accepted for publication by McClelland & Stewart before he even finished the degree. He would go on to teach at Concordia, UBC, and Queen's before settling into a 25-year stint with the University of Ottawa, publishing twenty-some books and becoming, at one point, the bestselling literary critic in the country. Following his retirement, he went on to write 11 mystery novels.

The hundreds of thinkers and ideas that Moss has encountered over a varied 50-year career seem to be folded into *To Set the Stone Trembling*. It is not always comfortable for the reader. The height of Moss's vertical sometimes exceeds my grasp. But this attribute, what Moss calls "page after page of [language] games and riddles," is the very heart of the argument Moss makes against writing with AI.

To date, debates about generative AI, particularly in relation to post-secondary education, have emphasized "the future." This "future" is a church whose singular object of workshop is speed. Like Amazon, Uber, and social media platforms such as X, speed is the name of generative AI's game. ChatGPT, for instance, can generate 1,000 words in less than 30 seconds. As a point of comparison, writing 1,000 words — now just as much as when I was an undergraduate — takes me days, weeks, even, if I count editing time. (This short piece you are now reading? I fiddled with it for more than six months.) Cognizant of this disparity in production time and, therefore, capacity for student output, university administrators politely suggest faculty like me incorporate AI skills-training into our curricula. If the future is about constant acceleration, we must teach our students how to keep their feet on the gas. Otherwise, they, and the organizations they work for, will get left behind. That is how the dominant narrative goes.

But by virtue of its many references, *To Set the Stone Trembling* tugs at an important and, as of yet, wholly underexamined thread in the conversation about generative AI: community. Writing slowly, *without* AI, gives us the opportunity to create it.

Talking about writing his book, Moss recalls what thrilled him the most: "I would get excited when I'd be trying to say something, and I'm pausing, there's something coming, but I can't quite get it, and then a line from Yeats comes to mind. And what I'm trying to say is, 'Who can tell the dancer from the dance?' How better to say it?"

Writing is about thinking alongside, with, and through other people. It is, for example, about reading Yeats's "Among School Children," mulling over its meaning, and then registering whether or not one agrees with the ideas the poem puts forward. In making that decision, one claims community, claims kin, and situates oneself in relation to, and in relations with, other writers.

Generative AI, such as ChatGPT, cannot enable this. ChatGPT can quote from other texts, but its algorithmically-selected references do not position a writer (nay, a text-generator) in relations with other writers. When a writer, that is to say a real person, alludes or cites, they situate another text in relation to their own in such a way that the nature of both is changed. To write in this way is to say, "That work preceded mine, and there is a sensible arc," or "These two things inflect one another," or "My line of thinking is indebted to and changed because of…" Or still yet, "My understanding of this person's text leads to a new interpretation of it." In contrast, when ChatGPT generates a reference, all we can reasonably deduce is that the AI identified a text that it was programmed to identify based on a formula. Generative AI makes of writers and writing heterogeneous compounds, things that exist in the same space without exchange or reaction. Therefore, the conditions for community-making are absent.

Of course, the community is imagined. Moss is no more speaking directly with Martin Heidegger, one of the people to whom *To Set the Stone Trembling* returns, than I am, following this paragraph's topic sentence, with Benedict Anderson. And yet the possibility of dialogue is real. Dialogue, after all, is conversation, the exchange of ideas, and both the aim and outcome of human writing is, precisely, to facilitate it.

This is a process that takes time. Cultivating an intellectual community requires careful, ongoing *un*algorithmic decision-making. It requires poring over books, making deliberate choices about whose ideas to engage with and whose to set aside, whose ideas to call forth in my own work and whose words to rely on to make my way through the world. In the era of generative AI, many are coming to think of this effort as a waste of time — redundant and unnecessary. But there is more at stake than speed and efficiency. To have the capacity to reference and allude and, therefore, to build intellectual community, is to have the ability to resist loneliness.

"Allusion is the most important literary device because what allusion means is I'm not writing alone," Moss says. "I'm writing with Yeats. I'm writing with all the other people who are writing, you know?" In other words, to write without AI is to experience a more-than-me-ness. It is to refuse to see writing as mere output — as a noun — and to reclaim it as a verb, as something that depends on *doing*, and depends necessarily on doing with others.

The stakes of this *doing* come to the fore in Paul Kalanithi's exquisitely-written book, *When Breath Becomes Air*, which *To Set the Stone Trembling* prompted me to revisit. At 36, Kalanithi, a neurosurgeon, was diagnosed with terminal lung cancer. In the 22 months between his diagnosis and death, Kalanithi says he turned time and time again to literature. Discussing one particularly gruelling day, Kalanithi recites Samuel Beckett: "I can't go. I'll go on." In the days leading to his death, Kalanithi looked to dozens of writers, seeking comfort and community in their words.

More recently, Roméo Dallaire, a retired military officer and former Canadian senator, wrote about what it has meant to him to draw on the words of others. In Dante Alighieri's *The Divine Comedy*, Dallaire, who has spoken both publicly and candidly about his struggles with post-traumatic stress disorder, says he found inspiration "to guide [his] thinking beyond the cycles [he] seemed to be stuck in." Dallaire writes of reading *The Divine Comedy* as both recognition and solace, of witnessing a story similar to his own and, thus, of feeling witnessed.

I am hazarding a guess that text generated by AI such as ChatGPT would not have bolstered either Kalanithi or Dallaire in the same way. For what is comforting about turning to machines when we are most alone? Kalanithi and Dallaire argue, as Moss and I do, that reading and repeating other human-written words make even the loneliest of journeys slightly more tolerable. This is communing. This is community.

Generative AI, like other technologies that have preceded it, has an isolationist impulse. Such is the condition of technologies focused exclusively on speed and efficiency. They ask us to generate, alone and fast, rather than to think, slowly and with. Moss, for his part, wants us to know that thinking slowly — vertically, semiotically — through the texts we have encountered in our lifetimes is both a pleasure and a responsibility we should not so easily cede and not so readily eliminate from our vision of "the future." While the tech-led discourse filtering its way down to industry and academia chants "go faster," *To Set the Stone Trembling* asks, "faster toward what? Are we sure about that?"

I, for one, am not. Like Moss, I worry about the ways generative AI alienates us from each other and from ourselves. Because, again like Moss, I am more concerned with relations than information, and about this, I could not say it better than him: "I am so much exhilarated by what language lets me do."

REFERENCES

Dallaire, R. (2024, March 23). "After Rwanda, I found a path to personal peace. Can the world find collective peace?" *The Globe and Mail.* https://www.theglobeandmail.com/opinion/article-after-rwanda-i-found-a-path-to-personal-peace-can-the-world-find/

Kalanithi, P. (2016). *When breath becomes air.* Penguin Random House

LIFE, IN SHORT

I close with what Crystal Chokshi in the preceding essay, "The End of Allusion," describes as my pseudo-obituary. *These are the words with which I chose to end my last novel,* To Set the Stone Trembling, *a work that drew from diverse parts of my life and literary experience to wrap everything up in a kind of magnum opus, appreciated for the most part by the few who read it, irritating to those who were baffled by its allusive erudition in a dystopian context. As with life, I accept its fate with forbearance.*

John Errington Moss. Arrived on Feb. 7, 1940; departure, to be determined. He will leave in his wake a life thoroughly, often fretfully, enjoyed. He grieved at the thought of separating from his beloved wife, Beverley Haun, but was grateful for the wondrous decades they shared. He vowed at eight to live a life of adventure and did his best to do so. Honoured with a BA, MA, MPhil, MSDT, PhD, and Fellowship in the Royal Society of Canada, he retired as *professor emeritus* to write eleven modestly acclaimed mystery novels, after publishing twenty-some books on Canadian culture, Arctic exploration, and experimental literature. He lectured from Rome to Tokyo, the Canaries to Greenland, throughout Canada and much of Europe, and held guest professorships in Berlin, Leeds, Mysore, Dublin, and Vienna. At various times he reared horses, raised dogs, kept swans, bees, chickens, and a few cats; redesigned, carpentered, plumbed, wired, and restored old houses; replicated colonial furniture. He was a scuba instructor (PADI and SDI), a fervid oenophile, a logophile with no musical sense but obsessed with the weight of words, an inveterate traveller, and an endurance athlete. He swam across the Hellespont in 1962, Abydos to Sestos; ran the Boston Marathon eleven times; completed the original Kona Ironman, 1987; did various loppets including the Canadian Ski Marathon, touring gold and coureur de bois, gold bar; did numerous treks in the Arctic, including twenty-eight days alone on the Barrens; and many long-distance ski and foot races closer to home. He enjoyed long treks with his redoubtable Beverley, including coast-to-coast walks across England (Hadrian's Wall in 2013, the Wainright Trail in 2017), The West Highland Way in 2023, and the Lake District Round, with mishaps, in 2025. In his youth he worked as a canoe tripper in Temagami, at the Aldwych theatre in London, and as a stand-in for the principal character in *Lawrence of Arabia*. In latter years, he renewed his passion for bees with Trembling Stone Apiary, and loved nothing more than to work on his '54 SeaBird, a gift from Bev named Corsair after the identical launch of his childhood summers with his beloved Aunt Beth in Muskoka. He grieved at leaving his beautiful daughters, Julia and Laura, after sharing with them the infinite joys and complexities of their childhood, enduring the terrible loneliness as they grew up and away, salving his sadness with pride in their achievements as they attained doctorates, professional stature, and had fine children (Julia's Clare, Maddie, and Olivia, with George Zarb; Laura's Simon, Owen, and Charlie, with Fred Cutler). He had no regrets at sharing thirty tumultuous and enriching years with their mother, Virginia, and honoured her achievement as a clinical psychologist; he revelled in Bev's Ph.D. in cultural theory and publication of a definitive book on Easter Island. He shared Bev's grief for the loss of their infant son, Jack Austen. He was saddened to leave her daughter Beatrice and son Joel, her husband Pedro de Silva and son Diego. Proud of his Moss, Clare, Pattinson, Cameron, and Erb heritage, he always thought of himself as lucky to have had such interesting parents as George Moss and Mary Clare, and such diverse siblings as Richard, Steve, Liz, and Erry, some of whom predeceased him but all who shaped his early life, mostly for the better. He grew up in Blair, Ontario, in a house not a hundred feet from his chosen burial site and even less from the grave of his ancestor Christan Erb, the founding father of Waterloo County, whose family purchased their land from the Mohawk Nation. John's life was touched by many. He accepted the end with forbearance.

www.ingramcontent.com/pod-product-compliance
Lightning Source LLC
Chambersburg PA
CBHW021144160426
43194CB00007B/689